Power Trading ◇ Power Living

By

Michael "Waxie" Parness

Power Trading ◇ Power Living

Printed in the United States of America.
First Printing: July 2004
Published by Trendfund Corp.
www.trendfund.com

EXAMPLES AND ILLUSTRATIONS

The examples and illustrations provided in this book are for illustration purposes only. Stock prices reflect the prices at the time of publication, or in some cases, may have been fabricated to better illustrate the concepts being presented. Similarly, stock or company names were chosen arbitrarily for illustration purposes only. The concepts presented could just as easily apply to any stock.

ISBN: 0-9743391-2-1

Dedication

This book is dedicated to all the people who have chosen to think "outside the market" and move to better themselves. You've helped me become a better person as well.

Acknowledgements

I would like to thank the following people who made this book possible:

Rodger Smith for all of his help in the production of this book.

Doug Koval, who has helped make 'Trend Trading To Win' the most successful stock market infomercial the world has ever known.

Michael "Tiny" Saul for helping to carry the message of Trendfund.com, and for being a great friend.

The staff of Trendfund.com and 'Trend Trading To Win' for being so good at what they do. It's allowed me to pursue my personal dreams.

Michael Parness, a.k.a. Waxie

About The Author

Michael Parness' first book, *Rule the Freakin' Markets* (St.Martin's Press, 2002), has been published in 6 languages and is a Financial Times Best Seller. He's been featured in the Wall Street Journal, Financial Times, NY Times, NY Post, Crain's Business and others. He's also appeared on CNBC, CNN FN, Reuters, Bloomberg Radio, Talk America Radio, Good Day, NY and others.

Michael was once homeless, living on the streets of Brooklyn, and riding the train back and forth from Manhattan to Brooklyn. After he put together a nest egg that his broker turned into nearly nothing, Michael turned roughly $33,000 into $7,000,000 and started Trendfund.com, the worlds leading online trading community. His infomercial package, Trend Trading To Win, has sold over 125,000 units in the 2-1/2 years it's been on TV. In 2001, Michael was honored for his charity work with children at the United Nations. In 2002 he co-hosted a benefit for Help A Mother, Save A Child with Susan Sarandon that raised over $100,000. His life story was optioned by Dustin Hoffman's Punch Productions, and in 2003 Michael started to fulfill his lifelong dream of being a filmmaker by writing and directing his first feature film, Max and Grace (www.maxandgrace.com), featuring; Natasha Lyonne, David Krumholtz, Lorraine Bracco, Rossana Arquette, David Paymer and Karen Black. He started a film production company, Full Glass Films, to help promote new and exciting independent films and filmmakers (including himself!).

Trendfund.com now has over 15,000 active clients, and it started with free emails and a part-time job with E*Trade! Though Michael doesn't recommend E*Trade any longer (contrary!), he has helped 1000s of traders pursue their own life's ambitions. He tries to carry his belief that anything is possible in all aspects of his life, and hopes you do the same!

Table Of Contents

Power Trading ◊ Power Living

Introduction

Welcome to "Power Trading ◇ Power Living", and thanks for your interest in this book! The trading techniques I discuss in *Power Trading ◇ Power Living* have proven to be quite profitable over the years; at least they have been very profitable for me, and my clients. Indeed, I have literally made millions from using them, and that's in both up and *down* markets! I hope that you find them equally as valuable and profitable as well!

For those of you that may not have heard of me, I'm Michael Parness, also known as "Waxie" among other traders and my clients. You can read the "About The Author" page for additional background information, and you can find out more about my online services at www.trendfund.com.

Power Living

Before I get into the trading aspect of this book, I think it's important to briefly discuss why the book is titled *Power Trading ◇ Power Living,* and not just *Power Trading*. One of the things that I've observed as a trader over the last 5 years in my own life, and in the lives of 1000s of others I've had the pleasure to meet and work with, is that trading, as well as any other business, in and of itself does not define success. Hence, money does not define the degree of success one can or should attain in life. It's one of the oldest clichés in books – "money isn't everything." The hardened among us would answer – "yes, you're right - it's the ONLY THING!" That has not been my experience.

For those of you who have seen my infomercial, or have read about me elsewhere, perhaps you know some of my story. I grew up in Queens, NY. When I was a teenager I dropped out of High School and ran away from what was a pretty abusive household. After exhausting all avenues, I lived on the streets for a while, riding the trains back and forth from the city to Brooklyn. I even lived in Prospect Park, sleeping on and under the proverbial park bench. Suffice to say; I know what it's like to be abused, to be poor and to struggle mightily.

Suffice to say also that once I had attained what many would consider "RICH" status in my life, I thought all my problems were solved. They weren't. They still aren't. At seminars, I like to say - "I've been poor and miserable, and I've been rich and miserable. Money does NOT cure everything." Having said that, I can also tell you unequivocally that I'd rather be RICH and miserable than poor and miserable. At least I know I can eat or sleep comfortably!

So, the first part of this book is going to deal with POWER LIVING, something that I've come to know over the last 5 years. Consider it prep work for when you yourself become financially independent so you don't encounter some of the same pitfalls that I did in my life. Ultimately, that's all one does when you read a book like this one. You hope to learn from the experts' advice and their mistakes so you don't have to make the same ones yourself. It's said that a smart person learns from his or her own mistakes, but a WISE person learns from others mistakes. I hope you learn from mine and it helps you to become the person you wish to be. That is POWER LIVING, living your dreams and BEING your potential to its fullest!

The second part, and meatiest part, of this book is Power Trading. I like to do things to the best of my ability, no matter what it is. I don't believe that we should do anything in life to lose. When I play my 3-year-old daughter a game of checkers, I cream her! How else is she going to learn how to win? Just kidding. However, the gist of that statement is true. When I play, I usually PLAY TO WIN! As a trader, I trade to win.

I dubbed my personal style of trading *Trend Trading*. Most daytraders lose money. That's because they scalp stock trades. They try to make small gains on large share lots. Since most of my clients don't start with a lot of money, scalping doesn't work for them, or me. I didn't start with a lot of money either, so it was never an option to be a typical daytrader. To this day, I don't think I'd ever want to be one.

So, I'm primarily a trend trader. That doesn't mean I gamble, not at all. I don't believe in the *gambling attitude*, and I don't see myself as a gambler. Gamblers lose money; trend traders make money. I look at trading as a business, as a way to make a good living, and as a way to potentially achieve financial independence and other personal goals. Besides being a professional athlete, I don't think there can be a more fun job in the world - IF you do it successfully!

Since I don't believe in gambling with my hard earned capital, I look for high percentage trades that tend to have a great risk/reward profile. The techniques that I'll be presenting in this book are generally based upon strong trends that meet those criteria.

Of course, that doesn't mean that all trades are successful and zero risk is involved. There is always risk associated with trading. However, the approaches I use minimize the risk and enhance the potential for a successful, profitable outcome over a period of time. Although some of your trades will be losers, if you can achieve greater gains on your winning trades than losses on your losing trades overall, then you will be successful over the long run.

Anyone that is interested in actively trading stocks or options could potentially benefit from the information contained in *Power Trading ◊ Power Living*. Whether you are an investor, a new trader, or seasoned trader, I think you will find *Power Trading ◊ Power Living* to be a valuable resource. It contains a variety of proven trading techniques that you can readily adapt to your own trading style and personal objectives. If you are a seasoned trader, you will likely come away with some additional tools in your arsenal that make the book well worth its cost. If you are just starting out, in addition to learning profitable trading techniques, you'll learn how to limit losses and how to avoid common mistakes that cause many first-time traders to fail.

If you are an investor relying on a stockbroker to manage your money, then I encourage you to proactively take charge of your own money, particularly if you aren't experiencing good results with whoever is doing it for you now. My experience with a stockbroker was — he made me *broker*! That doesn't mean that all financial advisors are bad but none have the same vested interest in your money that you do, and many have financial incentives to steer you in directions that aren't actually in your best interest. Still, by taking charge of your own money I don't mean that you should jump in head first without looking. Instead, learn as much as you can first then start out slowly using only a portion of your total funds until you gain experience and have a successful track record.

Regardless of your specific personal objectives, if you have an interest in learning more about trading the stock market, you'll find the information presented in *Power Trading ◊ Power Living* very helpful in your quest to learn more. And, if you have an interest in living your life to its fullest potential, then you're in the right place and you've picked up the right book.

By using this book, you've already made your first successful trade! What's that you ask? You bought it! Now you've begun a new journey in your life. There is no way then that you can do anything but WIN. I believe that if you practice the methods outlined in this book, you will succeed financially and potentially achieve financial independence beyond your wildest dreams. I have. What you do with that success will define who you are and what kind of person you wish to be in the world, which is part of what *Power Living* is all about!

The 3 D's - Dream, Define, Dream Realization

Dream Realization — Fulfillment Of Potential

One of the first things I have clients do at seminars or through the Trendfund.com website (or lecture about at universities) is write down and visualize their DREAMS. I believe that in order to truly attain that which we desire, we must know what it is we are, well - dreaming! Our dream page is very popular for this reason.

The great boxers visualize knocking out their opponents *before* they step into the ring. Ted Williams used to talk about dreaming of hitting line drives all over the field. Stephen Spielberg dreamed of making movies from when he was a small boy, and in fact got his first video camera before he was eight. There are literally 1000s of success stories that started with the 1st D - DREAMS. Our dreams *inform* who we are. Writing them down makes them real and helps us move in a direction that will hopefully enable us to attain them. Yet, before we attain them, we must know what they are. Our dreams are the roadmap that informs not just what we desire, but also our very core, the core of who we are and what we become.

Once we define our dreams, we can define who we are. I believe we all start from the same *perfect* place when we're born. We then go through a series of initiations that are bestowed upon us by our parents, and our environment. If you think of it in terms of language it really makes sense. If you were born in Spain, chances are your native language is Spanish. If you were like me, and you were born in the United States, then you probably speak English as your first language. There are exceptions, and those prove my point further, in that if your parents speak Spanish as their first language but you were born in the United States, your first language, the first language you learn just might be Spanish instead of English. However, once you start going to public school and the majority of your classmates speak English as their first language, you might and probably will soon end up speaking much more English than Spanish. Thus, English becomes, if not your first learned language, then at least the language that you use more than any other.

So, we start in one place of perfection and then we get a ton of things bestowed upon us by others. Some of these things we use to our advantage, some we learn to discard. The object is to get back to that "perfection." Have you ever heard the term "childhood dreams?" I certainly have, and I'm not referring to the ones where every boy wants to be a fireman and every girl wants to be a teacher. I'm talking about the childhood dreams that came to you when someone asked you what you REALLY wanted to do. Those are the dreams we all want to get back to, often desperately. I know I do. When I was five I dreamed of being a filmmaker and storyteller. Last year I wrote and directed my first feature length film, *Max and Grace* (www.maxandgrace.com). I'm planning a long and fortuitous career as a filmmaker now and in the future, hopefully just like Mr. Spielberg. That's my desire to get back to "perfection" and my core dreams.

For me, getting back to those dreams took a long time. I had a lot to overcome. Many people who overcome hardships have to take a longer route before they can accomplish the things they wished they had spent their entire life pursuing. I've read that Holocaust survivors have a much higher success rate once they overcome the trauma of what they went through, than the average population. I had a friend who was stabbed 3 times in front of his building, nearly fatally. When he overcame this near tragedy he was more focused, more determined and more unstoppable to realize his dreams. These events helped mobilize survivors and moved them closer to their core dreams. I know for me, when I was young, I felt immortal. I felt I had so much time to realize my dreams, why worry about it. In 2000, even after I attained great success as a trader, I took a vacation in Peru and contracted a rare heart ailment. I nearly died. I no longer think I will live forever. If I'm going to live my dreams, I'm going to do it, and I'm going to do it NOW. There is no time like the present and the present is NOW!

So, after you've defined your dreams, what do you do with them? The better question might be – "Who do you want to be?" What do you want to define you? Honesty? Integrity? Generosity?

Realizing your dreams should not just mean realizing your financial dreams. Success comes in many flavors, but in my book it always means that you spread the wealth of your success. For me that means giving time and money to help abused children. I've been honored at the United Nations and had the pleasure of co-hosting an event last year with Susan Sarandon to help a program focused on helping inner city youth and children that had the sort of childhood I had. One of my dreams as a child was that if I ever attained wealth, I'd be generous enough to remember my problems and help children that might otherwise fall into the same "traps" I had fallen prey to. I call that a dream of potential fulfillment as a person, as a human being. To me, that's another part of going back to that perfection of youth. Given the freedom, children laugh and play freely and generously. And, if given enough love and tender care, they share freely as well. Shedding the imperfection then involves getting back to the core that might have been if not for certain parental or environmental restrictions.

Does anyone really think that suicide bombers are born? No, they are raised and trained and brainwashed. So, the object then is to fulfill the promise and the potential that was who we were born to be. Fate? Sure, why not. Destiny? I don't believe so. We make our own destiny in life once we reach adulthood. It's up to us to visualize our dreams, define who we want to be, and realize our dreams and ourselves. Who you are is something YOU choose to become. Your heart, your mind, your soul, and your dreams are there for the taking. There is a reason they call it the PRESENT. It's a gift. Take it, own it and be grateful for it. One of the worst things you can do to children is tell them they can't live their dreams. If you take children's dreams, they are left with nightmares. As adults we have the power to make ourselves, to mold ourselves into who we always wanted to be. As you become successful as a trader you'll need to ask yourself, is this what I want to do? For me, it is a means to an end, toward realizing my dreams. For you, it might be the same thing, or it might be that you have dreams of a family life and trading is part of that since it allows you to be home with your kids. Regardless, welcome.

Beyond Self-Help

Have you turned on your television at 2 am lately? You might have, and it might have even introduced you to my infomercial, *Trend Trading To Win*. Every infomercial is selling you something that claims will better who you are, whether it's Carlton Sheets, Tony Robbins, or Moira Winsor's 'Pilades' program. Do you want to know what the top-grossing segment of the infomercial market is? It's weight-loss programs. In fact, the statistics show that most people who order one infomercial product to help them, order at least 1 or 2 more products in the same vein. Why? Well, it's because most of us are looking for help outside of ourselves. We're looking for answers that we don't feel we have inside of ourselves. And often, that is the case. So, you fail at one diet, why not buy 3 more until you get it right. The truth is, there is nothing wrong with that. I'd be the last person to tell anyone not to seek help with anything.

I'll give you another factoid; over 25% of all purchased infomercial products are NEVER even opened, and never returned either. They sit on a shelf and collect dust, or end up in garage sales years later. Yes, I'm sure even *Trend Trading to Win* has a similar collecting dust rate!

So, how do we go beyond self-help? How does the housewife who is 40 pounds overweight finally get the diet she needs? The reality is, there is no "right" diet. There are fad diets, like Atkins now, or the Scarsdale diet years ago, but in the end it comes down to creating the destiny of your choosing. You have to decide whether to turn that switch on that says – "I will succeed - PERIOD!" THAT is the right diet, or the right business opportunity. And, the funny thing is, it might be the worst diet for someone else, or the worst stock advice, but if you "get it" at the right time and you are ready to succeed, then nothing will stop you from that success. Again, this harkens back to visualizing your success and making it real for yourself. There is a saying in 12 step programs to help alcoholics stay sober and that is – FAKE IT 'TIL YOU MAKE IT! I tell my clients all the time – "dude, if you want to be a successful trader, let go of everything you learned as an investor and start from scratch." Yes, it's often easier said than done, but that's the challenge you must overcome. That's why you seek out help and take what you need in order to get to the place where you not only can succeed, but you WILL succeed, and you DO succeed!

That's beyond self-help. It's truly helping yourself! If you are ready for success, you will become a successful trader, but only IF that's what you want. I talk to clients all the time that tell me at some point a light bulb turned on in their head, or a switch turned on in their brains. They suddenly found they could understand the things they couldn't understand before. They were now ready for success! The question is – are you? The keys to financial freedom are here for the taking, if you are ready to let yourself in the door.

Living Powerfully

Living from your core means living powerfully. Knowing who you are means living powerfully. Being a man or woman of grace and dignity, of truth and integrity is living powerfully. Living powerfully is living without fear and knowing that you will and are being looked after in this crazy thing we call life. See, the thing is it doesn't matter what your belief system is. When I lived on the streets, I had to fend for myself and on occasion, I stole an apple or two from a deli. I was afraid I would starve, and it was a very real fear. Now, I'm not afraid of starving, and I don't steal anything. Was I right to steal way back when? Of course I wasn't. We can't justify taking things that aren't ours because we are afraid. I also begged for help, and often got some change or the offer of a warm meal. In the end, I was taken care of. Think about your life and how many times you've been afraid of something. There are likely times when that fear was well founded and healthy, but it's also likely that even when what you feared most happened, you survived, and possibly even thrived!

I talked about how as a child I wanted to be a storyteller, a writer and filmmaker. Well, when I was a teenager I had other dreams. I wanted to be a professional baseball pitcher. I was very good too. I even had scouts that were coming to see if I had the right stuff. It was all that I lived for, so much so that I pitched every day in some venue. It could be stickball or baseball. It didn't matter. I threw the ball as hard as I could competitively. Well, at 15 I threw my arm out and my dreams were shattered. I thought my life was over. I became depressed and fearful that the one thing that truly made me happy had been "taken" from me. It was soon afterwards that I ended up on the streets, homeless. At the time, I didn't realize my core dreams were still available to me.

When I was in my late 20s and bartending in NYC, I found myself back on a path toward that core dream. Like most other employees in bars and restaurants in New York, I was a writer and director (and actor!). I wasn't making any money at it, but I had dreams and was working toward them. My plan was to make enough money to make a movie, which I would write as well. I figured I needed $200,000 to make a very low budget movie, and I began saving toward that dream.

Later on, I started a baseball card business and after a couple of years, it really took off. After a few years of saving, I had just about enough money to realize my dream. That's when I gave my broker my money to invest, and that's also when he promptly helped me go broke! Once again, my dreams were smashed! I wondered if they would ever happen, and again I thought my chance at happiness was over. I was afraid again.

That's when I embarked on the path that has taken me here, with you reading my book right now. Irony is, not only did I get fairly wealthy; I also had my life story optioned by Dustin Hoffman! I was paid to write my own life story! In a million years, there is no way I could have imagined that happening. Yet, here it is and it's all true. And, all of that fear I once had turned out to be foolish.

The bottom line is we don't know all that the future holds for us, none of us, but we can work toward achieving and living our DREAMS! Even though we can't always control how they happen, I can tell you based on my experience that they do have a VERY good chance of success, if we work toward them.

Roberto Benini, when he accepted the Academy Award a few years ago for one of my favorite films, *Life Is Beautiful*, thanked his parents for the wonderful gift of poverty! Everyone laughed, but it wasn't a joke. All of the stuff we go through, as hard as it is sometimes, I believe it's all okay. I am grateful for what I've been through because it has helped define who I am, and it has helped me to make my own destiny, one of my own choosing. Our "job" is to keep our chin up, our mind open, and keep growing and moving toward our dreams.

As a trader, living powerfully means not only learning theory, but also applying it. Many traders paper trade. We recommend it wholeheartedly. Some find that once they start trading "live" with real money, it takes them time to make the leap. Why? Because trading with real money is always going to be different, if not more difficult, than trading with play money. It's a VERY valuable tool, but you'll still need to refine your skills once you make the switch to real 'cashola'.

When I make a trade, I always KNOW that I am going to make money on it. I am certain, 100% certain. Obviously, I'm wrong sometimes so I didn't really know, but it's the attitude that's needed to succeed at any endeavor in life. Do you think that Spielberg ever starts making a movie saying – "Ya know, I think this movie is going to SUCK but I want to direct it anyway!" Of course he doesn't. Yet, not every movie he makes wins an Academy Award, or is even good. Just go check out *Hook*!

Remember too that you need to eat healthy (always), and you need to take a break when you trade. Now, when I trade I always get up for at least an hour just to walk around, or to make myself lunch if nothing else. When I first started trading, I gained 20 pounds because I never left my screen. This harkens back to the fear factor. I was afraid that I might miss a profit opportunity. The truth is that there is no such thing. The market is open over 200 days a year! Do ya think there just might be another profit opportunity for ya over that time frame? Take a healthy lunch break, get up and exercise, make love to your wife, or husband, and make sure you shower!! Imagine how your neighbors feel when they smell you from two blocks down the street because you didn't shower for fear of missing a winning trade!

Knowing what your goals are, what your dreams are, and who you are gives you the best chance to succeed. In my first book, *Rule the Freakin Markets*, I discussed the "Inner Knucklehead." In short, it says that in order to succeed, you need to know both your strengths AND your weaknesses. In fact, I'd argue that knowing your Achilles Heel is always going to take you further in the long run.

I get asked all of the time what clients should do if they are making good money in the morning playing the gaps, and then giving most or all of it back during the afternoon trading. Of course, it's obvious from the outside looking in. If you are making money in the morning and losing money in the afternoon, stop trading the afternoon! That's logical, though, and logic doesn't always take into account our emotions. So, I usually tell them if they want to keep trading afternoons, to at least cut their lot sizes back at that time until they figure out how to make the trades profitable. Knowing your weaknesses not only helps empower you to overcome them, it helps you eventually master them as well.

You wouldn't think it, but the ability to take losses is a huge key to success as a trader, and a huge part of living powerfully. The ability to pick yourself up off the ground when you fail is invaluable. Believe me, as a Power Trader you will fail many times. Your ability to overcome those losses and maintain control of your emotions dictates your ability to be mediocre, or worse, or a stunning success. That's why we preach – plan your trade, and trade your plan! That helps take the emotion out of your trades and helps limit any losses you might incur. The statistics show that a good trader can hit on 40% of their trades and still be profitable. At Trendfund.com, we hit on a much higher percentage so Trendfund clients are in good hands, but I've seen traders hit on 60-70% of their trades and still LOSE money because they let their losers turn into investments – or turn into dust! You must be able limit losses by taking the loss and exiting the trade rather than hanging on, hoping it will come back your way.

Blaming others for your decisions will also hinder your ability to become a Power Trader (and Power Liver!). You are responsible for any trade you make, win or lose. Blaming someone else for a bad call is foolish and wastes your time. It's said that resentment is like peeing down your own leg; no one feels it but YOU! There are no victims, only volunteers – most of the time, once you get past the age of 21!

Power Trading and Power Living go hand-in-hand. To master one, you need to master them both. Mastering Power Living comes with time, practice, and the ability to self reflect. As humans we're never perfect, nor should we be. Hopefully we grow and stay open to the possibilities. I once heard Paul Newman say when asked how he got to be, well, Paul Newman, that he just accepted the gifts that were offered to him by life. Remember, life has many gifts. You may not see them at first but they are there nonetheless. Power Living is a way of life, so find your own Power Living and fulfill your destiny – POWERFULLY!

Power Trading

To me, *power trading* means full day trading. I think of a power trader as someone who is capable of trading the market successfully throughout the entire day, and when desired, before and after regular market hours as well.

If you already have trading experience, then you know that many diverse opportunities come and go each day in the market, and that trading them successfully requires a broad range of skills. To trade successfully throughout the day, you need to use a variety of tools, techniques and strategies. You also need to adapt quickly to changing market conditions. Trading AM gaps, PM laggards, breaking news events, or trading after-hours requires different strategies. Power traders have the experience, agility, and skills needed to recognize and take advantage of the various trading opportunities that come and go each day in the market.

Although it's not necessary to trade on a fulltime basis or all day everyday to be a power trader, power traders have the expertise to do so when they so choose.

Intraday Primer

For those of you that might be new to the term, *intraday* is associated with the period of time between the open and close of the market's daily session, though a more liberal interpretation might also include trading before the market opens or after it closes.

On a given day in the market, you'll encounter fluctuations in volume, trend continuations and reversals, changes in volatility, and more. Sometimes external events such as world news announcements, industry news releases, or even individual company news releases trigger intraday market swings. Rumors, general market perceptions, perceptions about the state of the economy, or simply the normal ebb and flow of supply and demand also cause intraday moves in the market. Regardless of the cause, a power trader needs to adapt to these changing market conditions.

A brief overview of the types of details that a trader may need to manage during a typical day follows. More in-depth information about these topics, and many others, are provided later in the book.

- Intraday Timeframes
- Intraday Overview
- News Events
- Swing Trades
- Gaps
- Laggards
- Market Close
- After-Hours

Intraday Timeframes

As previously mentioned, market conditions vary throughout the trading day. During the day, and depending on the time of day, different trading strategies apply.

Though many events such as unexpected news releases can move the market in unpredictable ways, there are also daily market rhythms that are predictable to some degree. Traders that become familiar with the market's daily rhythms can develop trading strategies to take advantage of them or to avoid their pitfalls.

The "Intraday Timeframes" chapter breaks down the trading day into a chronological sequence of separate timeframes, or time periods, and correlates them to market behavior. You'll find some useful trading tips there as well.

Intraday Overview

Preparation for the trading day generally begins with a check of the futures, latest news and overall market conditions. Next, open positions such as swing trades are reviewed, and throughout the process, traders are always on the lookout for specific stocks to trade.

Stocks that are gapping up or down from their prior day's closing price often provide great trading opportunities, but ideas may come from a variety of sources, including online news services or business news channels such as CNBC. The sections following this overview go into more detail about all of these topics.

As the trading day gets underway, traders watch for trade setups. The first few minutes after the market opens tend to be very volatile and active. Since this often results in exaggerated price moves, it can be a very profitable time for an agile trader. At this time, stocks that have gapped up or down are often turned over for a quick profit should they make a corrective price reversal. The specifics on how to trade gaps are covered later in the book.

As the day progresses and market conditions change, trading strategies are adjusted accordingly. Stop-loss orders may be tightened, positions may be exited, or new positions may be entered into. *Laggards*, stocks that are lagging behind the market or are lagging behind their peers, often provide new trading opportunities.

Throughout the day when appropriate, and as the end of the market's regular session approaches, traders plan exit strategies for their intraday trades. In most cases, traders exit all of their intraday positions by the close of normal market hours each day.

Of course, swing trades are also managed throughout the day and beyond according to the original plan for each trade, and depending on overall market conditions.

After the market closes, many traders quit for the day. Others continue to watch for after-hours trading opportunities, at which time, breaking news tends to become the dominant factor that influences stock prices and provides trading opportunities.

These topics are all discussed in more detail later in the book. Before continuing, though, I'll provide a few brief words of caution for those of you that may not have any experience trading outside of regular market hours. Due to lower volume, greater price spreads, and other factors, more risk is associated with after-hours trading. Consequently, you should be more cautious and use limit orders only when trading outside of regular market hours.

News Events

Traders generally follow the news closely. At least, I do, and I recommend that you do as well. Not only does the news provide trading ideas, it may also help prevent losses should breaking news have a negative impact on the market or stocks you are trading.

Typically, traders start the day by taking the market's pulse to determine whether there is an upside or downside market bias. The idea is to get a sense of whether anything has already begun to affect the temperament of the market, and if so, to determine what and why.

I begin by checking the S&P and Nasdaq futures to get a general sense of the overall market bias. If the futures are up, then the market at large will likely open higher as well. If the futures are essentially unchanged or they are down, the market will likely open flat or lower.

Once the overall market bias has been determined, it's time to check the online news wires and TV business news on CNBC or other business channels (you can also check the futures on CNBC). Generally, I just like to catch up on the news because it could influence my trading day, but I also want to see if there are any particular reasons for the market's bias. A variety of events could potentially influence the market and/or stock prices. Examples include breaking world news events, major company news releases, analyst upgrades or downgrades, earnings announcements, the release of economic data, and so on. However, in some cases there may not be any apparent reason for a bias. A bias could simply be the result of ordinary market fluctuations, trend continuations, or temporary imbalances between the overall supply and demand for stocks.

I also check to see if any particular stocks are being talked about in the news, or if any are moving in pre-market action, since as mentioned, major news about a large company could also influence the market. Maybe Cisco (CSCO) had a good or bad news announcement, or Intel (INTC) was downgraded. Whatever the reason, the idea is to determine why the market or certain stocks are up or down since it will influence the trading day, and could provide trading opportunities or affect the performance of positions I currently hold.

It's important to continue watching the news wires and CNBC throughout the trading day. Not only do you want to manage your trades if a major news announcement breaks, the news is a great ongoing resource for trading ideas.

More detailed information and examples of how news announcements can influence the market and individual stocks is provided in the "Trading The News" chapter.

Swing Trades

A stock that is held over a period of multiple days, but not as a long-term investment, is referred to as a *swing trade*. To minimize risk, I generally close out all of my trading positions at the end of each day. However, when a good reason justifies it, I do occasionally hold a stock over a longer time period.

On days when I am holding one or more swing trades, after getting a general sense of the overall market, I take any appropriate actions to manage my swing trades based on my original plan for a trade, and whether current market conditions, breaking news, or a desire to take profits justifies a modification of my original plan.

I generally remove all of my stop-loss orders before the close of trading each day. Since a breaking news event could cause a temporary exaggerated price swing, or a gap, I don't want to be arbitrarily stopped out of a position. For example, if I owned Siebel Systems (SEBL) with a stop-loss order placed $1 under its closing price and SEBL gapped down $2 the next morning, my stop-loss order would trigger but the order would fill $2 less than the prior close, or $1 less than my intended stop-loss limit for managing risk. I'd get filled based on the opening "tick" for the stock, even if it then bounced $3 or just to break even. Stop-loss orders should be lifted before the close of trading EACH DAY to avoid such possibilities. Remember that the first tick is often the low or high for the stock on any particular day.

Instead, I prefer to manage my trade and control how I exit a position so I can take into consideration overall market conditions, news announcements, or other factors that might influence my stock's price. Although I might not be happy about SEBL gapping down $2, if I'm in control, I have the option of holding out for a potential corrective snapback where I might be able to exit the position at a better price. Or, depending on the price action and market, I might still exit the position with a $2 loss, but at least I would have the option to choose rather than leaving it to a *market maker* to set the price at which my order fills.

Additionally, some market makers may try to intentionally trigger stop-loss orders by temporarily posting and retracting erroneous prices, particularly during after-hours trading. Or, due to low volume after-hours, wide price spreads between the best bid and best ask could trigger a stop-loss order. Removing stop-loss orders before the market closes each day also helps guard against these possibilities.

Since I begin each day fresh without stop-loss orders, one of the first things I do is either reset my stop-loss orders or exit positions, depending upon the strength of the market and my original plan for each trade. Alternatively, if I'm looking to enter into a swing trade, I evaluate the potential for that as well and plan accordingly.

Gaps

Great trading opportunities are presented when the market or individual stocks gap up (open higher than where they closed the day before) or gap down (open lower than where they closed the day before) significantly from their prior day's closing price. Therefore, before the market opens I start looking for stocks that are gapping up or down. The larger the gap, the better the potential trade.

I look for momentum stocks since they tend to gap more dramatically and provide the best opportunity for a corrective price reversal in the opposite direction. Though not always, momentum stocks often consist of technology or biotechnology (biotech) stocks. Most trade on the Nasdaq stock exchange, and therefore, they have 4 letters in their symbols such as INTC, CSCO, AMGN, and so on. Momentum stocks provide greater liquidity and price action, which makes it easier to get in and out of a trade fast, and hopefully, with a nice profit.

Once I've picked some good trading candidates, I add them to my watch list and start looking for potential trade setups. Then, it's just a matter of watching the price action and executing a trade, if the setup develops according to my plan for the trade.

Gaps offer so many potential trading opportunities that I've devoted two chapters of this book, "Trading Gaps" and "Trading Gaps Using Technical Analysis", to the topic. More detailed information and gap examples are provided in these chapters.

Laggards

Frequently, the prices of closely related stocks in the same sector or a similar industry move in sync with one another. Meaning, if the price of one goes up or down, the prices of other similar stocks may follow along.

Since the stocks are in a similar business, when an earnings announcement or other news event affects the performance of one, the other stocks are often impacted as well. If you watch these stocks, you may occasionally encounter an intraday price divergence where the prices of some stocks are making a significant move that leaves one or more of the others behind. The comparison could be between as little as two stocks, or it could be a larger group of similar stocks. Any stocks among the group that lag behind the price movement of the others are referred to as *laggards*.

A price divergence between a laggard and its peers will frequently correct itself at some point, either intraday, or sometimes during the following day or so. Depending on overall market conditions, and subject to stock specific news, often the laggard will take off and play catch up. However, the peer stocks could also be the ones that move back toward the direction of a laggard's price.

You can use the strength and direction of the overall market as an additional indicator as to which is most likely to make a corrective move. For example, if the market is moving higher and a laggard's peer stocks are moving higher, the laggard is more likely to make a corrective "catch-up" move at some point.

Laggards can provide nice intraday trading opportunities. The "Trading Laggards" chapter provides more detailed information and examples of laggards.

Market Close

In most cases, traders exit their intraday trades before the regular market session closes. Therefore, during the latter part of the trading day, traders begin watching for exit opportunities. Gains may be locked in with stop-loss orders or trailing stops, or positions are simply exited whenever an appropriate opportunity comes along.

At the same time, new trading opportunities may also appear near the end of the day. The types of opportunities that may show up are described in more detail in the "Intraday Timeframes" chapter.

After-Hours

In today's market, most online brokerage firms, and all direct-access brokers, let you trade outside of regular market hours. You can generally trade both after the market closes, and before the market opens. For purposes of discussion, I'm referring to both as after-hours trading. Since the type of support for after-hours trading can vary between brokers and changes frequently, you should check with your broker for specific information and the hours of operation.

Although many traders quit for the day when the market closes, many also continue to watch for after-hours trading opportunities. For the most part, breaking news tends to be the driving force of price action during after-hours trading.

While I occasionally trade after-hours (and once did virtually everyday), I don't do it as often now. Fortunately, I've reached the point in my career where I no longer need to work that hard at trading. When I do trade after-hours, I generally trade for about 30 minutes or so after the market closes, though it is possible to trade much later. Since after-hours trading is primarily news driven, and the bulk of companies release their news shortly after the market closes, a larger percentage of the trading opportunities take place soon after the market closes. Still, late breaking news does present opportunities at later times.

If you are new to after-hours trading, proceed cautiously at first because there is more risk associated with after-hours trading. Lower volume and/or larger price spreads, among other factors, can make it more difficult to get in and out of positions at a favorable price, particularly with thinly traded stocks.

2

Intraday Timeframes

In my opinion, one of the most important things about power trading is learning to trade the intraday timeframes.

At certain times of the day the market tends to be active and volatile. At other times, there may be a *lull,* or slow down, in the market's activity. While this behavior is not 100% certain to occur exactly the same each day, it does tend to occur with a reasonable degree of regularity.

Following is a chronological breakdown of the trading day based on observations I've made over the years.

Timeframe	**Potential Event**
09:30 AM – 10:00 AM	Gap Trades
10:00 AM – 1:00 PM	10:00 AM Rule In Effect
1:00 PM – 2:30 PM	Lunchtime Lull / Reversal
2:30 PM – 3:20 PM	Post-Lunch Activity
3:20 PM – 3:40 PM	Afternoon Lull
3:40 PM – 4:00 PM	Market On Close / EOD
4:00 PM+	After-Hours, News Rules!

Table 21: Intraday Timeframes

Referring to the preceding timeframes, it's easy to see why you need to adjust your trading strategies throughout the trading day. For example, trading gaps obviously requires different techniques than trading the lunchtime lull, and trading the lunchtime lull is different than trading after-hours.

Following is a more detailed description of each intraday timeframe.

Trading The Timeframes

Below is daily chart that shows how the Nasdaq Composite behaved during the various timeframes that are discussed in the following sections.

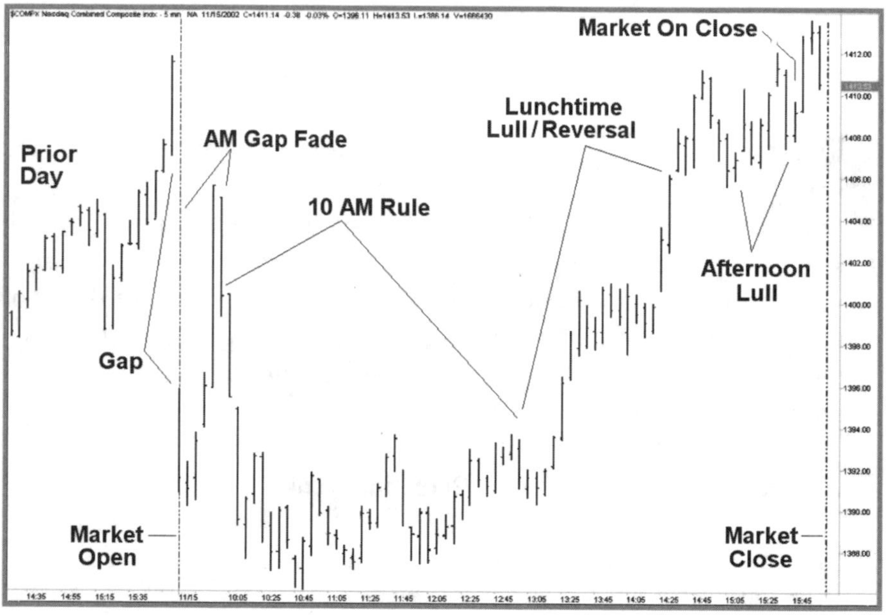

9:30 – 10:00 AM Gaps

As you can see on the preceding chart, the market is usually very active and volatile during the first 30-75 minutes of trading, which is great for traders. High volume and volatility often provide the best trading opportunities. In fact, if the morning goes well, after the first hour or so of trading, some traders may even meet their profit targets for the day and take the rest of the day off.

The first 30 minutes of trading is primetime for gaps, especially if the entire market is gapping large. Before the market opens, I look for stocks that are gapping up or down. If I find momentum stocks that are gapping significantly and otherwise look okay to trade, I start watching for a trade entry.

Large gaps often result from traders overreacting to news during after-hours (or pre-market) trading when volume is low. When the volume is low, any significant buying or selling pressure after-hours can move a stock's price more dramatically resulting in exaggerated price moves. Then when the market opens and volume returns to normal, there is frequently a corrective price reversal, or price snapback (see the preceding chart). When trading gaps, the snapback reversal is what I'm looking to trade. To further illustrate this concept, try pulling a rubber band further and further apart. Just when you can't pull it further without it breaking, let it go. What happened? If it's truly rubber, it will "snap back" and even better, it will often go much further in the OPPOSITE direction! This is what fading a gap equates to, the snapback of a rubber band.

If a stock gaps up significantly, I enter a short position anticipating a corrective pullback to the downside. Conversely, if a stock gaps down, I enter a long position anticipating a corrective snapback to the upside, as occurred on the preceding chart. Trading gap snapbacks in either direction is called *fading the gap*.

Of course, like everything else about the market, it does not behave exactly the same on any given day. Though gaps are high percentage plays, particularly in the case of large gaps, there are times when a stock gaps large and keeps on going the same direction without the usual snapback reversal.

You will also want to watch and manage your swing trades at this time. If you are holding a swing trade long and it gaps up large, you might want to consider taking advantage of the opportunity to take profits. The same is true if you are short and there is a large gap to the downside. Of course, you need to consider your overall plan for each trade, but if you have sufficient gains, a gap could provide a nice opportunity to take profits. Alternatively, if you want to remain in a position, you could consider taking profits and reenter the position at a better price should there be a snapback reversal of the gap. Although, since there is no guaranty that a corrective reversal will take place, you should take that possibility into account before exiting your position.

Examples and more detailed information about trading gaps are provided in the "Trading Gaps" and "Trading Gaps Using Technical Analysis" chapters of the book.

10:00 – 1:00 PM, 10 AM Rule In Effect

As discussed in the previous section, prices frequently snap back contrary to the direction of a gap. If you went long on a gap up and the price made a corrective pullback, you would likely take a loss on the trade. The same is true if you shorted a gap down and it made a corrective upside reversal. I created the 10:00 AM rule to help avoid getting caught on the wrong side of a trade when trading gaps.

The 10:00 AM rule is a simple guideline that can help you avoid losing money, and may help you make money, particularly if you are new to trading.

Here is the 10:00 AM rule:

> *If a stock gaps up, you should not buy it long unless it makes a new high after 10:00 AM. Conversely, if a stock gaps down, you should not sell it short unless it makes a new low after 10:00 AM.*

You may need to trade contrary to what your emotions are telling you to do in order to follow this rule, because when the market or stocks are gapping up there may be tremendous enthusiasm on the buy side. People frequently get caught up in the excitement and continue to jump in and buy the gap, or they may simply buy because they don't want to miss out on a potential rally. Alternatively, if it's a gap down, people may panic and sell initially.

Following the 10:00 AM rule can help keep your emotions in check and prevent a loss if a gap reversal occurs. Though a stock or the market may gap and keep on going, in most cases, there is at least a temporary snapback correction. If gaps are going to reverse, the reversal usually occurs before 10:00 AM.

Eventually, a dominant direction begins to emerge, which may only be temporary, or it could form a trend for the day. Regardless, after the initial gap trading is over, you can also use the 10:00 AM rule as a guideline to time potential entries for other trades.

If a stock makes a new high after 10:00 AM, it's a sign of strength. When this occurs, more often than not, an upside trend will continue. Therefore, I frequently enter a long position for a trade when a momentum stock makes a new high after 10:00 AM. After establishing a position, you should immediately place a stop-loss order to limit your risk then trail the price up if the trend continues, which it will often do throughout the morning, and possibly beyond on a strong up trending day. I'll discuss using the 10:00 AM rule in more detail and provide examples in the "Trading Gaps Using Technical Analysis" chapter, including the use of stop-loss orders.

In the case of new lows, you would take the opposite approach. If a stock makes a new low after 10:00 AM, it's a sign of weakness, so you could enter a short position and limit your risk by using a trailing stop-loss order.

1:00 – 2:30 PM Lunchtime Lull / Reversal

Some traders believe that lunch begins at 12:00 PM, however, the observations I've made while tracking the market's behavior over the years lead me to conclude that the majority of traders breakaway for lunch from 1:00-2:30 PM.

During the lunch timeframe you'll frequently see a slowdown, or lull, in market activity. Volume tends to taper off or dry up as traders take time off for lunch. As a result, the market and individual stock prices will often drift or move counter to the prior trend. It's also not uncommon for the market to reverse directions either during lunch or soon afterwards.

As always where market behavior is concerned, there are times when pullbacks don't occur, or new highs or lows are made over lunch, but I've observed this behavior for a number of years and a lunchtime lull occurs a large percentage of the time. For that reason, as the lunch timeframe approaches I either exit my intraday positions, particularly when I have nice gains from riding an AM trade, or I tighten my stop-loss orders.

Even though there are times when a trend continues right on through lunch and beyond, to me, it's just not worth taking the risk. I've experienced too many instances where gains slowly wither away while the market drifts aimlessly up and down through lunch. There frequently just isn't sufficient volume and momentum to sustain prices, and I don't want to risk giving back the morning's gains. However, if on a given day the market appears sufficiently strong, or weak if you are trading short, you could tighten your stop-loss orders as a safeguard rather than exiting your positions. You could also consider reducing your lot sizes by one-half to reduce your risk exposure. At the very least, you should watch your trades closely during the lunch timeframe.

On the other hand, if you are looking to enter a position, the lunchtime lull often provides a great opportunity to do so. It may also provide a great opportunity to enter a countertrend position. For example, if the market has been trading sideways or slowly trending down into the lunch timeframe, an impression may emerge that the market appears to have underlying strength and isn't likely to go much lower. As traders come back from lunch, they may think *what the heck* and take a long position. Since volume is low at lunch, it doesn't take a lot of buying to start pushing up prices. As momentum picks up and buying continues, it often results in a strong countertrend reversal. These types of days provide great opportunities for entering countertrend positions during the lunch time period.

2:30 – 3:20 PM Post-Lunch Activity

As traders come back from lunch, market activity generally begins to pick up. Initially, it may not be clear which direction the market will take but as described in the prior section, it's not uncommon for the market to reverse directions during lunch or shortly afterwards.

This is the timeframe when the market decides whether it's going to continue a lunchtime reversal or resume the pre-lunch trend.

3:20 – 3:40 PM Afternoon Lull

Later in the day, many traders begin taking profits and exiting intraday positions, while others may simply continue riding positions they opened during or after lunch.

Some traders may have already quit for the day by this time. In general, it's a time when the market tries to determine where it's going for the rest of the day. It may try to bounce or sell off during this time period as traders juggle their positions.

Regardless of the reasons, around the 3:20-3:40 PM timeframe, I've observed that an afternoon lull in market activity tends to occur with a high degree of regularity.

Similar to the lunchtime lull, this afternoon lull provides another opportunity to enter a position for a trade. For example, if you feel the day is going to close strong and there is a pullback during the afternoon lull, you can take advantage of the pullback to enter one or more long positions.

3:40 – 4:00 PM Market On Close / End Of Day

This is the timeframe when the market decides how it's going to close. Many institutions need to square away their positions by the end of the day. Any imbalances need to be balanced, hence Market On Close orders can provide some indication of what the market may do.

For example, if I'm watching the news wires or listening to CNBC and hear around 3:30-3:40 PM that there is strong institutional Market On Close buying due at the close, I'll likely be a buyer for a quick end-of-day trade since it often becomes a self-fulfilling prophecy. Meaning, when traders get the news of Market On Close buying they perceive the market is going higher so they start buying, which causes the market to go higher, even before the close.

It's similar to what happens with key moving average (MA) support levels, particularly the 200-day MA (but others as well). Since the 200-day MA is perceived as a strong level of support, when a price falls to the 200-day MA traders start buying, which once again creates a self-fulfilling prophecy by reinforcing the notion that the 200-day MA is a strong level of support.

Just because this timeframe is near the end of the day doesn't mean that I'm buying to hold overnight. If I do enter a position during this timeframe, such as a Market On Close *TRADE* as described above, it's typically for a quick 10-20 minute intraday trade only. While I may hold a Market On Close trade right up to the end of the day (or until the real Market On Close trades come in), in most cases, I will exit the trade before the market closes. Of course, as with all trades, there's no guaranty a given stock will go up, so you still want to employ reasonable risk management strategies and set stop-loss orders accordingly.

4:00 PM+ After-Hours, News Rules!

Even though the this section applies primarily to trading after the market closes its regular trading session, I'm using the term *after-hours* to refer to trading outside of the market's regular hours of operation, whether it is after the market closes for the day or before the market opens in the morning.

Though investors may occasionally buy or sell stocks during after-hours trading, their decisions are likely based on a long-term plan. Whereas, traders that trade after-hours are generally looking for a short-term trade that can be flipped for a profit during the current after-hours session, or at the longest, a potential gap the next morning. For a long-term investor, after-hours price action may be less of a concern but for a trader, some event must cause a substantial price swing in a relatively short time period, otherwise, there wouldn't be many, if any, after-hours trading opportunities. Fortunately for after-hours traders, there are events that cause the desired price swings. The main force that propels after-hours price moves is breaking news.

Examples include upgrades and downgrades, large company deals, stocks being added to a large index such as the S&P 500, earning warnings, earnings reports, major world news events, and others. Some news releases drive a stock, sector, or even the entire market up or down. For example, if a large company like Cisco (CSCO) comes out with an earnings report that substantially beats estimates, not only is CSCO likely to go up, it could take the futures and the entire technology market with it, particularly the stocks that are in the same sector as CSCO.

Here is another example. Suppose Applied Materials (AMAT) releases news that they've reached an inflection point, and orders are starting to pick up significantly. Since AMAT is a widely followed stock that could potentially influence the market, I would immediately start watching AMAT to see if the price takes off. More often than not, there isn't time to catch a ride on the specific stock for which the news was released, or AMAT in this case. If the price does take off, I would look for an opportunity to play other stocks in the same sector such as KLAC, INTC, NVLS, and so on. Mainly, I would just start watching competing companies.

In the case of big news releases that could potential move the market overall, I would also look at other popular momentum stocks like EBAY, AMZN, BRCM, RIMM, ERTS, and so on. Basically, I would take a look at any large momentum stock that is likely go up with an upside market move and as a result, could potentially be traded after-hours for a quick gain of $.50 to $1.00 or more.

If you set up your after-hours watch list with momentum stocks grouped by sectors, you can quickly check out competing companies when news breaks about a company, whether it impacts the entire market, a specific sector, or other companies in the same industry. For example, I group semiconductor companies such as INTC, AMAT, KLAC, NVLS, LLTC, MXIM, and etc. together. Similarly, I do the same type of grouping for other sectors.

Generally, I'm not looking to hold a position overnight. However, if the news is particularly good and I think the market may gap up the next morning, I may hold one-half of my position until the next morning. But if I do hold any shares, I will generally only do so when I am up on a trade and can close out half of my position with a profit to help offset a potential loss the next morning on my remaining shares. In most cases, though, I prefer to simply take my profits. I would much rather take a $1-$2 profit, even if it means leaving money on the table, than take the risk of turning a winning trade into a losing trade.

Additionally, if you are going to hold a position overnight based on news, you should make sure that you clearly understand the news and read it thoroughly. It's not uncommon for a company to release good news first to soften the impact of other bad news. For example, a company could announce that it beat the street and follow up 15 minutes later with an announcement that the CEO is retiring. A $1-$2 profit could evaporate in an instant during after-hours trading and turn into a $4 loss, especially considering prices can move quickly during after-hours trading due to relatively low volume and/or large price spreads.

As previously mentioned, if you are new to after-hours trading, I recommend that you proceed cautiously at first because there is more risk associated with after-hours trading. Low volume and/or larger price spreads, among other factors, can make it more difficult to get in and out of positions at a favorable price.

Timeframe Trading Examples

The following chart shows the price action of Expedia (EXPE) during various intraday timeframes. The price action was volatile on this particular day, which provided great trading opportunities.

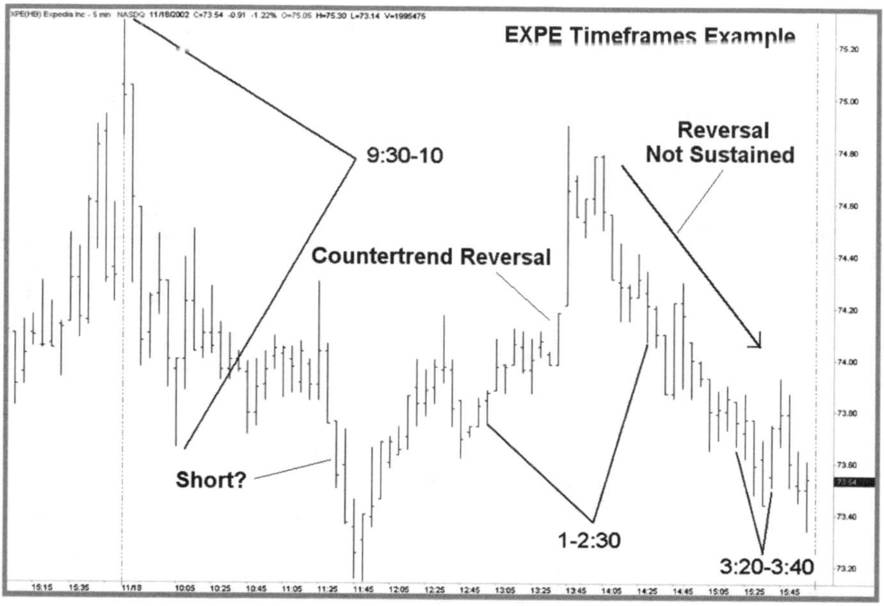

During the first 30 minutes, EXPE opened strong then pulled back. A nice trade would have been to fade the open with a short position.

After 10:00 AM, the price broke through its prior low, which provided another opportunity to enter a short position. Depending on how you executed the trade, you could have taken profits as EXPE made another new low. Otherwise, you would have likely stopped out if you were using a trailing stop and held the position longer.

Notice over the lunch timeframe, EXPE made a countertrend price reversal. If you had entered a long position in anticipation of a potential lunchtime reversal, you could have gotten out with some nice gains before the next pullback. However, the countertrend move wasn't sustained in this case and the stock eventually closed the day near its lows. Of course, this example applies to a single day only. In many instances, a lunchtime reversal continues throughout the rest of the day.

Here is another example that shows an intraday chart for the Dow Jones Industrials.

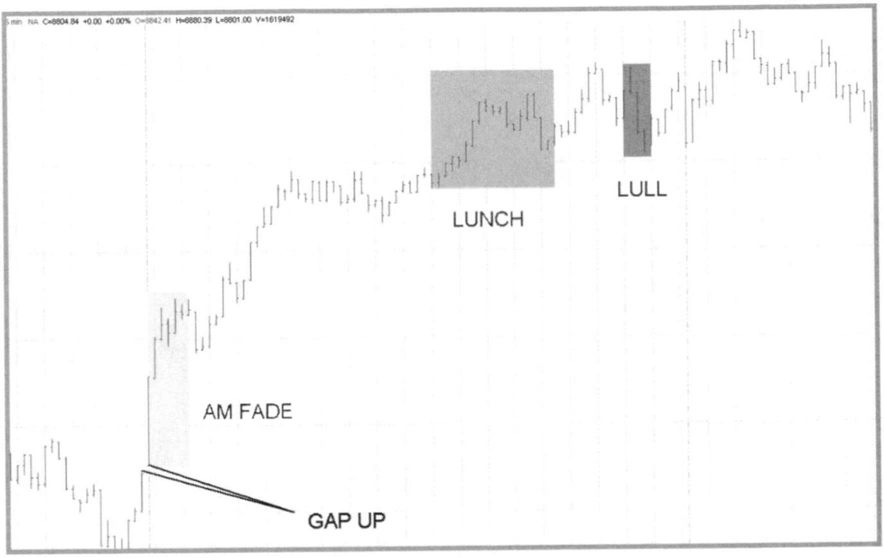

Notice in this case that the market gapped up by a small amount and kept going higher. After a brief pause around 10:00 AM, the uptrend continued into the lunch timeframe.

You could have potentially traded the trending day by using the 10:00 AM rule as a guideline. How to do this is discussed in the "Trading The Gaps Using Technical Analysis" chapter. Although there was a small pullback during the afternoon lull, a general uptrend continued throughout the day and beyond.

3

Shorting

Most people that are familiar with the stock market understand the general concept of buying stocks long with the expectation (or hope) that prices will go up, in which case, they make money.

But when the market and prices are trending down, most casual investors have limited, if any, idea of what to do to make money, or to preserve their existing capital. They may hold their investments expecting them to eventually come back and go higher. They may eventually sell at a loss and try again or wait for better times, or they may give up on the market entirely. Some may have heard about this technique called *shorting* where you are supposed to be able to make money when the market is going down, but they have very little concept about what it actually is, and they may be afraid to try it because they've heard that potential losses are unlimited. It seems too risky. Many of these preconceptions apply to new traders as well, at least initially.

As a trader, or even an investor, if your goal is to make money in both up and down markets then it's important not to limit yourself only to buying stocks long. In much the same way that you buy stocks in an up trending market to make money, you should be willing to sell stocks short in a down trending market. The best traders don't fight the market. They buy long or short depending on the relative strength of the market, or a particular stock, and take whatever the market gives them with no bias toward one direction or the other.

Since being able to successfully short stocks is such an important aspect of trading, this chapter discusses various issues related to shorting. It describes what shorting is, and discusses the fears and realities of shorting. Later in the chapter, shorting tips and examples are also included.

What is shorting?

When you buy a stock long, you buy it at a certain price hoping that it will go up in value so you can sell it at a higher price and make a profit. If the price goes down instead, you lose money.

Shorting is the opposite of buying a stock long. In this case, you sell borrowed shares of a stock at a certain price hoping that it will go down in value so you can buy it back at a lower price and make a profit. In other words, if you short a stock and the price goes down, you make money. If the price goes up instead, you lose money.

Basically, if you are a member of Trendfund.com, this is when you'll hear me say, "Die you dog - DIE!" We root for the stock we just shorted to go down into the bowels of the universe, or just to go down, if you don't want to be melodramatic!

To sell short, you borrow the stock's shares from your broker then sell them to another buyer. Your broker generally handles this transparently by simply allowing you to place a *sell short* order, or a *sell* order even though you don't currently own shares of the stock you are selling. At some point you must buy the shares back, which is called *buying to cover* your short position. This automatically returns the shares you borrowed to your broker, hopefully at a lower price. If the price is lower, you keep the profits the same as you would for a regular buy and sell order. Conversely, if the price is higher, you incur losses.

Before you can sell a stock short, your broker must have shares of the desired stock available for borrowing. A variety of factors can affect the availability of shares, including the volatility of a given stock and the demand for shares. The method for determining whether shares are available to short varies between brokers. Some brokers let you check whether shares are available in advance while others inform you at the time you place a short order. You can check with your broker if you need help with determining the availability of shares for shorting.

At first, the process of selling stocks short may seem somewhat convoluted but it's really fairly simple. At most direct-access brokerage firms, the process for executing short orders is generally as straight forward as buying a stock long, although there are a few additional rules that apply to shorting. An example is the uptick rule. These are discussed in more detail later in this chapter.

Why sell short?

When the market is up trending virtually anyone, including investors, can buy stocks long and make money. But what happens when the market is down trending?

Conventional wisdom says that you should buy the dips, or hold onto to your stocks and wait for them to come back. While this may work for investors when a short-term correction occurs in a long-term bull market, it doesn't work in a true bear market, and it certainly doesn't work for short-term traders. A true bear market can last for years. Investors that follow the conventional wisdom in a bear market may lose not only all of their hard-earned gains; they may lose a large percentage of their original capital as well.

Similarly, traders can't sit on their hands for months or years waiting for the next uptrend or bull market. They must be able to make money consistently regardless of whether the market is going up or down, which is why they must be capable of selling stocks short. All *serious* traders, and certainly all power traders, must be capable of shorting stocks!

Initially, when traders are just starting out, they tend to resist shorting. And some try to trade bounces or short-term trends (such as earnings runs) in a down trending market. It's even possible to make money by doing this. However, it's much more difficult to consistently make good money day-to-day unless you are willing to sell short as well. Successful traders soon realize that you shouldn't fight the market. Meaning, if the market is going up, you want to go with the market and buy into strength, or buy the pullbacks. Similarly, if it's going down, you should go with the market by selling short. A key trading rule to keep in mind is *don't fight the market (or the TREND!)*.

Another reason to short stocks is that prices tend to fall much faster than they rise, which presents great profit opportunities for traders. If you only attempted to trade the bounces in a down trending market, you would miss out on all of these other excellent opportunities. I've seen occasions when the market has dropped by 1000 points in three days. While the market can rally quickly as well, generally, it takes much longer to achieve similar gains.

People tend to panic when they think they may lose money, which causes prices to fall faster than they rise. The same is true of individual stocks. In many instances, when a company misses earnings estimates, it's not uncommon for its stock to plunge 15%-25%, or even 50% or more in some cases. On the other hand, it's rare to see a stock go up by 50% after a positive earnings announcement, except possibly for a small cap stock. But even in the case of small cap stocks, the large upside moves don't happen with the frequency and vigor of the downside moves. Therefore, when prices are falling, shorting provides some great opportunities to generate nice profits in a relatively short timeframe.

The Fear And Reality Of Shorting

Fear is the number one reason why people don't like to short stocks. Since there is no inherent limit to the amount of potential losses when shorting stocks, people think the stock price could go up to infinity, causing them to lose all of their money, or worse yet, even more than the amount of their original capital. Of course, the reality is different but overcoming the fear associated with shorting is initially an issue for many traders.

Here is an example that illustrates the fear people have about shorting stocks. If the stock price of XYZ is $50 and you buy it long, the most you can lose is $50 per share, and that's only if the stock's price drops all the way to zero. If you sold XYZ short at $50, it could theoretically keep going up indefinitely, that is, to infinity! As a result, the amount you could potentially lose when selling short has no upside limit.

However, there is the theoretical, and there is – *the reality*. The reality of shorting is, as I like to say in jest:

> *Infinity is a long way away and even the Starship Enterprise didn't get there in its five-year mission, so it's doubtful your stock will either.*

The reality is no stock will go to infinity. If you employ good money management and use stop-loss orders to limit risk, the most you can lose is the amount of your predefined risk. For example, if you shorted the hypothetical stock XYZ at $50, and then placed a stop-loss order at $51, typically, the most you will lose on the trade is about $1.00. By predefining your risk, you would have a $1.00 downside risk with a maximum potential profit of $50, if the price were to fall to zero.

About the worst that could happen is that you hold the stock short overnight and when you wake up the next morning, your stock has gapped up because of good news, such as another company buying it out, a new sales contract, a positive earnings announcement, or whatever. In that case, maybe it would gap up to $52, $53, or whatever, before you could get out of the trade and you would take a bigger hit. However, the same thing could happen if you hold a long position overnight. It could gap down as a result of bad news.

Of course, this isn't as much of an issue for intraday short trades, just as it isn't for intraday long trades. Regardless of whether you are trading short or long, holding positions overnight increases your potential risk. In any case, as a trader, you are less likely to hold positions overnight or long-term, and when you do, you would generally only do so after carefully weighing the potential risks and rewards of the trade beforehand.

Even in a worst-case shorting scenario, the stock won't go to infinity and you'll generally be able to exit your position with acceptable losses, or at least, with losses that are comparable to the potential losses associated with buying stocks long.

To summarize, although you can lose money when shorting stocks, if you predefine your risk and use stop-losses, you can limit potential losses when shorting the same as you would when buying a stock long. You would simply get out of a trade when it goes against you by a predetermined amount.

If you are serious about trading then you need to be capable of making money in both up and down trending markets, which means you need to be capable of shorting. All good traders short stocks.

If you haven't ever shorted stocks and still have trepidations about shorting, even though the concept of shorting may feel uncomfortable to you initially, I suggest giving it a try using a small lot size. Shorting small lots initially is a good way to overcome the *fear factor*. You can try 100 shares, or even 10 shares, if that feels more comfortable. Then, once you've experienced the reality of shorting, you'll likely be wondering why you waited so long. Besides, it can feel really good to yell - *DIE YOU DOG - DIE!*

Shorting Rules And Restrictions

There are a variety of restrictions, SEC rules, and rules imposed by individual brokerage firms that cover selling stocks short. Examples of these include the following:

- Shorting requires a margin account
- You can short a stock only on an uptick or zero-plus tick
- You can short post- or pre-market without an uptick at some direct ECN brokerages
- You can short Amex Holders, Exchange Traded Funds (ETFs), and indexes such as QQQ, SPY, DIA, etc. without an uptick
- You may not be able to short stocks that are under $5
- You can't short penny stocks

This section covers some general rules that frequently apply to shorting stocks, however, some requirements may vary between brokerage accounts, and rules change over time. Therefore, you should check with your broker for the most up to date information and their specific requirements before actually selling stocks short.

Margin Account

In most cases, a margin account is required to short stocks. A margin account also lets you leverage your money by increasing your buying power.

The amount of leverage can vary between brokers and the size of your account. For smaller margin accounts it may be about 2 to 1, though some brokers may allow more or less. A large daytrading account might be 4 to 1, or even more. A 2 to 1 margin ratio simply means that if you deposit $5,000 into your account, you will be able to purchase up to about $10,000 worth of stock (subject to maintenance requirements, etc.). Since this can vary between brokers and accounts, you'll need to check with your broker for their specific margin account requirements.

Be aware that buying, or shorting, stocks on margin also increases your potential risk. When trading on margin, your broker loans you the money to buy more stock than you would normally be able to purchase using your own funds. Since you can buy more shares, if you decide to do so (you don't have to use your margin buying power), your potential losses could be greater if your trade(s) go against you.

For example, suppose you only have enough money to buy 1000 shares of INTC long using your own funds. However, you really feel that AMD is going to go up as well. So, you decide to use your margin leverage and buy 1000 shares of AMD as well. Obviously, if a major news event suddenly caused the whole market to plunge, you could lose money on both trades rather than only one. The losses on any margin purchases, such as AMD, come out of your original capital as well. Still, if you employ reasonable money management techniques and use stop-loss orders, you can manage risk such that it makes sense to use your margin leverage in some instances. Later in the book, I'll discuss using stop-loss orders to limit risk in greater detail.

You should also take into consideration the risk/reward of a given trade, or trades, when deciding whether to trade on margin. If there is a particularly strong, high percentage trend in your favor, then you may want to consider using some of your margin buying power. On the other hand, in cases where the outcome is less certain, it's generally best to limit your margin exposure.

Uptick Rule

SEC rules allow you to short stocks only on an uptick or a zero-plus tick. These rules were implemented in part to prevent the driving down of stock prices from heavy shorting, and then buying the shares for a large profit.

An uptick means a stock's price is quoted higher than its preceding price. For example, if a stock last traded at $20.02, an uptick occurs when it subsequently trades at higher price such as $20.03 (or higher). A move as small as $0.01 higher can generate the required uptick. A zero-plus tick occurs when the price is the same as the last price, but it is higher than the preceding price.

Virtually all brokerage quote displays show whether a stock's current price is the result of an uptick or downtick. I'll provide some complete Level II quote screen examples later, but for the moment, following is an excerpt from one that shows the current tick indicator. An up-arrow indicates a price uptick, and a down-arrow indicates a price downtick. An arrow such as this is commonly used for displaying the current tick; however, keep in mind that the precise method could vary between trading platforms.

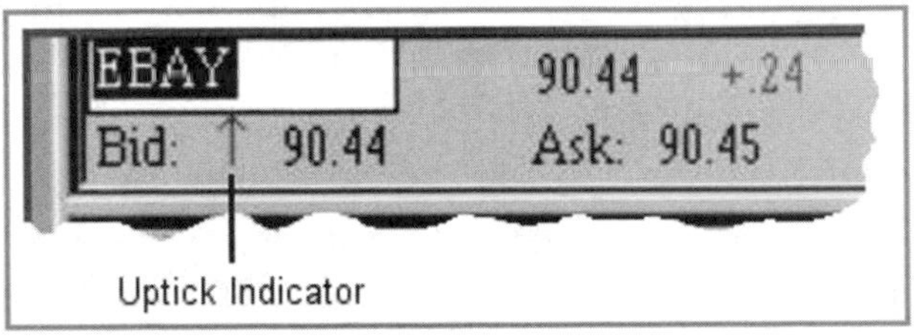

Regardless of the stated purpose of the uptick rule, it makes sense from another point of view as well. In order to short a stock, you must not only be able to borrow the desired number of shares from your broker, you must be able to sell them to someone else, which means there must be buyers present. Since a stock's price up-ticks due to buying at the best asking price, it's more likely you will be able to sell your shares short on an uptick. Conversely, a downtick occurs when there are no buyers at the prior asking price, or when there are more sellers than buyers.

Note that there are exceptions where shorting without an uptick is allowed. These are pointed out, as applicable, in the sections that follow.

After-Hours

Most direct access brokerage accounts let you to sell stocks short during after-hours trading. During after-hours trading (i.e., after the market closes and before it opens), an uptick is not required to sell short. If the desired quantity of shares is available, you can simply sell short at the current best bid. Later, I'll discuss this more under "Shorting Tips".

Holders, ETFs, and Indexes

You are allowed to short Exchange Traded Funds (ETFs), AMEX holders, and indexes without an uptick.

Similar to indexes, holders and ETFs are generally comprised of a collection of companies related to specific sectors or industries such as the Semiconductors, Internet, Biotechnology, and so on. Example indexes, holders and ETFs include QQQ, SPY, HHH, DIA, SMH, BBH, BHH, SOX, OEX, and OIH. There are many more than the few examples I've listed here just for illustration purposes. ETFs and holders have become quite popular in recent years so new ones are constantly being introduced as their popularity continues to grow.

The following chart is an example of the Diamonds (DIA), which is representative of the overall Dow Jones Industrial Average. Since no uptick rule applies, you could short the DIA at the current best bid.

If you can't get shares of a specific stock that you want to short, you could consider using ETFs, holders or indexes instead. They can also be useful in situations where you think an entire sector or the overall market is going lower but you need to act quickly and don't have time to pick specific stocks to short.

Another reason you might use them is to further reduce risk. If you feel strongly that an entire industry or sector is likely to go lower but are uncertain about which specific stocks will go down, you can spread your risk across a collection of companies by using ETFs, holders, or indexes.

Stocks Under $5

At one time, you could rarely short stocks that were priced under $5.00. However, more brokers are beginning to allow this. You'll need to check with your specific broker regarding their policies related to this.

Though I might occasionally short a stock that is priced under $5.00, such as when I think a company could be going out of business, generally the stocks I short are priced higher.

Penny Stocks

Due to their high-risk, speculative nature, shorting penny stocks is not allowed, regardless of the price. Most penny stocks sell for less than $1 but even if they are over $5, shorting penny stocks is generally not permitted.

Shorting Tips

Limit Orders

Generally, you should use limit orders rather than market orders when shorting stocks. Using market orders increases the risk of getting shares at unfavorable prices, particularly when prices are changing quickly.

If the price is dropping and you place a market order to sell short, your order may not execute until the price bottoms and buyers step in to generate the required uptick. As a result, your market order could fill at the worst possible price.

However, there are a few instances when you could consider using a market order to ensure your order will be filled, if you use reasonable care and discretion. In the case of indexes, holders, and ETFs, which were discussed earlier in this chapter, since the prices tend to move more slowly, you could consider using a market order. Once again, you should take into account the specific conditions that exist at the time you place your order, such as how volatile and fast the price action is, and then decide the best course of action accordingly.

In general, you need to use limit orders to also ensure your trade is executed as planned. The risk/reward for a trade is based upon your planned entry and exit prices, so using limit orders ensures your orders will fill according to your plan. If you use a market order and get filled at an unfavorable price, then the risk/reward of the trade may no longer be in your favor. Even worse, it could now be a very poor trade that you have virtually no chance to recoup on.

Level II Quotes

You should use a good direct access broker and Level II quote system to accurately gauge the buying and selling pressure concerning your trades, and consequently, to determine where to place your limit orders to get the best fills. This not only applies to shorting, it applies to trading in general.

When you place an order, you need to know how it fits in with the overall order flow. This simply isn't possible using Level I quotes consisting only of the best bid, best ask, and last price. As you'll see in a moment, a Level II quote display shows how orders are stacking up on each side of the market beyond the best bid and best ask. This lets you see whether there are more buyers or sellers present, not only at the inside bid and ask, but at prices further away from the best bid and best ask as well.

Many web-based brokers may advertise fast order executions or lower commissions, but after slippage, lost profits, and 3rd party handling tradeoffs are factored into the costs, you will generally pay more over time than any additional upfront costs associated with using a direct access trading platform that supplies Level II quotes. More importantly, in order to compete with other traders, you need the split-second execution speeds that a good direct access broker provides. Regardless of which broker you use, it should be one that gives you direct access to the market. You are invited to visit www.trendfund.com for our latest recommendations.

The following illustration shows a Level II quote snapshot for INTC. However, it's important to keep in mind that the Level II quotes shown in this book are for illustration purposes only. They reflect snapshots of prices that occurred at the specific instant the screens were captured. A Level II quote screen is constantly changing so a few minutes later, or even seconds later with volatile stocks, the quotes could be completely different.

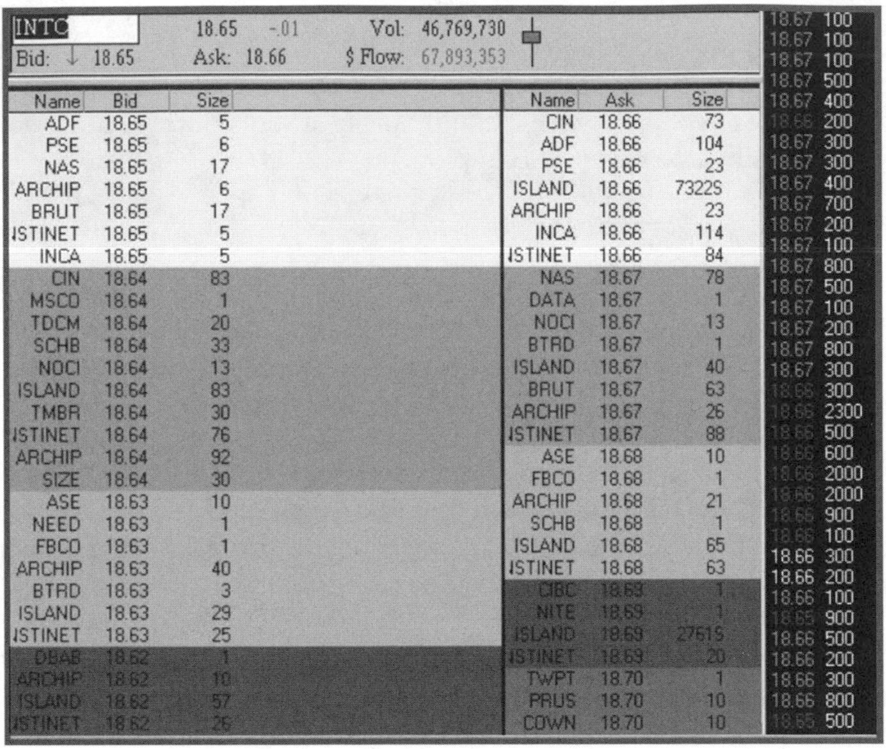

INTC 18.65 -.01 Vol: 46,769,730
Bid: ↓ 18.65 Ask: 18.66 $ Flow: 67,893,353
Name Bid Size
ADF 18.65 5
PSE 18.65 6
NAS 18.65 17
ARCHIP 18.65 6
BRUT 18.65 17
ISTINET 18.65 5
INCA 18.65 5
CIN 18.64 83
MSCO 18.64 1
TDCM 18.64 20
SCHB 18.64 33
NOCI 18.64 13
ISLAND 18.64 83
TMBR 18.64 30
ISTINET 18.64 76
ARCHIP 18.64 92
SIZE 18.64 30
ASE 18.63 10
NEED 18.63 1
FBCO 18.63 1
ARCHIP 18.63 40
BTRD 18.63 3
ISLAND 18.63 29
ISTINET 18.63 25
Name Ask Size
CIN 18.66 73
ADF 18.66 104
PSE 18.66 23
ISLAND 18.66 7322S
ARCHIP 18.66 23
INCA 18.66 114
ISTINET 18.66 84
NAS 18.67 78
DATA 18.67 1
NOCI 18.67 13
BTRD 18.67 1
ISLAND 18.67 40
BRUT 18.67 63
ARCHIP 18.67 26
ISTINET 18.67 88
ASE 18.68 10
FBCO 18.68 1
ARCHIP 18.68 21
SCHB 18.68 1
ISLAND 18.68 65
ISTINET 18.68 63
TWPT 18.70 1
PRUS 18.70 10
COWN 18.70 10

For those of you that might not be familiar with Level II quote displays, here's a brief overview of the key elements, keeping in mind that the specific layout might vary slightly between brokers. At the top of the screen, you'll see the stock ticker symbol, or INTC in this case; the best bid and best ask (the inside quotes); the last price; the volume; and the order flow.

Of particular importance for shorting, notice the small arrow next to the word "Bid". This reflects the current tick. The arrow points up for an uptick, and down for a downtick, as in this case. The tick arrow needs to be pointing up to satisfy the uptick rule that applies to shorting stocks.

The price list in the left pane shows the buy orders, and the price list in the right pane shows the sell orders. The order lists are grouped chronologically and according to price. The inside prices, or the best bid and the best ask, are at the top of the lists. Though this illustration is shown in gray, each quote list is actually color-coded. This is done so you can easily see at a glance how many orders exist at each price level. Each price level is displayed using a different color. Most brokers let you customize many of these features to your own liking.

Each price list shows the name of the market maker or electronic exchange network (ECN), the price, and the size of the order. The size of the order is typically the number of shares in hundreds, meaning, you need to add two zeros to the end of the displayed size to get the total number of shares. For example, 5 would be 500 shares.

On the far right, you'll see the *time and sales* pane. It shows the time and size of executed orders (this can usually be customized and may include other information), which can be very useful for tracking the order flow. You'll want to pay attention to whether orders are predominately executing at the best bid, which could indicate selling pressure, or at the best ask, which could indicate buying pressure. Of course, this should also be used in conjunction with the size of the orders and the amount of pending orders at a given price in the price list panes as well.

I'll provide more Level II quote screen examples later in this chapter that illustrate various issues related to shorting stocks. Meanwhile, hopefully you can see the many benefits of using a Level II quote display over Level I quotes. If you are currently using a web-based broker, I strongly encourage you to consider switching to a direct access broker and a Level II quote system. After all, it's your money that's at stake, so you should use the best tools available and play to win!

Buyers Wanted

As I mentioned earlier, in order to sell short you need buyers for your shares. Therefore, it's easier to enter a position when shorting into strength. If you wait for a sell-off to begin, it may hard to sell short due to both the uptick rule, and the lack of buyers.

A short trade may require a bit more courage and conviction at times. You may need to enter a trade sooner than you would when buying long, and you may need to trade contrary to everyone else. For example, when shorting into strength, you are entering a short position betting that a stock's price will subsequently go down at the same time other people are buying betting the price will go even higher. Since I'm primarily a trend trader, I'm generally playing a strong, high-percentage trend that provides a great risk/reward potential. Trusting the trend makes it easier to go against the crowd. Shorting a gap up, which is covered in the "Trading Gaps" chapter, is only one example of this. When shorting gap ups, you are frequently going against the crowd and shorting in the midst of a flurry of buying activity.

As I discussed in the preceding section, to help determine when to enter a short, you really need to use Level II quotes. On your Level II quote screen, you can watch for indications that buying is beginning to taper off and selling is beginning to increase. As this occurs, you'll notice the overall quantity and sizes of sell orders increase while the quantity and sizes of buy orders decrease. The time and sales display shows trades beginning to shift from the best ask to the best bid, or to a more evenly divided mix between the two. When the timing looks most favorable for a price pull back, but without waiting too long, enter your short position. With a little practice and experience, the timing of your entries and exits will improve. Later, under "How To Short", I'll provide some additional Level II quote information and examples.

Since you must short into strength, and since no one can pick the exact tops or bottoms every time, it's more likely that a short trade will go against you a little at first. As always, you should still protect yourself against losses with a stop-loss order. However, taking into consideration the need to short into strength, and depending on the circumstances and your risk tolerance, you might want to give the price a little extra room to fluctuate. If using a wider stop exceeds your risk tolerance, you can also consider using a smaller lot size to reduce risk.

When shorting outside of regular market hours under reduced liquidity conditions, and when shorting thinly traded stocks, remember to consider the quantity of shares on the best bid. If someone is bidding to buy 300 shares and you are trying to short 1000 shares, you aren't likely to get your 1000 shares, not unless other buyers come along at the same price. Later, I'll provide specific examples pertaining to shorting thinly traded stocks.

Shorting After-Hours

An uptick isn't required to short stocks outside of regular market hours. You can simply short at the current best bid when using a direct access broker (some web-based brokers may not allow you to short during after-hours trading).

I especially like to take advantage of this when shorting gap ups. Since gaps are such high percentage trends, I will frequently enter a short position on a large gap up by placing an order at, or slightly below, the best bid during pre-market trading without being subject to the uptick rule. For example, if EBAY is gapping up by a $1.50 in the morning, you could go short pre-market for the full $1.50 at the best bid. Generally, you won't have trouble getting filled on large volume stocks such as EBAY. The "Trading Gaps" and "Trading Gaps Using Technical Analysis" chapters provide detailed information about trading gaps.

Similar to trading pre-market, you can also trade post-market without being subject to the uptick rule. For example, frequently stocks that report earnings "run up" during after-hours trading. If you know that historically a particular stock you are tracking does this, and then subsequently pulls back, you might consider taking a short position during after-hours trading. Since no uptick rule applies, once again, you can enter a short position at the best bid.

Volume And Liquidity

Though you can profit from shorting both low and high volume stocks, the easiest stocks to short are those with high liquidity, or high volume. The higher the volume is, the greater the liquidity.

This is intended to be just a general guideline rather than a firm rule, because I do like to short low volume stocks as well. You can make good money trading thinly traded stocks, but the risks can also be greater. Therefore, it's important to understand what you are doing, and to take into consideration a variety of issues that apply to trading low volume stocks. I'll discuss these in more detail and provide some specific examples later in this chapter under the "Shorting Thinly Traded Stocks" section.

Generally, I prefer highly liquid stocks, particularly when I'm trading a large lot size. It's just much easier to get in and out of positions when the volume is high because a larger number of shares are changing hands. I consider highly liquid stocks to be those that tend to trade over a million shares a day. Examples include stocks such as INTC, MSFT, DELL, and IBM, but there are many others as well.

Another benefit to trading highly liquid stocks is that they tend to have tighter point spreads and more gradual price changes (though not always). The spread between the bid and ask might only be one or two cents while a low volume stock could be ten cents, twenty cents, or even larger.

When trading low volume stocks, a potential advantage, or disadvantage depending on which side of the trade you happen to be on, is the price can change very rapidly once it begins to move. This is great if the trade is in your favor but you can also take a huge hit before getting out when the trade goes against you. You could have a hard time finding sellers, which could make it difficult to *buy to cover* your short position. It really comes down to the overall risk/reward of a given trade. Though there is the potential for greater gains, there is also the potential for greater losses.

Still, many traders, including me, play low volume stocks as well as high volume stocks. You can take into consideration the pluses and minuses of each and decide according to your own preferences and risk tolerance. As mentioned, I'll provide specific examples that apply to trading low volume stocks later in this chapter.

Falling Prices

If prices are falling quickly, it can sometimes be difficult to enter a short position using limit orders. You may no sooner place an order than the price falls below your limit price. That doesn't mean you should use a market order, however.

A technique I use to help ensure my order fills is to set the limit price for my order a reasonable distance below the current best bid according to the minimum price that I'm willing to accept as an entry for the trade. This lets me get ahead of the rapidly falling price and provides a reasonable range in which the price can temporarily uptick so my order can fill. Of course, the risk/reward for a given trade should remain favorable even after allowing for a somewhat lower entry price.

For example, suppose that I believe a stock currently priced at $25.50 is going to decline by about $1.50, and the price has already begun fall. I might put in a limit order to short the stock with my limit price set at $25.35. Since the potential upside for the trade (or the downside move on the stock) is still far greater than the additional $0.15 risk, the risk/reward for the trade remains favorable. And, my order could fill at a higher price, such as $25.48 or whatever. But even if it doesn't, I would be satisfied with entering the trade at $25.35 or better. If my order still doesn't fill, so be it. I'll wait and watch for another opportunity or pass on the trade altogether.

Short Squeezes

Whenever you are shorting stocks, you should take into consideration the potential risk of getting caught in a *short squeeze*. A short squeeze can occur when the price of a stock that is heavily shorted, and/or the overall market, starts to rise. As the price goes up, people rush to buy to cover their short positions. This additional buying causes the price to climb even higher, which in turn compels more short sellers to cover their positions.

Depending on how the market is trending and the quantity of shorts, a short squeeze can sometimes take on a life of its own, feeding on itself as more and more short sellers cover their positions in conjunction with other investors jumping in on a perceived rally. As you might imagine, a short squeeze can result in very rapid price increases.

Here's an example of what can occur. Suppose the market has been trending down for a somewhat lengthy period of time. During this time, more and more people decide to take advantage of the downtrend by selling stocks short. The longer the downtrend lasts, the greater the number of shorts. Finally, the selling dries up, then the market bottoms and starts to bounce. At this point, short sellers rush to cover their positions, which can be the initial catalyst for a short squeeze.

By diligently using stop-loss orders, you can alleviate some, but not all, of the risk associated with a short squeeze. If the trade goes against you due to a short squeeze, your stop-loss order will trigger and limit your losses. However, in the case of short squeezes, the use of stop-losses can actually exacerbate the problem. Since many other traders use stop-losses as well, the triggering and execution of the stops can propel prices even higher, causing more stops to trigger, and so on until everyone is stopped out. Still, I recommend that you diligently use stop-loss orders to predefine and limit your risk on all of your long or short trades. Since risk management is such an important aspect of trading, I'll discuss the use of stop-loss orders in more detail in the next two chapters, and at other appropriate times throughout the book.

Later in this chapter, under "Shorting Thinly Traded Stocks", I'll provide additional information about short squeezes and examples that are applicable to trading low volume stocks.

How To Short

Placing Orders

The specific method of placing a short order varies between brokers but here is a general introduction for those of you that might be new to trading, or more specifically, new to shorting.

To sell short with some brokers, you simply place a sell order for a stock that you don't already own. The broker's system interprets this as a sell short order. Other brokers provide specific features for selling short. You might click an on-screen button labeled "Short" or select a "Sell Short" order type.

To exit a short position, you buy back the same amount of shares of the stock that you sold short. This is referred to as *covering* your short position with a *buy to cover* order. Again here, how this is accomplished can vary between brokers. It may be as simple as placing a regular buy order, or you might need to specify the type of order by selecting "Buy To Cover" or by clicking an on-screen button for that purpose.

If you are still uncertain about how to place an order, you should seek additional information from your broker.

Entering Short Positions

Now that you have a general background about shorting, I'll provide some Level II quote examples and discuss various factors that could affect your ability to enter a short position. In the next chapter, I'll also discuss how you can use technical analysis techniques to plan your short entries.

Generally, how easy it is to enter a position comes down to the amount of buying and selling pressure, the directional price bias, and the availability of shares at a given price.

The following illustration shows a Level II quote snapshot for INTC.

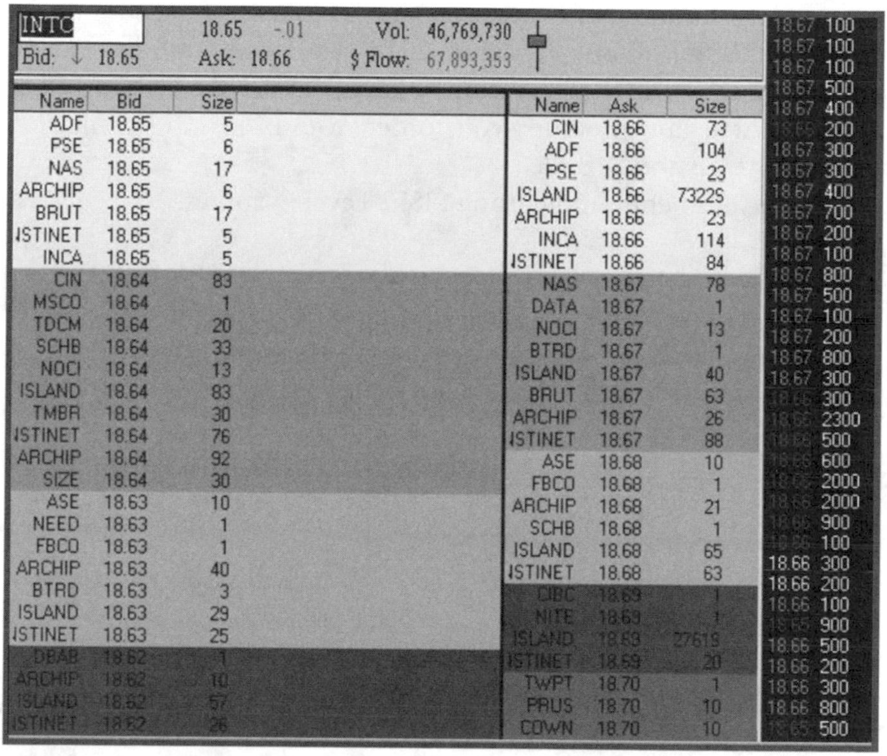

INTC
Bid: 18.65
18.65 -.01
Ask: 18.66
Vol: 46,769,730
$ Flow: 67,893,353
Name Bid Size
ADF 18.65 5
PSE 18.65 6
NAS 18.65 17
ARCHIP 18.65 6
BRUT 18.65 17
ISTINET 18.65 5
INCA 18.65 5
CIN 18.64 83
MSCO 18.64 1
TDCM 18.64 20
SCHB 18.64 33
NOCI 18.64 13
ISLAND 18.64 83
TMBR 18.64 30
ISTINET 18.64 76
ARCHIP 18.64 92
SIZE 18.64 30
ASE 18.63 10
NEED 18.63 1
FBCO 18.63 1
ARCHIP 18.63 40
BTRD 18.63 3
ISLAND 18.63 29
ISTINET 18.63 25
DBAB 18.62 1
ARCHIP 18.62 10
ISLAND 18.62 57
ISTINET 18.62 26
Name Ask Size
CIN 18.66 73
ADF 18.66 104
PSE 18.66 23
ISLAND 18.66 7322S
ARCHIP 18.66 23
INCA 18.66 114
ISTINET 18.66 84
NAS 18.67 78
DATA 18.67 1
NOCI 18.67 13
BTRD 18.67 1
ISLAND 18.67 40
BRUT 18.67 63
ARCHIP 18.67 26
ISTINET 18.67 88
ASE 18.68 10
FBCO 18.68 1
ARCHIP 18.68 21
SCHB 18.68 1
ISLAND 18.68 65
ISTINET 18.68 63
CIBC 18.69 1
NITE 18.69 1
ISLAND 18.69 27619
ISTINET 18.69 20
TWPT 18.70 1
PRUS 18.70 10
COWN 18.70 10

Looking at the preceding Level II quote screen, you can see that the best bid is $18.65 and the best ask is $18.66. Also notice the quantity of shares is biased toward the sell side, meaning there is currently more shares for sell at the best ask than there are buyers at the best bid. In determining this, remember to consider more than just the topmost order only. You need to consider all of the orders at a given price. For example, at the best bid price of $18.65, there are orders for the following quantities of shares (they are shown in lots of one hundred): 500, 600, 1700, 600, 1700, 500, and 500 for a total of 6100 shares. It's easy to see there are considerably more shares on the sell side. At the moment, the downtick arrow reflects the downside bias as well.

At this point in time, since you need the stock to uptick and there are currently more sellers on the best ask than buyers on the best bid, you would likely have trouble shorting the stock at $18.66. Additionally, if you placed a short order at $18.66, your order will follow the other orders that are already lined up to sell at that price, so unless a large number of buyers stepped up to buy up all of the other shares that are ahead of you in line, your order wouldn't fill. Instead, if you wanted to short INTC, you could place a limit order around $18.63. If the required uptick occurs, your order would likely fill somewhere between $18.63 and $18.66.

Here is another example using MSFT Level II quotes.

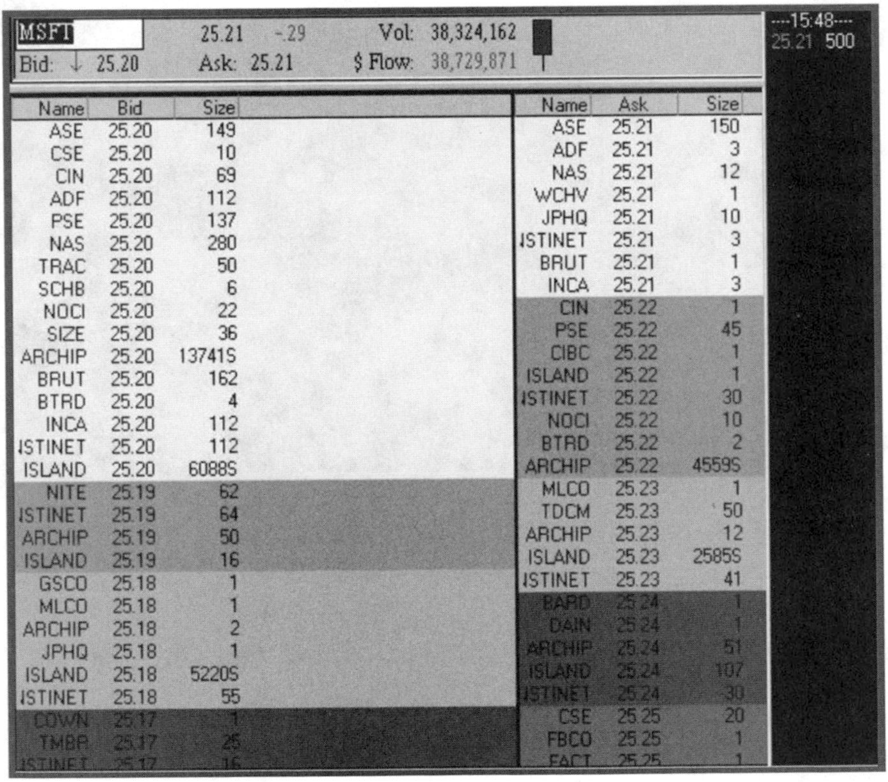

MSFT 25.21 -.29 Vol: 38,324,162
Bid: ↓ 25.20 Ask: 25.21 $ Flow: 38,729,871
----15:48----
25.21 500

Name	Bid	Size	Name	Ask	Size
ASE	25.20	149	ASE	25.21	150
CSE	25.20	10	ADF	25.21	3
CIN	25.20	69	NAS	25.21	12
ADF	25.20	112	WCHV	25.21	1
PSE	25.20	137	JPHQ	25.21	10
NAS	25.20	280	ISTINET	25.21	3
TRAC	25.20	50	BRUT	25.21	1
SCHB	25.20	6	INCA	25.21	3
NOCI	25.20	22	CIN	25.22	1
SIZE	25.20	36	PSE	25.22	45
ARCHIP	25.20	13741S	CIBC	25.22	1
BRUT	25.20	162	ISLAND	25.22	1
BTRD	25.20	4	ISTINET	25.22	30
INCA	25.20	112	NOCI	25.22	10
ISTINET	25.20	112	BTRD	25.22	2
ISLAND	25.20	6088S	ARCHIP	25.22	4559S
NITE	25.19	62	MLCO	25.23	1
ISTINET	25.19	64	TDCM	25.23	50
ARCHIP	25.19	50	ARCHIP	25.23	12
ISLAND	25.19	16	ISLAND	25.23	2585S
GSCO	25.18	1	ISTINET	25.23	41
MLCO	25.18	1	BARD	25.24	1
ARCHIP	25.18	2	DAIN	25.24	1
JPHQ	25.18	1	ARCHIP	25.24	51
ISLAND	25.18	5220S	ISLAND	25.24	107
ISTINET	25.18	55	ISTINET	25.24	30
COWN	25.17	1	CSE	25.25	20
TMBR	25.17	25	FBCO	25.25	1
ISTINET	25.17	16	FACT	25.25	1

Unlike the prior INTC example, you could most likely enter a MSFT short position at the best ask of $25.21 due to the large number of orders on the best bid at $25.20, and the relatively low number of shares available at the best ask. Even though the illustration currently shows a downtick, if you could see the price action in realtime, you would see the arrow flip to an uptick periodically as buyers step in at $25.21.

Referring to the best bid and ask on the preceding MSFT chart, at first glance, it might appear that there is a relatively large order on the sell side. Notice the best ask shows ASE is offering 15,000 shares at $25.21. However, with further examination, you can see that ASE is also on the best bid as well.

Most stocks have a dominant market maker, referred to as the AX, who is responsible for making a market for the stock. The AX is generally the most active and influential market maker for a stock. Consequently, the AX has considerable influence on the direction of a stock's price, depending on whether he/she has a lot of shares to buy or sell. As a general rule, if you can spot the AX for a stock, you should trade on the same side as the AX, rather than against him. Since many of the larger firms like Lehman Brothers, Goldman Sachs, Solomon Smith Barney, and so on, are now hiding behind popular ECNs such as ISLD, ARCA, and BRTD, it's somewhat less important than it once was to determine the AX for large stocks (like MSFT, etc.). Many of the popular ECNs used to be traded primarily by daytraders, but now when large firms have a large amount of buying or selling to do, they will frequently place their orders through an ECN to hide their actions. When firms trade through an ECN, their names don't show up as the market maker in the LEVEL II quote list. Instead, you'll see the name of the ECN.

Referring back to the preceding illustration, on this day, ASE appears to be the AX for MSFT. Though it's beyond the scope of this discussion on shorting stocks to go into more detail about the role of market makers and the AX, I provided this general explanation because the quantity of shares being offered by ASE on the best ask is probably meaningless. Unless the stock is being accumulated, it's likely ASE would pull the ask and/or bump the price higher, if any significant buying began.

Following is an example Level II quote screen for IBM, a stock that is listed on the NYSE rather than the Nasdaq.

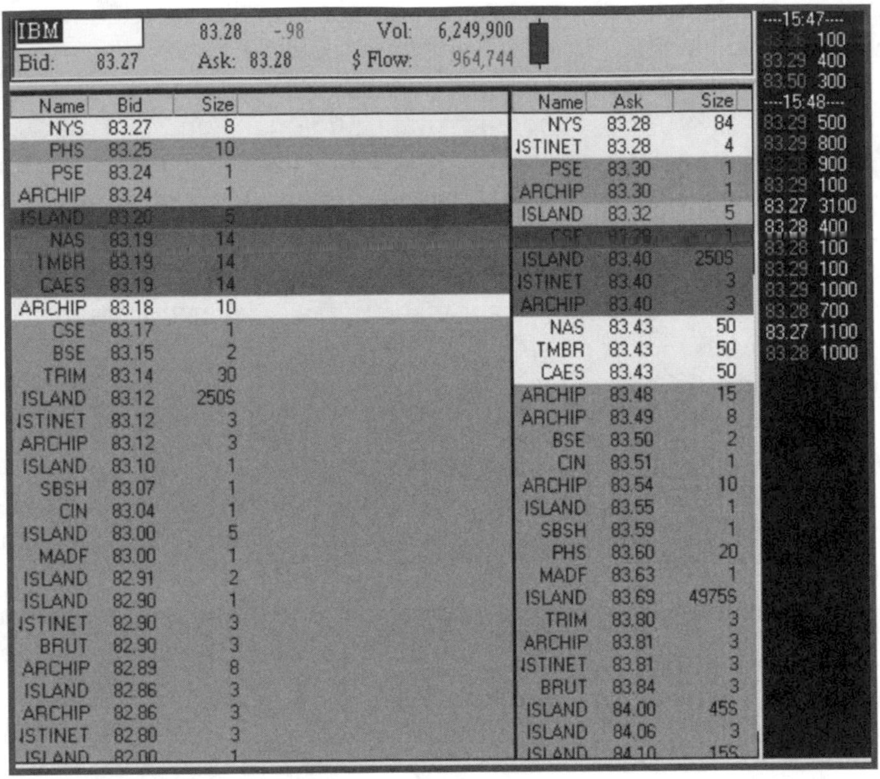

IBM	83.28	-.98	Vol:	6,249,900
Bid: 83.27	Ask: 83.28		$ Flow:	964,744

Name	Bid	Size
NYS	83.27	8
PHS	83.25	10
PSE	83.24	1
ARCHIP	83.24	1
ISLAND	83.20	5
NAS	83.19	14
TMBR	83.19	14
CAES	83.19	14
ARCHIP	83.18	10
CSE	83.17	1
BSE	83.15	2
TRIM	83.14	30
ISLAND	83.12	250S
ISTINET	83.12	3
ARCHIP	83.12	3
ISLAND	83.10	1
SBSH	83.07	1
CIN	83.04	1
ISLAND	83.00	5
MADF	83.00	1
ISLAND	82.91	2
ISLAND	82.90	1
ISTINET	82.90	3
BRUT	82.90	3
ARCHIP	82.89	8
ISLAND	82.86	3
ARCHIP	82.86	3
ISTINET	82.80	3
ISLAND	82.00	1

Name	Ask	Size
NYS	83.28	84
ISTINET	83.28	4
PSE	83.30	1
ARCHIP	83.30	1
ISLAND	83.32	5
CSE	[illegible]	1
ISLAND	83.40	250S
ISTINET	83.40	3
ARCHIP	83.40	3
NAS	83.43	50
TMBR	83.43	50
CAES	83.43	50
ARCHIP	83.48	15
ARCHIP	83.49	8
BSE	83.50	2
CIN	83.51	1
ARCHIP	83.54	10
ISLAND	83.55	1
SBSH	83.59	1
PHS	83.60	20
MADF	83.63	1
ISLAND	83.69	4975S
TRIM	83.80	3
ARCHIP	83.81	3
ISTINET	83.81	3
BRUT	83.84	3
ISLAND	84.00	45S
ISLAND	84.06	3
ISLAND	84.10	15S

----15:47----	
[illegible]	100
83.29	400
83.50	300
----15:48----	
83.29	500
83.29	800
[illegible]	900
83.29	100
83.27	3100
83.28	400
83.28	100
83.29	100
83.29	1000
83.28	700
83.27	1100
83.28	1000

Looking at the preceding Level II quotes, once again, it's not likely a short order would fill at the $83.28 best ask since fewer shares exist on the top level bids than are being offered on the best ask. Notice that there are currently 8400 shares being offered at $83.28 and only 2500 shares on the bids all the way down to $83.20 (800+1000+100+100+500). Upon further examination of the Level II quotes, you can see there are quite a few bids at $83.19. So, if I wanted to short IBM, I would place a limit order at $83.20. If an uptick occurs, my order would likely fill somewhere between $83.20 and $83.28.

Here is a Level II quote screen for the Diamonds Index (DIA).

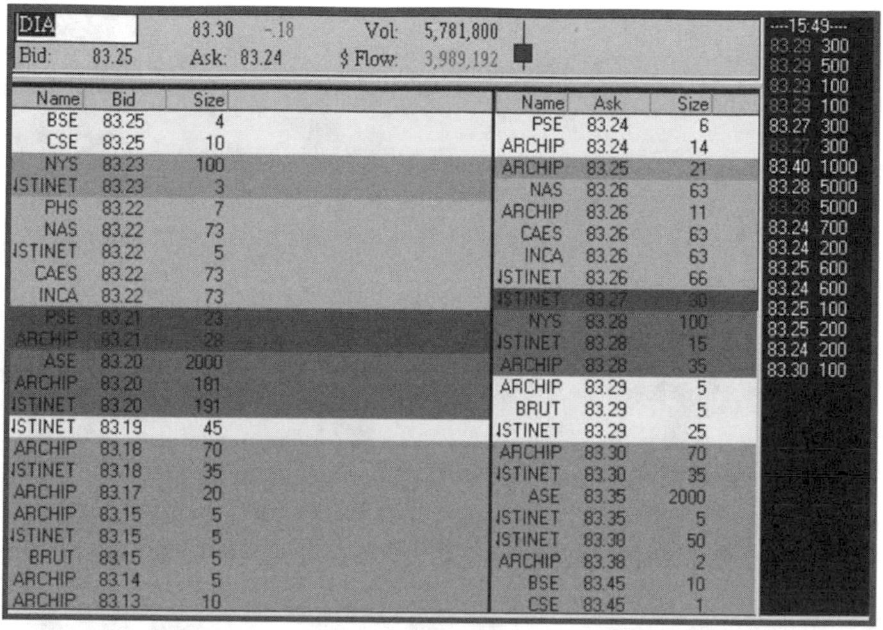

DIA
83.30 -.18
Vol: 5,781,800
Bid: 83.25
Ask: 83.24
$ Flow: 3,989,192
Name Bid Size
BSE 83.25 4
CSE 83.25 10
NYS 83.23 100
ISTINET 83.23 3
PHS 83.22 7
NAS 83.22 73
ISTINET 83.22 5
CAES 83.22 73
INCA 83.22 73
PSE 83.21 23
ARCHIP 83.21 28
ASE 83.20 2000
ARCHIP 83.20 181
ISTINET 83.20 191
ISTINET 83.19 45
ARCHIP 83.18 70
ISTINET 83.18 35
ARCHIP 83.17 20
ARCHIP 83.15 5
ISTINET 83.15 5
BRUT 83.15 5
ARCHIP 83.14 5
ARCHIP 83.13 10
Name Ask Size
PSE 83.24 6
ARCHIP 83.24 14
ARCHIP 83.25 21
NAS 83.26 63
ARCHIP 83.26 11
CAES 83.26 63
INCA 83.26 63
ISTINET 83.26 66
ISTINET 83.27 30
NYS 83.28 100
ISTINET 83.28 15
ARCHIP 83.28 35
ARCHIP 83.29 5
BRUT 83.29 5
ISTINET 83.29 25
ARCHIP 83.30 70
ISTINET 83.30 35
ASE 83.35 2000
ISTINET 83.35 5
ISTINET 83.38 50
ARCHIP 83.38 2
BSE 83.45 10
CSE 83.45 1
----15:49----
83.29 300
83.29 500
83.29 100
83.29 100
83.27 300
83.27 300
83.40 1000
83.28 5000
83.28 5000
83.24 700
83.24 200
83.25 600
83.24 600
83.25 100
83.25 200
83.24 200
83.30 100

Since an uptick isn't required for holders, ETFs, and indexes, you could short the DIA at the $83.25 best bid shown in the preceding illustration, as long as the amount of shares you are selling short doesn't exceed the number being offered at the best bid. If they do exceed the amount of shares available at the best bid, you could get a partial fill. To help ensure your order fills entirely, you could adjust your limit price lower to also include shares that are being offered at lower price levels, such as the 10,000 shares being offered at $83.23 in the preceding example.

You may have noticed that at the moment the quotes were captured, the best ask temporarily displayed as $83.24, which is lower than the best bid. This is referred to as a locked market. The quotes/trades are generally updated quickly to resolve the discrepancy. At any rate, you shouldn't have any trouble getting a limit order filled to sell short at the current best bid, or $83.25 in this case, if the desired number of shares are available.

Following is another momentum stock example that shows a Level II quote screen for EBAY.

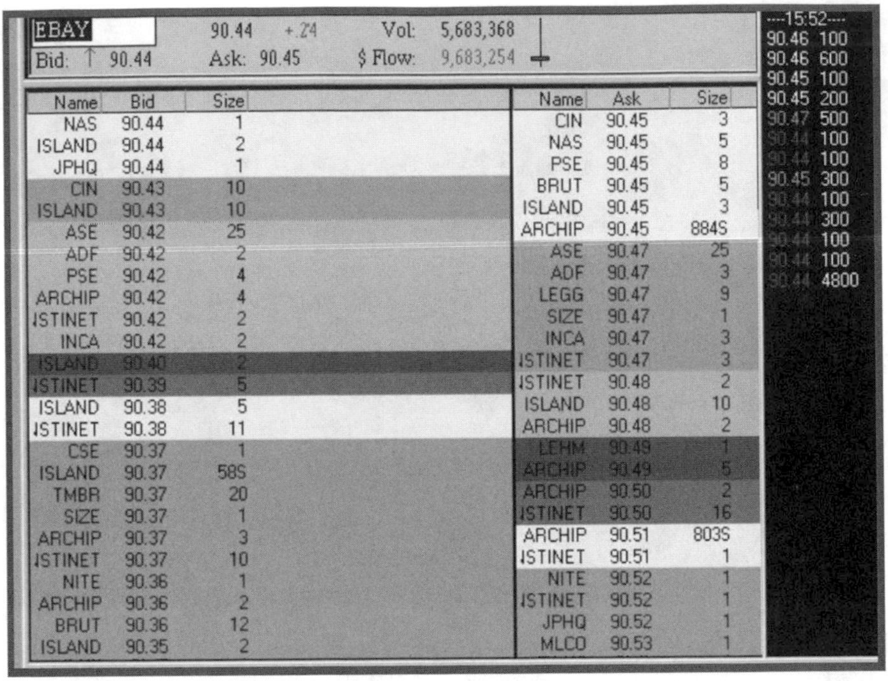

EBAY
90.44 +.24
Vol: 5,683,368
Bid: 90.44
Ask: 90.45
$ Flow: 9,683,254
Name Bid Size
NAS 90.44 1
ISLAND 90.44 2
JPHQ 90.44 1
CIN 90.43 10
ISLAND 90.43 10
ASE 90.42 25
ADF 90.42 2
PSE 90.42 4
ARCHIP 90.42 4
ISTINET 90.42 2
INCA 90.42 2
ISLAND 90.40 2
ISTINET 90.39 5
ISLAND 90.38 5
ISTINET 90.38 11
CSE 90.37 1
ISLAND 90.37 58S
TMBR 90.37 20
SIZE 90.37 1
ARCHIP 90.37 3
ISTINET 90.37 10
NITE 90.36 1
ARCHIP 90.36 2
BRUT 90.36 12
ISLAND 90.35 2
Name Ask Size
CIN 90.45 3
NAS 90.45 5
PSE 90.45 8
BRUT 90.45 5
ISLAND 90.45 3
ARCHIP 90.45 884S
ASE 90.47 25
ADF 90.47 3
LEGG 90.47 9
SIZE 90.47 1
INCA 90.47 3
ISTINET 90.47 3
ISTINET 90.48 2
ISLAND 90.48 10
ARCHIP 90.48 2
LEHM 90.49 1
ARCHIP 90.49 5
ARCHIP 90.50 2
ISTINET 90.50 16
ARCHIP 90.51 803S
ISTINET 90.51 1
NITE 90.52 1
ISTINET 90.52 1
JPHQ 90.52 1
MLCO 90.53 1
----15:52----
90.46 100
90.46 600
90.45 100
90.45 200
90.47 500
90.44 100
90.44 100
90.45 300
90.44 100
90.44 300
90.44 100
90.44 100
90.44 4800

Looking at the preceding quotes for EBAY, you would likely be able to fill a short position if you placed a limit order at $90.42. Since it would be $0.03 under the current best bid and the stock is currently upticking, your order would likely fill. Even though there are slightly more sellers at the best ask, if you take into consideration the price levels just beyond the inside prices, the buyers and sellers are actually fairly evenly matched. Additionally, EBAY tends to be a very liquid stock, so a sell order placed below the best bid will likely fill.

When liquid stocks, such as in the case of the preceding EBAY example, are essentially trading flat or moving higher, you generally don't have much trouble getting a fill on a short position. However, many traders frequently wait until stocks are selling off, or have already sold off, to short them. At that point, it's easy to see they are going lower, so everyone wants to jump in for a ride. The problem is, the reason they have gone down is because there were either no buyers at higher prices, or there were many more sellers than buyers. As a result, it can be difficult to get shares once the selling begins. Traders trying to get in on the move will frequently get filled after the stock has already sold off, hoping it will go even lower. Instead, they often end up getting filled near the bottom then the stock reverses and they get blown out of the trade.

I tend to trade contrary to what everyone else is doing. Usually, when everyone else is overly bullish, that's when we are nearing a top. Everyone is in a position so the buying dries up, and only sellers remain. Similarly, when everyone is bearish, we could be nearing a bottom for the same reason. Since I'm a trend trader, I'm usually also playing a strong, high percentage trend in this context, which enhances the potential risk/reward even further.

As with any trade, once you have entered a short position, you should immediately place a stop-loss order to define and limit your risk on the trade, according to your own predetermined tolerance for risk. I'll provide more specific information about managing risk and using stop-loss orders in later chapters.

Shorting Using Technical Analysis

Though it's beyond the scope of this book to explain the extensive range of tools that are used to perform technical analysis, there are a few well-known charting techniques you might find beneficial for planning short trades. I'll discuss those here then if you would like to learn more about charting and technical analysis, there are many good books you can explore that are devoted solely to the topic. You can also check our web site at www.trendfund.com for our latest book recommendations. In the "Trading Gaps Using Technical Analysis" chapter, I discuss some additional techniques that can also be applied to shorting.

About Support And Resistance

You can use levels of support and resistance to help determine entry and exit price targets for short trades. For those of you that might be unfamiliar with these terms, a brief description of each follows.

As a stock's price increases, it eventually reaches a point where the majority of people that are interested in buying the stock feel it has gotten too expensive, so they put off buying it. Additionally, people that already own the stock may decide to take advantage of the high prices and take profits. Regardless of which is the dominant factor, the end result is the stock's price resists going any higher. This is referred to as a *resistance.*

Alternatively, the same is true when the price of a stock falls. At some point, it becomes sufficiently inexpensive that people interested in the stock start buying it, and/or sellers that want out have closed their positions. The stock's price quits falling and is said to have *support* at the price where this occurs.

The following chart shows examples of support and resistance.

Shorting Into Resistance

You can use levels of resistance as potential entry points for short trades. When resistance is encountered, the price often reverses, even if the reversal is only temporary. The following chart of MMM shows an example of resistance.

The line that appears across the top of the preceding chart connects a series of price swing point highs. Since MMM's price repeatedly tried but could not substantially break through this price level, a strong level of resistance is established and confirmed. Generally, the more times a level of resistance holds, the stronger it becomes.

Notice on the chart that each time the price reached the prior level of resistance, the price declined shortly afterwards. When you see levels of resistance such as this for stocks that you intend to short, you can use them as potential entry targets. Looking at the preceding chart, if you had entered a short position each time the price hit the resistance level, you would have had a series of very profitable trades.

After entering a short position based upon resistance, you should immediately place a stop-loss order slightly above the level of resistance. If the resistance is broken through, you will stop out of the trade with a small loss. A break through resistance is an indication of strength, which means the price could go higher. Give your stop a bit of wiggle room, though, since the price may occasionally go above the resistance a bit before pulling back.

The risk/reward for this type of trade is great because your risk is limited and predefined according to the placement of your stop, which is typically only a short distance above the resistance. You also have an established trend on your side. Resistance that has been tested and confirmed is more likely to hold than to break, which further enhances the risk/reward of the trade. As I mentioned earlier, the more times resistance has been tested and successfully held, the stronger it becomes. However, if the resistance is broken through, you'll stop out of the trade according to your predefined risk.

Though this example applies to shorting stocks, you could reverse this strategy and use a stock's support level for entering long a position, and as a potential exit point for a short position. You should use caution and watch your shorts closely as the price reaches prior levels of support, since the price could bounce at this point. If you aren't yet ready to take profits, you may want to at least tighten your stops to help ensure your gains are preserved. Always remember that Pigs get slaughtered and NO ONE ever went broke taking profits!

Shorting Support Breakdowns

A breakdown of support is a sign of weakness. It indicates buying pressure is declining and/or selling pressure is increasing. Therefore, you can use support breakdowns as potential price entry targets for short trades.

Looking at the preceding chart, notice that after the price broke through support, the downside momentum continued.

To trade a break of support, enter a short position after the breakdown occurs then place a stop-loss order slightly above the support level. You'll want to stop out of the trade if the price bounces back through the support significantly, since the breakdown could have just been an aberration and the price may continue higher. At any rate, it indicates the price isn't falling as anticipated, and whenever a trade isn't going according to the plan you should limit losses and stop out.

Similar to shorting resistance, it's a good idea to leave a bit of wiggle room with your stop-loss settings. Price swings may not stop precisely at support and resistance levels, so you don't want to prematurely stop out of a potentially profitable trade because support or resistance levels are exceeded slightly before holding.

Here's another example using DNA that shows a support breakdown of a range trend.

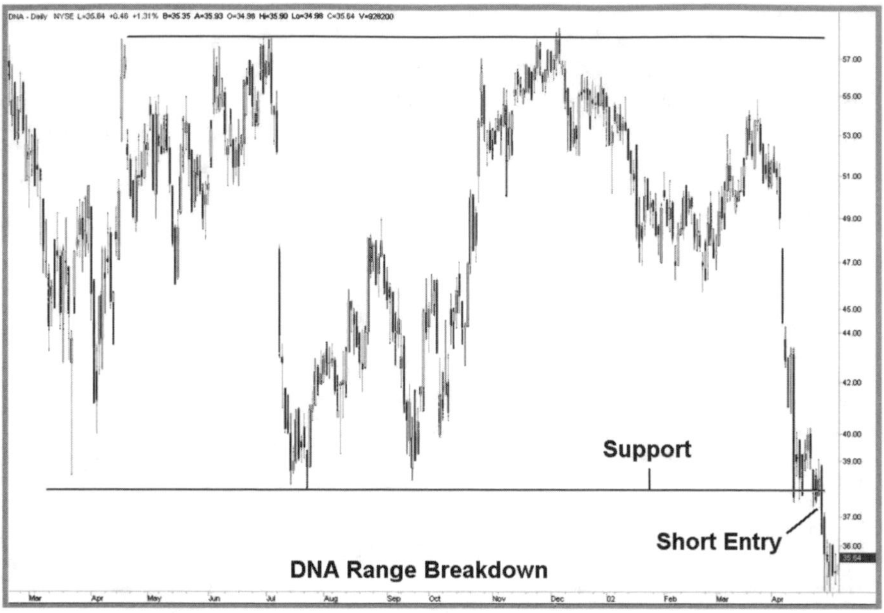

On the preceding chart, you can see how DNA was range bound for a period of time. You could enter a short position once the range is broken through to the downside, and as before, place a stop-loss order just above the prior support level in case the downside momentum doesn't continue as expected.

As with resistance, the more times support is tested and held, the stronger the support becomes. However, it's also why a breakdown of strong support indicates weakness and presents nice shorting opportunities. The risk/reward for this type of trade is also good, because once again, your risk is limited and predefined according to the placement of your stop-loss order.

Shorting Thinly Traded Stocks

Thinly traded stocks are stocks that trade on relatively low volume. For the most part, the frequency, quantity, and size of the trades tend to be low. As I mentioned earlier, thinly traded stocks offer nice profit opportunities. However, the potential risks are greater as well.

Here are some key points to consider when deciding whether to short thinly traded stocks. Some of these points are good, some are bad, and some can be downright ugly when you get caught on the wrong side of a trade.

- Prices have the potential to move very fast
- You have less control over order fills
- It's possible to *fake out* other traders and market makers
- It can be difficult to cover your position
- Spreads are often wider
- Short squeezes trigger easier

About Low Volume Stocks

Since the volume on thinly trades stocks is relatively low, any substantial buying or selling pressure can move the price more dramatically in a shorter period of time. If the price is moving in your favor, it's great! You can reap substantial profits in a very short timeframe. On the other hand, if the price goes against you, it can be difficult to get out of the trade, and you can take a huge hit in the effort. Unlike large volume stocks such as MSFT, which generally tend to move more slowly (unless there is a major news event or other catalyst), thinly traded stocks are capable of moving several points in a matter of minutes or hours. Later, I'll provide Level II quote examples to further illustrate these points.

Buyers and/or sellers may not always be present when trading low volume stocks. As a result, you have less control over your fill as opposed to trading stocks with higher volume and liquidity. The larger the lot sizes you trade, the more problematic this can become. For example, if a stock trades 20,000 shares a day, while you might be able to short a small 100-share lot, if you desire to short a reasonably large number of shares like I frequently do, you risk driving the price up or down just by going in and out of the trade. Similarly, if a sufficient number of shares aren't available at a reasonable or acceptable price, you could have trouble entering and/or exiting your position.

Another factor to consider when trading thinly traded stocks is the price spread. The spreads between the best bid and best ask tend to be wider. For example, the spread on highly liquid stocks, such as MSFT or INTC, might only be one or two cents. On thinly traded stocks, the spread might be in the range of ten cents, twenty cents, or even more. After entering a position, you can take a sizeable hit getting out due only to the size of the spread. On the other hand, there are times when you can take advantage of the spread and capture the difference for a profit.

Following is an example Level II quote screen for PRX, a thinly traded stock listed on the NYSE.

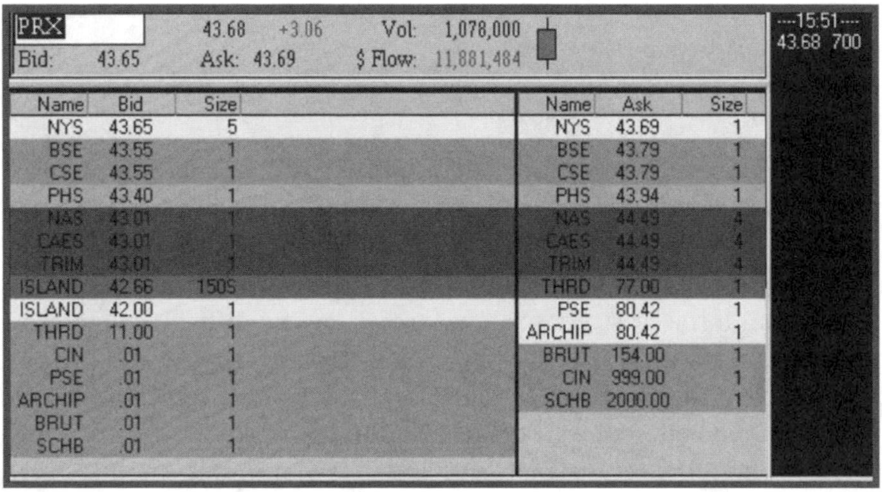

PRX 43.68 +3.06 Vol: 1,078,000

Bid: 43.65 Ask: 43.69 $ Flow: 11,881,484

----15:51----

43.68 700

Name	Bid	Size	Name	Ask	Size
NYS	43.65	5	NYS	43.69	1
BSE	43.55	1	BSE	43.79	1
CSE	43.55	1	CSE	43.79	1
PHS	43.40	1	PHS	43.94	1
NAS	43.01	1	NAS	44.49	4
CAES	43.01	1	CAES	44.49	4
TRIM	43.01	1	TRIM	44.49	4
ISLAND	42.66	150S	THRD	77.00	1
ISLAND	42.00	1	PSE	80.42	1
THRD	11.00	1	ARCHIP	80.42	1
CIN	.01	1	BRUT	154.00	1
PSE	.01	1	CIN	999.00	1
ARCHIP	.01	1	SCHB	2000.00	1
BRUT	.01	1			
SCHB	.01	1			

As you can see by looking at the preceding Level II quotes, the quantity of shares being offered on each side is low. Though the current bid is $43.65, only 500 shares are being offered at the bid, and less than 1000 shares are offered on the bids all the way down to a price of $43.01. Conversely, only four 100 share lots, or 400 shares total, are being offered on the sell side all the way up to $43.94. After which, the price jumps to $44.49.

Looking the preceding quotes, suppose you were in a 3000-share short position and needed to quickly cover your position. There are currently only 1600 shares being offered up to $44.49. Therefore, it's anybody's guess as to what price you could get out of the trade. You would essentially be at the market maker's mercy. If you put out an order to buy 3000 shares on the bid, it's very unlikely that it would fill. Once the market maker saw your large order appear, he would likely remove the current inside asks and the price would go up, probably to over $44.00. Regardless, as you can see by the low quantity of shares for sell, you would have to pay-up substantially to get out of your position. So, it's important to use more discretion and not overdo it when trading low volume stocks, or you could end up burying yourself in the trade.

Here's another thinly traded example using a Nasdaq stock, INFY.

INFY 43.50 -.30 Vol: 92,590
Bid: 43.43 Ask: 43.55 $ Flow: -1,173,316

Name	Bid	Size	Name	Ask	Size
NAS	43.43	1	NAS	43.55	2
BTRD	43.43	1	BRUT	43.55	2
BRUT	43.32	1	ADF	43.60	1
CIN	43.25	4	ISTINET	43.60	1
ISLAND	43.25	431S	INCA	43.60	1
ISLAND	43.20	1	NITE	43.70	4
ISLAND	43.11	5	FBCO	43.85	1
ISLAND	43.10	10	CIN	44.00	16
ISTINET	43.05	50S	JPHQ	44.00	1
SCHB	43.05	5	ISLAND	44.00	16
ISLAND	43.00	1	SCHB	44.00	10
NITE	43.00	5	MONT	44.10	1
MSCO	42.95	1	SIZE	44.20	1
ISLAND	42.51	10	SWST	44.25	1
SIZE	42.50	1	BTRD	44.30	1
ISTINET	42.11	20S	MSCO	44.50	1
WIEN	42.00	1	SBSH	44.50	1
ISLAND	42.00	35S	SUSQ	44.60	1
BERN	41.65	1	ISLAND	44.75	3
ISLAND	41.53	2	BERN	44.80	1
ISLAND	41.50	10S	HILL	45.00	1
ISLAND	41.00	210S	UBSW	45.00	1
UBSW	41.00	20	ISLAND	45.00	2875S
JPHQ	41.00	1	ABNA	45.50	1
MONT	40.35	1	BEST	45.65	1
SBSH	40.22	2	ISLAND	46.00	50S
SUSQ	40.05	1	LTCO	47.00	1
BEST	40.01	25	ISLAND	47.52	23S
HILL	40.00	1	ISLAND	47.90	50S
MLCO	40.00	1	WIEN	48.00	1
ABNA	39.00	1	ISLAND	48.00	17S
LTCO	39.00	1	ISLAND	49.00	50S
SWST	38.40	1	DBAB	50.00	1
ISTINET	38.00	10S	ISLAND	53.99	2
DBAB	37.00	1	ISLAND	55.72	1
FBCO	37.00	1	TWPT	58.00	1
TWPT	35.50	1	MLCO	65.65	1
ADF	35.00	500	ISTINET	67.67	5S
GSCO	35.00	1	GSCO	67.85	1
ISTINET	35.00	500	ISTINET	68.00	6S
INCA	35.00	500	ALLN	94.50	1
ISTINET	20.20	1	OTAA	100.00	1
ALLN	20.00	1			

----12:38----	
43.43	1000
43.50	200
43.43	300
43.43	600
----12:39----	
43.42	600
43.43	300
43.42	300
43.42	200
43.50	900
----12:40----	
43.50	100

As you can see on the preceding quote screen, INFY is another relatively thinly traded stock. There isn't any significant volume showing up on either side at, or near, the inside prices. Also notice the $0.12 spread between the best bid of $43.43 and the best ask $43.55. Even if you were able to get a fill on your short at the best bid, you would need to make up the $0.12 spread to break even.

As you can tell from examining these two prior examples, if you are on the right side of the trade, it could potentially move substantially in your favor. That's the advantage of playing thinly trade stocks. Conversely, if you are on the wrong side of the trade, it could just as easily move against you by 0.50, $1.00, or even more. And that's the downside.

Subject to your tolerance for risk, whether to trade low volume stocks is mainly a matter of personal preference and what works best for you. As is often the case in life and with trading, the greater the risk, the greater is the potential reward.

Faking It

You may recall that one of the key points I mentioned earlier is that you can sometimes fake out other traders or market makers when trading low volume stocks. A trick that I have sometimes used, and made money with, is called a *press*. However, using this technique and at the same time, remaining within your risk limit on a given trade, generally requires a large portfolio.

For those of you that might like to give it a try, here is how a press works. Using the preceding INFY Level II quotes as an example, suppose I currently hold 3000 shares of INFY short at $43.55 and would like to get out of the position. What I could do is put in a sell order at a somewhat higher price than the current inside price. It depends on the specific trade, but using this example, I might put in a sell order to sell 5000 shares at $43.56 or $43.57. I use a price slightly higher than the current best ask, which is $43.55 in this case. Even though I really don't want my order to fill, meaning I don't want more shares on the short side, there is always a possibility that my order could fill. Therefore, I only try this technique in situations where I am prepared to take the additional shares in the event my order actually fills. This is why I indicated it's a technique most suited to larger accounts.

The idea is to give everyone that is watching the quote screen the impression that selling pressure is increasing. It's not uncommon for someone else to jump in on the action with me, and put in additional sell orders.

If all goes well, buyers will think the selling pressure is increasing and cancel their buy orders. As a result, the price will subsequently decline and let me get out of my position, possibly with a nice profit.

This trick often works but you do need to be careful, and as I said, you need to be prepared to take on the additional shares short, just in case your order fills. Additionally, since your intent isn't really to add to your position, you need to watch the best ask closely. If the best ask moves higher and your order suddenly becomes the inside ask, then you should immediately cancel your order, or reset it to a higher price. Conversely, if the price does fall, I will frequently reset my order and follow the price down as well, just to keep the illusion going for as long as possible. But when doing so, I continue to stay slightly higher than the inside price.

This technique works best in a slow market. I don't recommend using it when prices are already moving quickly. Of course, you still need to exit your original short position at an appropriate point after *pressing* prices lower. The precise timing of your exit depends on the circumstances but it wouldn't be uncommon to get $0.50 or more out of the preceding trade using this technique.

The Big Squeeze

Although there is a potential for short squeezes to occur anytime you are shorting stocks, they can be particularly disconcerting when shorting thinly traded stocks. Should you get caught on the wrong side of a short squeeze while trading a low volume stock, things could get very ugly in a hurry!

All of the factors described earlier that apply to thinly traded stocks become even more exaggerated. A short squeeze can quickly become a feeding frenzy–at your expense. Prices could move dramatically against you. Plus, there will likely be even fewer shares available to buy, making it that much more difficult to cover your position and exit the trade. After all, if you were long the stock, why would you want to sell when the price is racing higher? You would likely wait until the price appears to be topping out.

The following chart of RMBS shows the kind of price action that can take place during a short squeeze.

As you can see by the preceding chart, a short squeeze can result in a dramatic price move. RMBS, having been somewhat controversial in recent times, was heavily shorted when positive news came out about the company. The price more than doubled in a matter of days. As the price went up, traders were either stopped out or otherwise forced to cover their short positions, which drove the price even higher. Adding to the momentum, investors and other traders were rushing in to buy the stock long based on the positive news.

If you happen to be long the stock when a short squeeze such as this occurs, you can reap the benefits of the squeeze. Fortunately, we were playing RMBS long for an earnings trend at the time of this short squeeze, which made for some very nice profits indeed! In fact, one of the reasons I chose to trade RMBS is because I knew it was heavily shorted at the time, which created the potential for a short squeeze if the stock ran into earnings according to its historical trends. The positive news that became the catalyst for the squeeze was an unexpected bonus. As you can see, the payoff on the trade in this case was great. Traders that were caught on the other side of the trade, however, were surely feeling the pain.

Of course, getting caught in a short squeeze is a worse case scenario but it is a factor you should consider when shorting stocks. And when shorting thinly traded stocks, it's even more important to take it into consideration due to the additional inherent risk that is associated with low volume trading.

4

Trading Gaps

I first touched on the concept of trading gaps in the "Intraday Primer" and the "Trading The Timeframes" sections of this book. This chapter provides more detailed gap related information. It explains what gaps are, what causes gaps, when gaps occur, and more. Suggestions and examples for trading both gap ups and gap downs are included.

The next chapter, "Trading Gaps Using Technical Analysis", supplements the information presented here with additional techniques for trading gaps that are based primarily upon charts and technical analysis. You'll find charting techniques there to determine specific price targets for entering and exiting gap trades.

As previously discussed, trading morning gaps is a great way to trade the market on a part-time basis. If you desire to trade part-time and can spare an hour or so in the mornings when the market first opens for trading, then I suggest you give trading gaps a try. And for full-time traders, gaps often provide some of the best trading opportunities of the day. I know many traders who merely trade the gap and "go home," having made their daily goals in an hour or less most days.

What Are Gaps?

There are essentially three ways that the price of a stock can open for trading relative to its prior closing price. It can open higher, lower, or at the same price.

When there is a difference between a stock's closing price and it's opening price, it is called a *gap*. If the opening price is higher than the prior closing price, it's called a *gap up*. If the price is lower, it's a *gap down*. When a stock opens at essentially the same price as the prior close, or the difference is very small, then it's considered to be a *flat* open.

The following table shows some price examples of gaps (chart examples are provided later).

Stock	Close	Open	Difference
INTC	$24.00	$24.62	$0.62 gap up
INTC	$25.00	$24.00	$1.00 gap down
INTC	$24.20	$24.22	$0.02 ~ flat

Table 41: Price Gap Examples

A stock that has a reasonable degree of liquidity rarely opens at exactly the same price as its prior close. Whether it is large, medium, or small, a stock generally gaps by some amount. However, if the price difference is so small that it is essentially a flat open, you generally shouldn't try to trade the open as a gap play since a price reversal is less certain (there's more about this later).

Gaps not only apply to individual stocks, they apply to the overall market as well. Since the market is a collection of individual stocks, if the market is gapping up or down significantly then a large number of individual stocks are likely gapping up or down as well.

The following chart shows a gap down of the Nasdaq Composite.

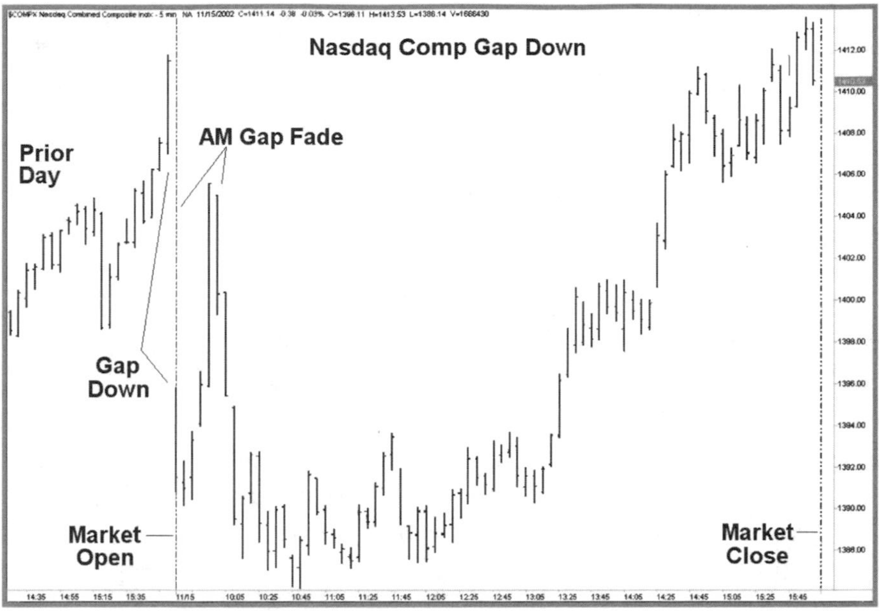

Chart examples with more detailed explanations are provided later. For the moment, just notice on the preceding chart that the Nasdaq Composite opened considerably lower, or gapped down, from where it closed the prior day, which means that a large number of technology stocks within the Nasdaq likely gapped down as well.

What Causes Gaps?

A variety of factors can cause the market or individual stocks to gap. Examples include late breaking news on specific stocks, earnings reports, analyst upgrades or downgrades, overnight futures trading, economic news, major world events, or simply an imbalance between supply and demand.

Regardless of the specific catalyst, gaps occur due to excess demand on the buy or sell side, which is further exaggerated by low volume trading that takes place outside of regular market hours. Since the total number of buyers and sellers is lower during post- and pre-market hours, any significant buying pressure pushes stock prices higher than would normally occur during regular market hours. The opposite is true when there is more selling pressure.

Emotions play a role as well. Large gaps often result from traders overreacting to news in after-hours trading. Not wanting to miss out on a big move, people get excited and buy or sell impulsively causing the prices to move even more dramatically.

Once the market opens and liquidity returns to normal, the exaggerated prices tend to correct themselves with a snapback price reversal. For an example, take a look at what happened on the prior chart of the Nasdaq Composite. After the large gap down, there was initially a snapback price reversal to the upside.

Understanding this, agile power traders can potentially profit by anticipating and trading these snapback price reversals. This is also called *fading the gap*. As the buying or selling pressure that caused the gap subsides, prices tend to *fade* in the opposite direction.

Filling the gap is when a stock, or the market, ends up retracing the entire gap at some point. A stock that closed at $25.50 and gapped up to $26.10 only to retrace the move back to $25.50 has *filled the gap.* Many technical analysts will tell you they believe that almost all stocks (and the market itself) will invariably fill their gaps. I don't necessarily agree with this statement, as I've seen too many gaps over the years NOT filled. However, it's worth noting that many, if not most, INTRADAY gaps do fill. Those are the ones we are keying on here, so it's an important statement.

When Do Gaps Occur?

Although the size of gaps varies, they occur almost everyday. On a given day, gaps are generally traded during the first 30 minutes of the day. The short timeframe for trading gaps is why they provide such a great part-time trading opportunity. The length of a gap trade can range from seconds to minutes, to hours, or occasionally, all day if a gap reversal gains momentum in the opposite direction and you decide to trail the move for as long as possible.

On a weekly basis, it's been my experience that the best days for gaps tend to be Mondays and Fridays, though any day of the week could turn out to be a good day. Increased uncertainty is one of the reasons. Going into a new week, no one knows for certain how the market will behave, either that day or for the rest of the week. Similarly, the uncertainty going into the weekend is a factor on Fridays, though less so than for Mondays. The increased uncertainty often causes more volatility, which results in larger gaps.

Although there are occasions when a stock is halted during the day due to pending news or for other reasons then gaps when it re-opens for trading, it's the morning gaps that we are interested in as traders because they provide the most predictable and consistent trading opportunities.

Planning The Trade

Even though gap plays are generally quick, short-term trades, a reasonable amount of preparation is still needed in order to achieve the best results. Obviously, you'll need to determine which stocks are gapping and which of those may offer the best trading opportunities. Additionally, to properly prepare you should review the overall news and market conditions, news pertaining to individual stocks of interest, pre-market activity and price action, volume and order flow, what type of setups to use for potential trade entries, how to best manage risk and take profits, what lot size to use on a given trade, and so on.

Following are some general tips and techniques that I use when trading gaps. In the "Trading Gaps Using Technical Analysis" chapter, I'll discuss a variety of other techniques you can use to help plan entry and exit strategies that are based upon charts and technical analysis.

Since there are a variety of tools and techniques from which to choose, I suggest that you read both chapters about trading gaps and try out the approaches that seem to work best for you. If one doesn't work out well, you can try another. As is often the case, techniques that work well for one person may not work as well for someone else, so after some experimentation and as you gain more experience, you'll be in a better position to determine which techniques best suit your personal goals and trading style.

If you do decide to use the technical analysis techniques that are discussed in the next chapter, I highly recommend that you still take into account the information provided in this chapter when planning your trades. The information provided in the next chapter is intended to supplement the information presented here.

Daily Profit Goals

Many traders set daily profit goals. Whether or not to do so is really a matter of personal choice, but I personally believe it's beneficial not only to have trading goals, but also, to have general life oriented goals as well. After all, before you can realize your dreams you need to know what they are. I suggest that you create a written list. Then, you can define the series of steps needed to accomplish each item on your list by breaking them down into smaller, more easily achieved goals. Before you know it, many of your seemingly out of reach dreams may become your new reality!

Of course, your goals should be reasonable and realistic, but that doesn't mean that they can't be far reaching, even to the point of becoming a multi-millionaire! While you may not be able to achieve such lofty goals overnight, you very well could at some point in the future.

I'm including a discussion of this topic here because if you do set a daily profit goal, the exit strategy for your gap trades could be affected. For example, if your daily profit goal is $300, you'll need to decide what you will do if you are still holding positions when you hit your daily goal. On a good day, you could potentially hit such a daily goal with a single gap trade. If you bought 1000 shares of XYZ stock on a large gap down and it moved by $0.30 in your favor, you would hit your daily goal. If that happens, what will you do? Will you immediately close out all of your positions and quit for the day, or will you continue trading?

Many traders consider their job done once they hit their daily goal. Not wanting to risk giving back any of their hard earned profits, they immediately close out positions, quit, and enjoy the rest of the day off. Other traders go for all they can get and continue trading after meeting their daily goal. And yet others may use the remaining time for learning or experimenting. You can use the time to try out new tactics by paper trading or trading in demo mode rather than risking your real capital. If you discover new techniques that work well, they can be incorporated into your trading strategies.

Once again, this is really a matter of personal preference and what works best for you. If you find that you tend to make a good profit in the mornings and end up giving it back later in the day, then it might be best to quit once your daily goal has been met. As discussed in the "Intraday Timeframes" chapter, there are frequently lulls in the market at certain times of the day. Attempting to trade these could result in a churning of your account with little or no gains, or even worse, losses.

If you intend to set a daily profit goal, you must first determine what amount is reasonable and realistic, taking into consideration the size of your trading account. Obviously, it's not realistic to expect to make 50% on your account each day. And, the amount that is reasonable for a $5000 account won't be the same as for a $10,000 account, a $50,000 account, and so on.

While the specific amount is subjective, and in-part dependent upon your level of experience, the size of your account, as well as other factors, generally, I feel a daily goal that is about 2% of your account size is realistic, especially once you've mastered trend-trading techniques. Therefore, if you have a $10,000 account, your daily goal based on 2% would be $200.

Of course, you are not likely to achieve your daily goal every day. Some days, and possibly even some weeks, you will lose money. But hopefully, and in order to be successful over the long-term, you will have more winning days overall than losing days, and the upside potential of having a daily goal of just 2% can be quite large on average over a period of time. As the size of your account increases, the size of your daily goal will increase.

Expectations And Objectives

Your expectations and objectives for a trade can influence both how you manage the trade, and how you exit it. If you have realistic expectations and objectives going into a trade, you will be less likely to make impulsive decisions that are based on emotion rather than a predetermined plan. You'll also be in a better position to plan entry and exit strategies, manage your risk, and consider strategies for taking profits.

With that in mind, what are some realistic expectations for gap trades? Well, you should anticipate any of the following. A gap trade can be fast and volatile, so you may need to react quickly to rapidly changing conditions. A gap trade can be short and easy, or it can last well into the morning, and in some cases, it can even last all day. This, at least in many instances, depends on your objectives for the trade, how you manage it, and how much time you have available to devote to trading on a given day. Gaps create opportunities to achieve nice profits in short timeframes, but it's also possible to lose money in short timeframes.

The objectives you set for a trade will likely affect the outcome of the trade as well. Do you plan to take profits and quit once your daily profit goals have been met, even if there could potentially be additional gains left in a trade? Are you prepared to trade throughout the morning? All day? Or, do you need to quit trading within the first hour, and perhaps go to another job? Do you have predetermined price targets, or do you plan to simply play it for what you can get? Of course, another obvious objective is to make a profit, but what if the trade goes against you? Since that's a possibility, another objective should be to predefine and limit losses as well.

These are only a few examples of how your expectations and objectives could potentially affect the outcome of a trade but as you can see, if you think about them in advance, you'll at least be in a better position to factor them into your trading plan. More specific ways of doing this are provided later in this chapter, and in the next chapter.

Watch The News

The news can play an important role in planning and tracking your trades. Before the market opens each morning, I look for momentum stocks that are gapping up or down without a good reason, meaning *on no substantial news*. The larger the gap, the better the potential trade.

Since the preference is to find stocks that are gapping without a good reason, you should always review the news before planning your gap trades, and then keep an eye on the news while executing your trades as well. Initially, you'll want to determine whether stocks are gapping for a good reason based on substantial news, or whether the gaps are overly exaggerated on no news and as a result, are more likely to reverse direction. You should take into account any news that could affect the market at large, and news related to the individual stocks you choose, including any news related to their sectors or other stocks within their sectors.

If there is some type of major news propelling the market one way or the other, you may want to wait a little longer for confirmation of a gap reversal before entering a trade. If an individual stock is gapping up on news such as a major analyst upgrade or an upside earnings announcement, then it is a riskier play. Why would you risk selling it short? It has positive news that could propel the price even higher, or that could keep the price propped up, making a pullback less certain.

Instead, you can generally achieve better results by looking for a stock that is gapping up large on no news. Preferably, a weak stock in a weak sector that appears overbought. Conversely, when entering a long position on a gap down, it's usually best to look for strong stocks and avoid stocks that have bad news associated with them, or with their sectors.

Some of the best opportunities occur when stocks in one sector gap on major news that doesn't apply to stocks in other sectors, but the unrelated stocks gap as well. Stocks that gap for no reason or on news that doesn't pertain to them are good candidates for potential gap reversals.

Interpreting the news, and the reason for gaps, can be subjective and dependent upon a large variety of factors, so you should take all of the circumstances into consideration and use your own judgment, preferably with a historical perspective about what has occurred previously under similar conditions. Dramatic gaps will frequently reverse even when they were triggered by a substantial news event, particularly when gaps push stocks further into an oversold or overbought condition. With time and experience, you'll get better at judging which set of conditions provide the best trading opportunities (a touch of instinct about market behavior doesn't hurt either).

Finding The Gaps

As is often the case, there are a variety of methods and tools you could potentially use to ferret out stocks that are gapping.

One approach is to use your broker or quote provider. Some services have features that show which stocks are moving the most in premarket activity. For example, you can try checking the largest percentage gainers and losers, and which stocks are the most active.

You can also check the broader markets such as the Nasdaq

Composite, the Nasdaq 100 Stock Index Futures, and the S&P 500 Stock Index Futures. For example, if the Nasdaq is gapping down but the S&P 500 is up slightly, then I would narrow the field by looking for technology stocks that are gapping down.

And as just discussed in the preceding section, the news can also be a good source for gap trading ideas. Often, stocks that are gapping based on substantial good or bad news impact other stocks in the same business or sector, so you can check the news for potential trading opportunities.

Typically, I look for popular momentum stocks since they tend to gap more dramatically and provide the best opportunity for a corrective price reversal. However, depending on the circumstances, I do play other stocks as well, such as S&P 500 stocks. The idea is to find stocks that will provide the most "bang for the buck". I would rather play a $1.50 EBAY gap down than a $0.30 Citicorp gap down. Since the EBAY gap is considerably larger, the potential price movement on the trade is likely to be considerably larger as well, and the larger the price movement, the greater the potential for a nice profit.

Another advantage to using momentum stocks is that they provide greater liquidity and price action, which makes it easier to get in and out of a trade fast (an important consideration for traders). Though not always, momentum stocks generally consist of technology or biotechnology (biotech) stocks that trade on the Nasdaq stock exchange. As a result, they usually have 4 letters in their symbols such as INTC, CSCO, AMGN, and so on. Note that I'm only using these particular symbols to illustrate Nasdaq ticker symbols. I'm not suggesting that you use these specific stocks to trade gaps. There are many potential momentum stocks to consider. Which stocks are best varies on a day-to-day basis and is subject to overall market conditions and the specific circumstances of a given trade. Also, I do trade stocks from other exchanges at times.

Once I've picked some good trading candidates, I add them to my watch list and start looking for potential trade setups.

Watch Order Flow

As I previously mentioned, the timeframe for trading gaps is frequently short, and as a result, the price action can be fast and volatile. Although a gap trade may last for minutes, hours, or even all day, it can also be over in a matter of seconds. In some instances, the action can be so fast that even fractions of a second in order execution speeds can affect the outcome of a trade.

For that reason, you really need a fast order execution system and a Level II quote display. As I discussed in the "Shorting" chapter, in my opinion, you need a direct access brokerage account to trade gaps. You can check www.trendfund.com for our current recommendations.

On the whole, web based brokers simply don't have the consistent, reliable execution speeds you need to get in and out of gap trades quickly enough, even those brokers that advertise fast ten-second execution speeds. Waiting ten seconds for an order to execute can be an eternity when trading gaps, and can turn a winning trade into a losing trade. Although any system is subject to occasional technical problems or unanticipated demand loads, generally, order executions are virtually instantaneous (fractions of a second) when using a good direct access broker with broadband Internet access.

Once you are set up with a good broker, you'll want to pull up your Level II quote screen and watch the price action and order flow for any stocks of interest.

On my Level II quote screen, I pay attention to who is buying or selling my chosen stocks and judge when to get in based on the overall buying or selling pressure. I wait for signs that the buying (for gap ups) or selling (for gap downs) is beginning to subside. To help determine this, I watch the overall size, volume, and quantity of orders on each side for signs that the order flow is stabilizing, or beginning to dry up on the buy side for gap ups, or the sell side for gap downs. If this doesn't occur as expected or as desired for a particular stock, then I look for a different play and don't force the trade. I don't want to take on additional risk by going against particularly heavy buying or selling on the opposite side of my trade.

If I'm shorting, however, I may act sooner than when I'm buying long, particularly if the gap is large and appears to be very exaggerated. Since you must short into strength, if you wait too long, you might not be able to get shares to short (not after the selling begins from a snapback price reversal). That's why I prefer gap downs. They are typically easier to play. You can wait longer for confirmation of a reversal and still get in on the move. Still, since the risk/reward for the trade is so favorable, you may not want to wait too long on *large* gap downs either.

I discussed using Level II quotes and provided general information, as well as examples that apply to selling stocks short, in the "Shorting" chapter. If you haven't yet read the "Shorting" chapter, you can go there for additional information about Level II quote screens. A screen snapshot is provided there as well.

Managing Risk

Managing risk is a key element to succeeding as a trader, so much so that in addition to this specific discussion, I will frequently include reminders and suggestions for limiting risk throughout the book, most often by suggesting the diligent use of stop-loss orders. In a sense, managing risk is also having a preplanned exit strategy for your trade. It is a preplanned exit strategy for what happens when a trade goes against you. Similarly, taking profits could be thought of as a preplanned exit strategy for what happens when a trade moves in your favor. I'll discuss this more in the next section, "Taking Profits".

One of the benefits of playing gaps is that they have unlimited upside potential with limited downside risk. The downside risk is limited because you can predefine and limit the amount of risk you are willing to accept with the disciplined use of stop-loss orders. And when the price moves is in your favor, you can adjust your stop-loss order, or use a trailing stop-loss order and let it run, taking profits along the way according to your plan for the trade.

A good approach is to sell ? of your shares when your initial profit target is reached, then move your trailing stop-loss order to at least breakeven on your remaining shares. This ensures that you can't lose on the trade. If an upside move continues, you'll capture additional gains on your remaining shares until the price reverses and you are stopped out of the trade. I'll discuss this more and provide an example in the next section.

Although gaps are high percentage trends, it always pays to use due diligence and a reasonable degree of caution. Like everything else about the stock market, there are no guarantees. There are days where the market gaps up large, or gaps down large, then just keeps on going the same direction and never looks back. This is when you should use the 10:00 AM rule as a guideline. How to trade days like this is discussed in more detail in the next chapter. Other days, although there is almost always some type of a gap, the gap may be modest, making the play more risky. Similarly, if a gap is quite small, the market is considered to be essentially flat from the prior day, in which case, it's advisable to wait until the market reveals a direction and not play the gap at all.

On the other hand, large gaps are such high percentage plays that when uncertain, I will often just go ahead and play the gap. If a stock has gapped down *large* on no news, the risk of it going down considerably further in such a short period of time is relatively low. Since gaps are usually very short-term intraday plays the risk/reward is even more in your favor, because shorter timeframes decrease the time-based risk. Though the price could go down further after a large gap down, if you employ good risk management and use stop-loss orders, your downside risk will be defined and limited.

To determine a maximum risk limit, I recommend using the 2% rule as a guideline. Meaning, you shouldn't let any single trade go against you by more than 2% of the total value of your account. Using the 2% rule, if you had a $10,000 account, you shouldn't lose more than $200 on any single trade. Of course, that doesn't mean that you should base all of your stop-loss settings solely on your maximum risk limit. It's intended to be the *most* you will lose on any given trade. You should still take into consideration the specific circumstances of each trade.

For example, with a $200 maximum risk limit, if you bought 200 shares, you couldn't let the trade go against you by more than $1.00 ($1 x 200 shares = $200 maximum limit). Depending on the price range of a given stock, a $1.00 stop-loss setting might be too much, or too little. Here's another example. Suppose you bought 1000 shares. Now, your stop-loss setting would need to be $0.20 to remain within your $200 maximum limit ($0.20 x 1000 = $200). When trading gaps, you would likely get stopped out of most trades with such a small stop-loss setting. Therefore, on any given trade, you need to adjust your lot size such that you can use a reasonable stop-loss cushion and still remain within your maximum risk limit for the trade.

I'll discuss using stop-loss orders from a technical analysis perspective in the next chapter. In general, if you are playing a gap down without using technical analysis, after entering a position you should place an initial stop-loss order slightly beneath the stock's low for the day. Conversely, if you are playing a gap up, place a stop-loss order slightly above the stock's high for the day. Of course, if setting a stop-loss at these points exceeds your maximum risk limit then you should make appropriate adjustments to either your stop-loss setting, or your lot size.

Since gap trades tend to be more emotional and volatile, be careful not to set your stops overly tight or you could be stopped out of a profitable trade prematurely. The price might retest the low (or high as the case may be). In doing so, it could go a bit beyond the prior low or high before reversing. Many traders have a tendency to set their stop-losses too narrow for gap plays. They stop out with a small loss then miss a multiple point move that follows. Give the stock a bit of breathing room, but if a sell off continues after a gap down, or if a run continues after a gap up, you'll want to limit losses and stop out of the trade.

As previously discussed, remember that you can also limit risk by reducing your lot size. If you are frequently getting stopped out of trades prematurely, meaning you would have subsequently profited if you had not stopped out, try reducing your lot sizes so you can use wider stop-loss settings.

Taking Profits

Equally as important as managing risk on a trade is planning how you will take profits. You've likely heard the common adages that apply to this topic, which are — *pigs get slaughtered* and *no one ever went broke taking profits!* If you get greedy and wait too long to take profits, you risk giving back your gains and even worse, you risk turning a winning trade into a losing trade. Once again, this is such an important aspect of trading that in addition to discussing it here I will occasionally provide suggestions and reminders about it at other appropriate times.

As mentioned in the preceding section, taking profits is in a sense having a preplanned exit strategy for your trade. In this case, you might think of it as an exit strategy for what happens when a trade moves in your favor. I'll discuss a general approach that I frequently use, and prefer, for taking profits here. The next chapter, "Trading Gaps Using Technical Analysis", provides other methods of planning specific entry and exit price targets that are based on technical analysis. Of course, there are many potential variations for when and how to take profits. As always, you should take the specific circumstances of a trade into consideration as well.

Many traders set hard and fast price targets for taking profits, and then when their price targets are hit, they close out their positions entirely. Depending on the circumstances, I may occasionally do this as well but generally, I prefer to lock-in profits a piece at a time as I achieve any significant gains.

For example, suppose I buy 1000 shares of a stock at $50 a share. If the price breaks $50.50 (the specific amount depends on the situation), I might sell 1/2 of my shares, or 500 shares in this case, and then move my stop-loss setting to breakeven on my remaining 500 shares, or to $50.06 in this case, allowing for commissions. This not only locks in a portion of my gains, it ensures that I can no longer lose on the trade. In other words, it ensures that a winning trade will not turn into a losing trade, which is a key rule you should strive to enforce. Ideally, you should *never allow a winner to turn into a loser*.

Extending the preceding example further, there are a couple of ways that I might finish out the trade, depending on how I feel about the strength of a particular trade. If I achieve additional gains but the move appears to be running out of steam, I may just take profits and close out my position entirely at that point. Alternatively, if I achieve substantial additional gains and it appears there could still be more upside movement in the play, I may once again sell 1/2 of my remaining shares and continue to trail the move with a stop-loss order, possibly tightening my stop-loss setting. At this point, I will frequently just continue trailing the move with what shares remain until the price eventually reverses and triggers my stop-loss order, thereby, closing out my position.

What approach works best also depends on the specifics of a given trade, the stock price, the number of shares being traded, and so on. If I have a large quantity of shares and the momentum is particularly strong in my favor, I may continue slowly taking profits off the table and stay in the trade longer. On the other hand, if there is a huge unexpected move in my favor, possibly due to breaking news or even for no apparent reason, I may just immediately take all of the gains and close out the position. In my opinion, if a price move unexpectedly exceeds your expectations, you should take the money and run. Yes, there could be some hot news that you haven't heard about yet and you could leave money on the table, but it could just as easily go the other way and often does, so you should at least lock in a portion of your profits. After all, you are a trader. If you made money then you did your job well, regardless of what happens after you exit the trade. And, you can always consider entering a new position later, if you subsequently discover reasons that justify doing so.

As mentioned, there are many variables to take into consideration when deciding how to take profits. The actual quantity of shares and stock prices are different for each trade. I simply used the amounts in the preceding example for illustration purposes. Obviously, if you buy a $2.00 stock rather than a $50.00 stock, you wouldn't likely wait for a 50-cent move before taking profits. Similarly, on any given trade you might own more or less than 1000 shares. Therefore, take the specifics of each trade into account when deciding when and how to take profits.

The main points are you must take profits when you have any significant gains, and you should never allow a winning trade to turn into a losing trade. Once you are ahead sufficiently, move your stop-loss to at least breakeven. If the price subsequently pulls back and stops you out, so be it. It's much better to stop out flat without any gain than to stop out with a loss because you didn't trail a favorable move with your stop-loss order.

As you can see from reading this and the prior section about managing risk, the way you use stop-loss orders to manage risk and how you choose to take profits could determine how you exit a trade. However, you can have more specific preplanned exit strategies as well. The "Trading Gaps Using Technical Analysis" chapter shows additional techniques you can use to plan entries, exits, and stop-loss settings for your gap trades.

Believe In The Trend

Successfully trading gaps often requires you to overcome emotions and trade contrary to what other people believe. Therefore, you should take market psychology into consideration, and believe in the trend.

Regardless of the initial event or news that triggers a gap, a large gap up occurs in part because people think they may miss out on a big run, so they buy impulsively. It's the reason many people will continue to buy a gap up, only to sell at a loss a short time later when, to their dismay, a snapback reversal occurs. Conversely, people panic when there is a large gap down and continue to sell rather than wait for the market to stabilize or bounce back.

Trading a gap may require you to short the market when everyone else appears to be buying, or it may require you to buy long when everyone else appears to be selling. To do this, you must be able to overcome the excitement of the moment, set your emotions aside, and trust the trend.

Though a gap trend is not 100% (no trends are), more often than not the market will pull back when it gaps up *large* or will bounce when it gaps down *large*, even if only temporarily. Therefore, you should play the trend by shorting large gap ups, and by buying large gap downs. As previously mentioned, for modest or small gaps you should take into account all of the circumstances and use more discretion.

You generally should not buy a large gap up or sell a large gap down at the open of the market. Either trade the gap trend or use the 10:00 AM rule as your guideline. For your convenience, here is a restatement of the 10:00 AM rule (this is covered more in the next chapter and in the "Intraday Timeframes" chapter):

> *If a stock gaps up, you should not buy it long unless it makes a new high after 10:00 AM. Conversely, if a stock gaps down, you should not sell it short unless it makes a new low after 10:00 AM.*

Don't Panic

You can rarely catch the exact top or bottom of a gap trade, or any trade for that matter. No one does on any kind of consistent basis. When it happens, great, but you shouldn't count on it.

Therefore, you should anticipate that the trade might go against to some degree at first. If you plan your trade using appropriate lot sizes and stop-loss cushions, you will be less likely to panic as the price fluctuates. You can relax knowing that you will stop out of the trade if it goes against you by your predefined risk limit. Additionally, with your stops in place you will be less likely to make rash, impulsive decisions that are based upon emotion rather than your original plan for the trade.

As mentioned under "Managing Risk", it's best to give your stops a bit more breathing room when trading gaps because there is often some leftover buying or selling pressure initially. If necessary, you can reduce your lot size to allow for wider stop-loss settings without exceeding your maximum risk limit.

When a trade does go against you and you stop out, don't beat yourself up over it! You will have both winners and losers. It was a good risk/reward play and you traded your plan. By stopping out of the trade, you preserved your capital for the next trade.

As I frequently say, *trading is a marathon, not a sprint*. And since trading is a marathon, preserving your capital is key to succeeding over the long-term.

Trading Gap Downs

As discussed earlier, a gap down occurs when a stock's price opens lower than it closed on the previous day. The follow chart of NVLS shows a gap down.

Notice on the preceding chart that NVLS gapped down by $1.52, and then after a brief period of consolidation, the price of NVLS reversed direction and retraced all of the losses from the gap down, which illustrates the profit potential of fading gaps.

To trade a gap down, you buy the stock long once the initial selling pressure subsides. Afterwards, you should place a stop-loss order slightly beneath the low of the day, or according to your own tolerance for risk, to limit losses in the event the price continues to move lower.

The next chapter, "Trading Gaps Using Technical Analysis", discusses additional techniques you can consider using to time the entries and exits for your gap trades based upon charts and technical analysis.

Gap downs are powerful, high percentage trends that provide consistent moneymaking opportunities. In fact, they are one of my favorite trades. During the years that I've tracked gap downs; they have been one of most consistent, profitable trends that I've used.

Gap ups provide nice trading opportunities as well, but between the two, gap downs present the best opportunities. When shorting gap ups, you must sell short on strength due to the uptick rule (i.e., you must short on a price uptick), so if you wait too long to enter a position, you might not get shares. When playing gap downs, if you are unsure about the trade, you can wait longer for confirmation of a reversal before entering a position. And since sellers are virtually always present on gap downs, it is generally easier to enter a trade.

Following is another example that shows QLGC gapping down.

Though the QLGC gap isn't as large as the NVLS gap, it still provided a nice opportunity to profit in a very short period of time.

As before, to trade the gap down, you enter a long position once the initial selling pressure subsides, and then place a stop-loss order slightly below the low of the day, subject to your own tolerance for risk.

Also notice on the preceding chart that after the gap down reversed directions, the price continued higher and eventually surpassed the prior close. It actually moved about $2.00 from the low point of the morning.

One way to take advantage of this type of move is to take profits on 1/2 of your shares once the gap fills (there is more about this in the next chapter), then you can trail any further upside movement on your remaining shares with your stop-loss order. If the upside move continues, you can continue adjusting your stop to trail it higher. If/when the price pulls back, you'll stop out of the trade with any additional gains intact.

Trading Gap Ups

A gap up occurs when a stock's price opens higher than it closed on the previous day.

The following chart of EBAY shows an example of a gap up. Notice that EBAY closed at $89.21 and opened the next day at $89.79 for a $0.58 gap up.

Looking at the preceding chart, you can see that the price reversed direction soon after EBAY opened for trading. The price not only retraced the distance of the entire gap, it continued moving even lower. You could have faded the gap for a nice profit in a very short timeframe.

To trade a gap up, you sell the stock short once the initial buying pressure subsides. Afterwards, you should place a stop-loss order slightly above the high of the day, or according to your own tolerance for risk, to limit losses in case the price continues to move higher.

A gap reversal usually occurs within the first 30 minutes of trading.

Initially, however, there may be some left over buying interest after a gap up from people not wanting to miss out on a perceived rally. Therefore, when placing your stop-loss order, it's a good idea to leave a bit of breathing room in case the price does move slightly higher before pulling back.

As mentioned earlier, due to the uptick rule you should be prepared to short into strength. You might not be able to get shares to short if you wait until the selling begins before placing an order. Although the preferred approach is to wait for signs that the buying pressure is subsiding, this is such a high percentage trade that if the market gaps up *large*, with large being the key word, you can consider simply shorting the gap right away. If you manage risk by using a stop-loss order afterwards, the potential upside reward for the trade typically outweighs the downside risk.

You should use more discretion with small gaps since price reversals are less certain. You might consider using tighter stops and reducing your lot size. When uncertain about a small or modest gap, it may be best simply to wait it out and use the 10 AM rule as a guideline.

Following is another example chart that shows IBM gapping up.

Notice on the preceding chart that after IBM gapped up by $1.05 the buying interest continued initially. A short time later the upside momentum subsided, which resulted in a price reversal that subsequently retraced the entire gap.

This example also illustrates why it is best to give your stop-losses a little breathing room, even if it means using smaller lot sizes to limit your total risk exposure. As you can see on the chart, the price initially moved higher after the gap. If you had entered the trade soon after IBM opened for trading and your stop-loss setting was too tight, you could have potentially stopped out of the trade prematurely. If you stopped out too soon, you would have missed the price reversal and a very profitable trade.

As before, to trade the gap, you would enter a short position once the buying pressure subsided. You should then place a stop-loss order slightly above the high of the day, or according to your own tolerance for risk.

5

Trading Gaps Using Technical Analysis

In addition to the approaches described in the preceding "Trading Gaps" chapter, you can use charts and technical analysis to help determine entry and exit price targets for your gap trades. This chapter describes many of these techniques but before continuing, I would like to point out that I often don't use technical analysis to trade gaps.

Although I do occasionally use charts for additional confirmation of a gap trade, in cases where there is a large gap down and I'm confident about the trade, I will frequently just buy the gap right at the open as described in the "Trading Gaps" chapter rather than wait for confirmation using technical analysis. Conversely, if I'm shorting a large gap up, I might even short a stock during pre-market trading.

Large gaps are such powerful, high-percentage trends that I generally don't feel the need to wait for technical confirmation. However, many traders prefer to use technical analysis to help pick their entry and exit points, so for those of you that might have such an interest I'm including a variety of charting techniques that are useful for trading gaps.

The following strategies help you pick exact entry and exit points for your trades, but which techniques to use is really a matter of personal preference and what works best for you. You'll likely find that as you gain more experience and develop your own intuition about trading gaps, you'll discover other short cuts and tricks to use in addition to these.

Reversal Bars

Reversal bars, or candles, are just a few among many well-known candlestick chart formations that are used when performing technical analysis. They frequently signal a change of trend is on the way. Since some of the sections that follow employ the use of reversal bars to set entry and exit price targets for gap trades, for your convenience, a brief introduction to reversal bars is provided here.

Just keep in mind that technical analysis and candlestick charting involves much more than is practical to include here for gap trading purposes. If you would like to explore technical analysis and/or candlestick charting further, there are many good books devoted entirely to these topics. You can visit www.trendfund.com for a list of our current recommendations.

Doji

The appearance of a Doji candle indicates the price opened and closed within a tight range for the candle's time period (I generally use 5-minutes when trading gaps). It means the bulls and bears were in a tug of war.

If a stock has been in a directional trend, either up or down, a Doji could signal a potential change of direction is on the way.

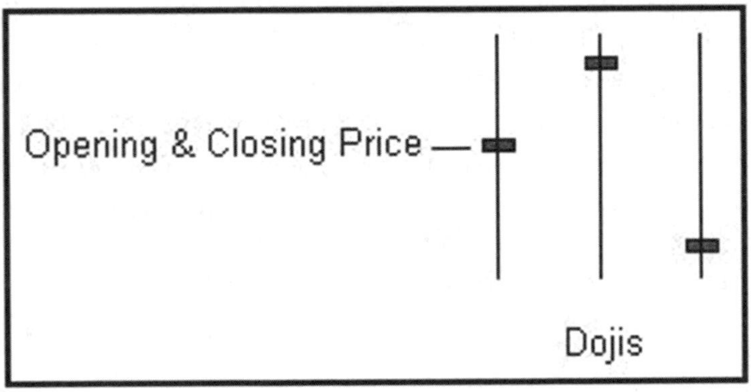

Dojis are very powerful indicators. When you see one, you should at least consider it a red flag. Some traders will even enter a trade or tighten stops based solely on seeing a Doji, particularly when a stock has been in a strong directional trend up to that point.

Hammer

A Hammer has a very small stub as the upper shadow (the thin line above and below the rectangular body of the candle), and a long lower shadow. It has a short real body that is positioned at the top of the candle.

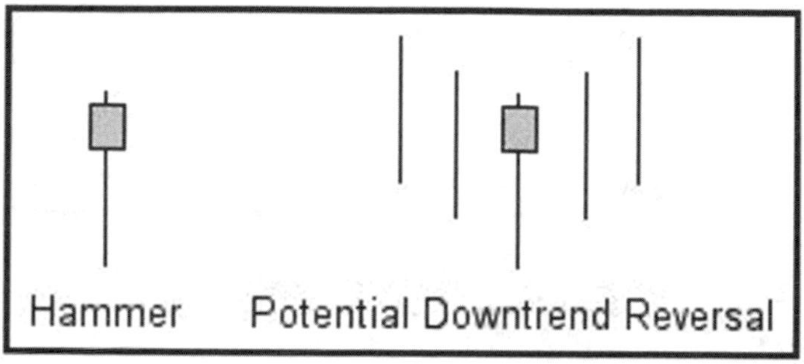

A Hammer is another powerful indicator of strong support, and often indicates the end of a significant downtrend. Confirmation occurs when the price breaks above the top of the Hammer.

While you don't necessarily want to jump in and trade a Hammer when in a sideways range, in a downtrend it is a great low risk, high percentage trade, especially when it occurs at a support level. You can enter a long position with defined risk by buying a break of the high of the hammer and putting a stop-loss order just below the bottom of the hammer.

Shooting Star

A Shooting Star looks like an upside down Hammer, or Inverted Hammer. It has a long upper shadow with a short stubby shadow underneath.

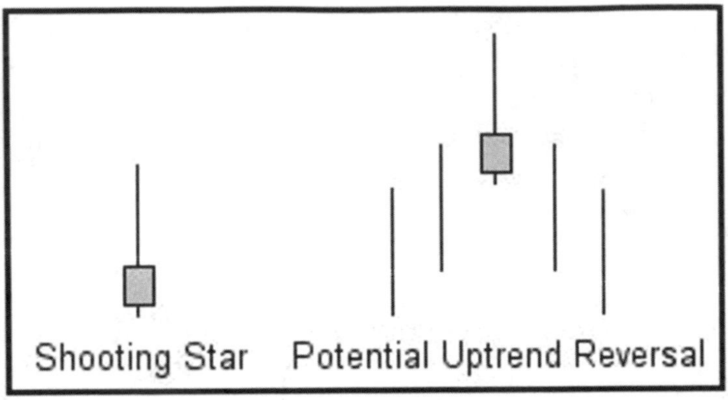

A Shooting Star is a powerful bearish indicator, and a very reliable indicator of an uptrend reversal.

Entry Strategies

Following are a variety of technical analysis strategies that you may find useful for timing the entries to gap trades. After the entry strategies are explained, exit strategies are also discussed.

First Bar High/Low Entry

One entry technique for trading gaps is to use the high and low of the first bar of an intraday chart. The high is used to set an entry for gap downs, and the low is used for gap ups.

Though some traders use 1-minute or 3-minute charts, I've achieved better results trading gaps with 5-minute charts. Therefore, I generally use 5-minute charts. Following is 5-minute intraday candlestick chart of MXIM that shows a gap down.

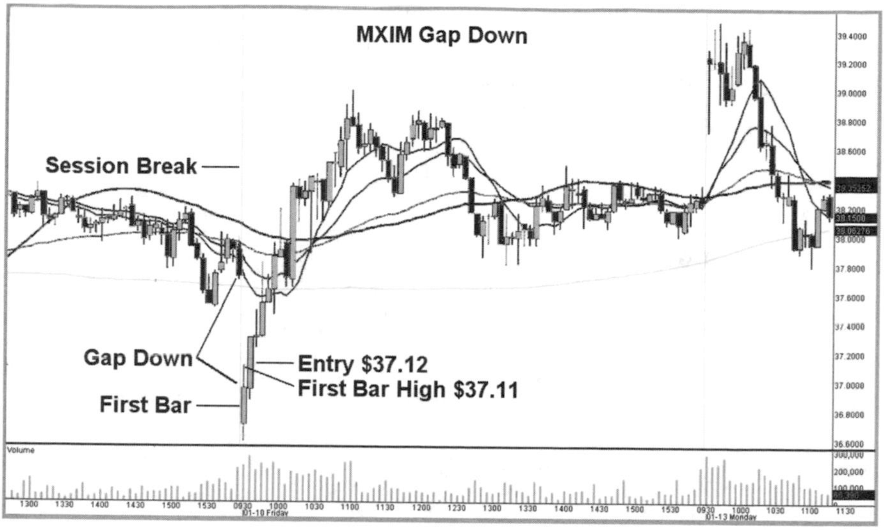

Notice on the chart that the high price of the first bar after the gap down is $37.11 (see the next illustration for a close-up view of the bars). If the stock's price breaks the high of the first bar, or moves higher than $37.11 in this case, it's a sign of buying interest, which indicates the gap down could be reversing. Therefore, you could use $37.12 as an entry price target for the trade.

Here is a close-up view of the first two candlestick bars that followed the gap down on the preceding chart.

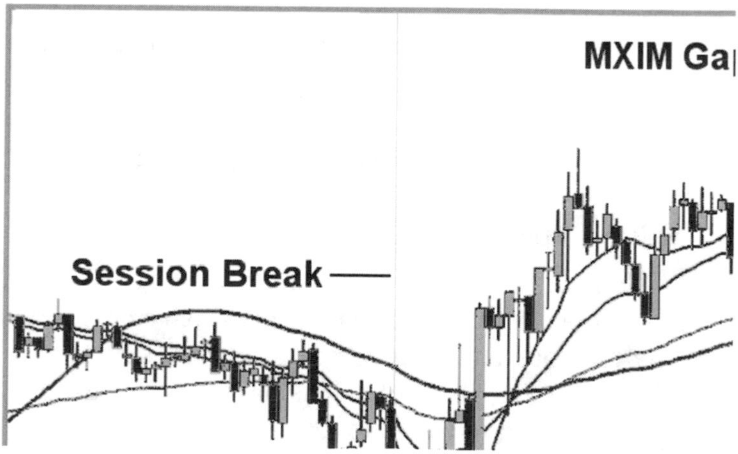

You would buy the stock long when the price reaches $37.12, and then place a stop-loss order slightly beneath the low of the first bar, which is generally the low of the day as well.

The next chart shows another first bar entry based on a gap down of MSFT.

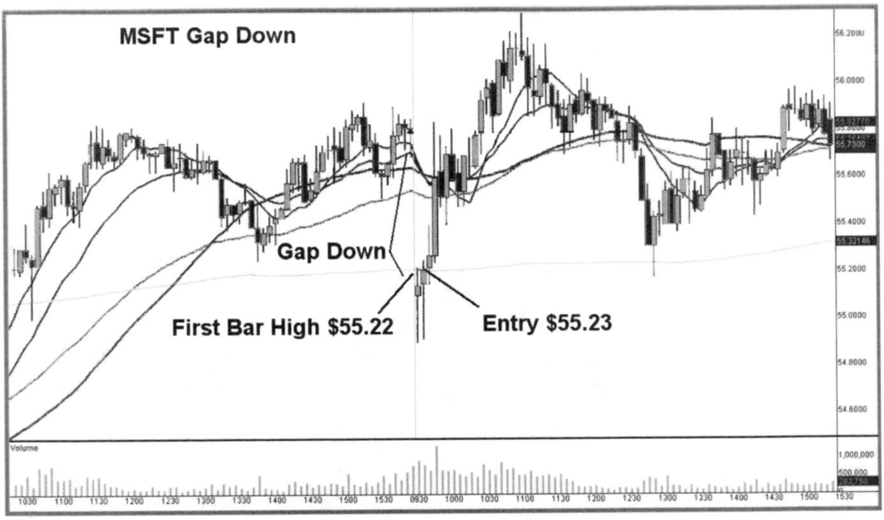

Since the high of the first bar after the gap down on the preceding MSFT chart is $55.22, you could enter the trade long once the price hits $55.23, and then place a stop-loss order slightly beneath the low of the first bar.

You can also use the first bar to determine entry targets for gap ups. In the case of gap ups, you simply reverse the process and sell short when the price breaks through the low of the first bar. You would then place your stop-loss order slightly above the high of the first bar.

Inside Bar Entry

Another way you can set an entry price target for a gap trade is by using an inside bar. An inside bar occurs when a bar's high price is lower than the previous bar's high, and it's low is higher than the previous bar's low. The price range of an inside bar is "inside" the range of the prior bar, as shown in the following illustration.

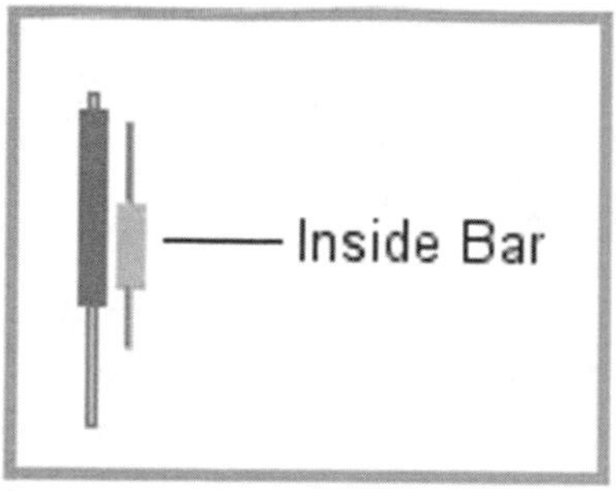

Inside bars indicate contracting range and volatility, which also indicates the selling pressure is subsiding. And as mentioned earlier, since emotions also play a role in causing stocks to gap, inside bars can indicate that the emotional selling may be coming to an end.

The following chart of MERQ shows how an inside bar can be used to set an entry price target for a gap down trade.

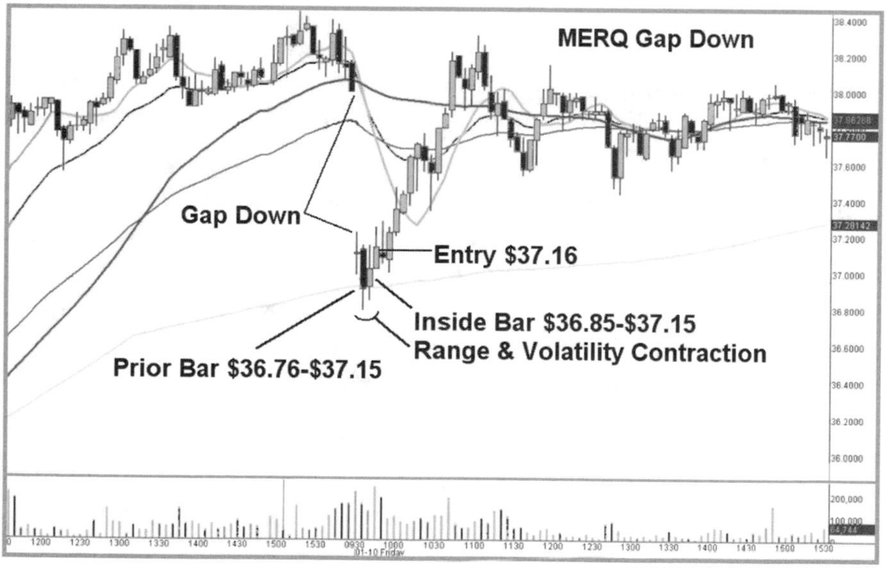

A close-up of view of the inside bar on the preceding chart follows.

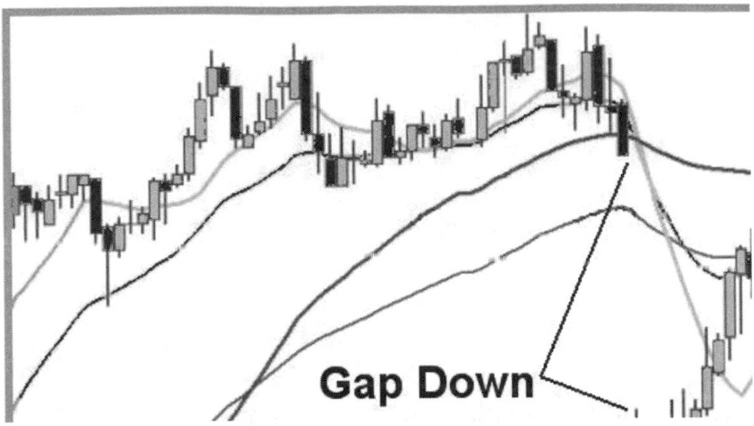

Inside bars are my favorite indicators for determining entry targets when I'm using technical analysis confirmation of gaps. I particularly like inside bars when the bars that precede the inside bar are trending in the direction of the gap, as in the preceding example. Meaning, the gap is to the downside and the bars preceding the inside bar are trending downward as well. Inside bars are such powerful indicators that I generally don't wait for any additional technical confirmation after seeing one (e.g., like a break of the first bar's high).

You can set your entry price target slightly above the high of the inside bar. In the prior example, the inside bar price range is from \$36.85 to \$37.15 so you could enter the trade long when the price hits \$37.16. Upon entering the trade, place a stop-loss order slightly beneath the low of the inside bar to limit your risk should the trade go against you. Should the inside bar's low be too close (and unreasonably narrow) for a stop-loss order, you can consider using the lowest low of the bars that preceded the inside bar, or the low of the day. See the "Using Stops" section later in this chapter for additional stop-loss guidelines and suggestions.

Inside bars can also be used to trade gap ups. The following chart shows a gap up of GNSS.

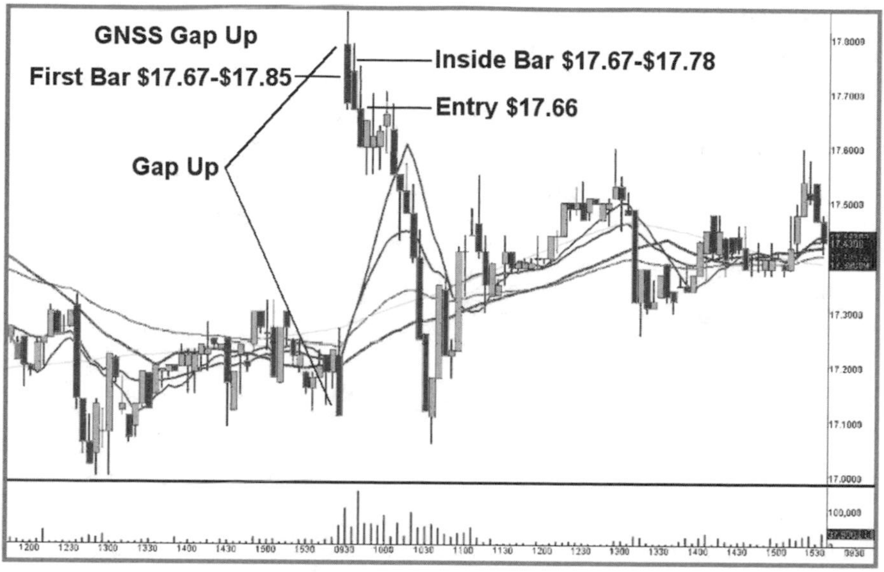

Notice on the preceding chart that the first bar's price ranges from $17.67 to $17.85. The next bar is an inside bar, because it's range of $17.67 to $17.78 is inside the range of the first bar. Since this is a gap up, the price target is just under the low of the inside bar, or $17.66, which in this case, just happens to be the low of the first bar as well. If the price hits $17.66, you could sell the stock short then place a stop-loss order slightly above the bar's high, or once again, you can consider using another nearby level of resistance in situations where you might need to widen your stop slightly.

Reversal Bar Entry

You can also use reversal bar formations to set entry price targets for gap trades, although this strategy does tend to be a bit more aggressive. If you need a general refresher about reversal bar candlestick formations, please see "Reversal Bars" earlier in this chapter. Later, I'll provide examples of using reversal bars as potential warning signs for exiting trades as well.

Following is a chart of KLAC that shows a Shooting Star reversal bar, which appeared soon after the stock gapped up.

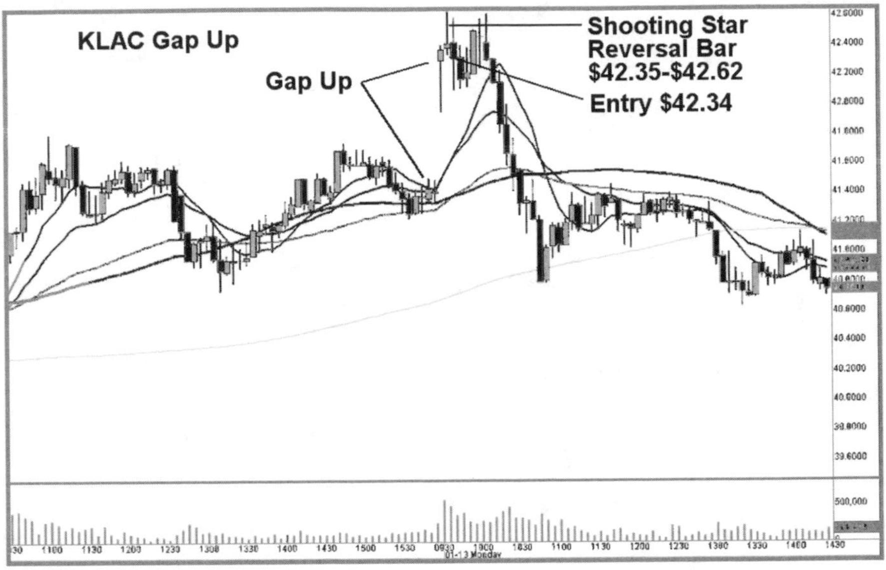

The next illustration shows a close-up view of the Shooting Star reversal bar from the previous chart.

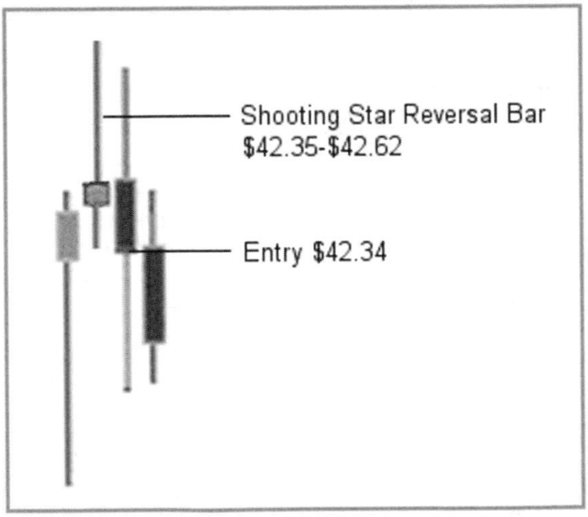

As mentioned earlier, a Shooting Star often signals the end of an uptrend, or a gap up in this case. Looking at the preceding chart, notice that the price fell a short time after the appearance of the Shooting Star.

Upon seeing a Shooting Star after a gap up, you could sell the stock short when the price breaks through the low of the Shooting Star. In the preceding example, the price range of the Shooting Star is from $42.35 to $42.62, so the entry price target is $42.34. After entering a position, place your stop-loss order just above the high of the Shooting Star, which is $42.62.

When using reversal bars, your stop-losses should generally be fairly tight. If the indicator fails, which is the case if the price subsequently breaks the high of the preceding Shooting Star; you should stop out of the trade. A related tidbit that you can keep in mind is that another potential trading opportunity occurs when a pattern formation fails. You can frequently enter a profitable trade in the opposite direction based upon the failure of a pattern setup.

As is discussed later in the "Trading Laggards" and the "Trading The News" chapters, stocks in similar businesses or sectors will often move in sympathy with one another. The following chart of EXPE shows an example of this. Bad news came out about ROOM, which is in a similar business as EXPE, so EXPE also gapped down on the bad news. The stock closed on a Friday at $70.85 then open at $63.28 the following Monday, which was a huge $7.57 gap down. This chart also illustartes a trade entry that is based upon a Hammer reversal bar.

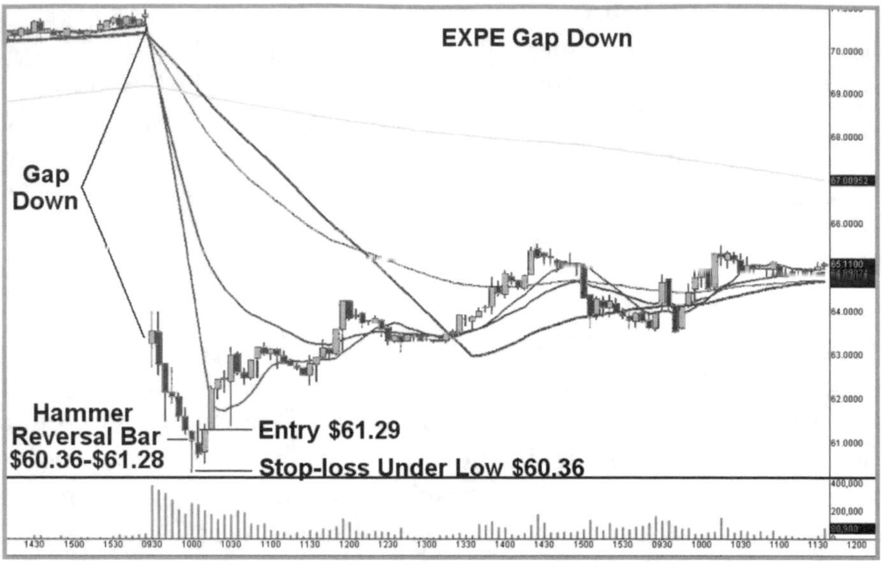

Here is a close-up view of the Hammer reversal bar.

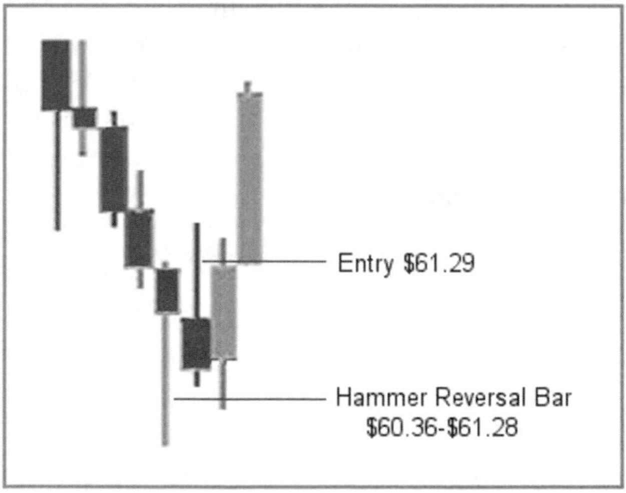

As discussed earlier, a Hammer frequently signals the end of a downtrend. Notice on the preceding chart how EXPE was initially trending lower after the gap down. Shortly after the Hammer appeared, the stock reversed direction and moved higher.

The range of the Hammer reversal bar is $60.36 to $61.28, so you could set a potential entry price target for the trade at $61.29, or just above the high of the Hammer reversal bar. If the price breaks through the high of the Hammer, then there is a good chance the downtrend may be reversing. After entering a position, you would place a stop-loss order slightly beneath the low of the reversal bar, or slightly below $60.36 in this case. As before, if the reversal bar fails, you should limit losses and exit the trade.

The OOPS Entry

Larry Williams, a systems/commodity trader, coined the term "OOPS" and invented the OOPS setup in the 1970s, though his usage of the setup includes more variations than presented here for our purposes. He noticed when the market gaps up, people tend to get caught up in the buying frenzy and continue to buy the gap up, then when the selling begins, they realize the mistake with an "OOPS", so he called the setup "OOPS"!

An OOPS setup occurs when a gap up opens higher than the previous day's high price, rather than simply opening higher than the previous day's closing price. Or, conversely, in the case of a gap down, when the price opens lower than the previous day's low price, rather than its closing price.

Actually, if a gap is strictly defined from a technical point of view, true gaps are as just described in the previous paragraph. That is, a gap up is when the price opens higher than the previous day's high, and a gap down is when the price opens lower than the previous day's low. When a gap is based upon the closing price only, and doesn't exceed the prior high or low, as the case may be, it is technically referred to as a *lap*. Still, most people refer to either as a gap, and I generally do as well. However, for the purpose of discussing an OOPS entry, it seemed appropriate to make the distinction.

In the case of a gap up, an OOPS entry price target is the breach of the prior day's high. And for a gap down, it is a breach of the prior day's low. The following QLGC chart shows an OOPS gap up that provides two potential entry targets, an inside bar entry, and an OOPS entry.

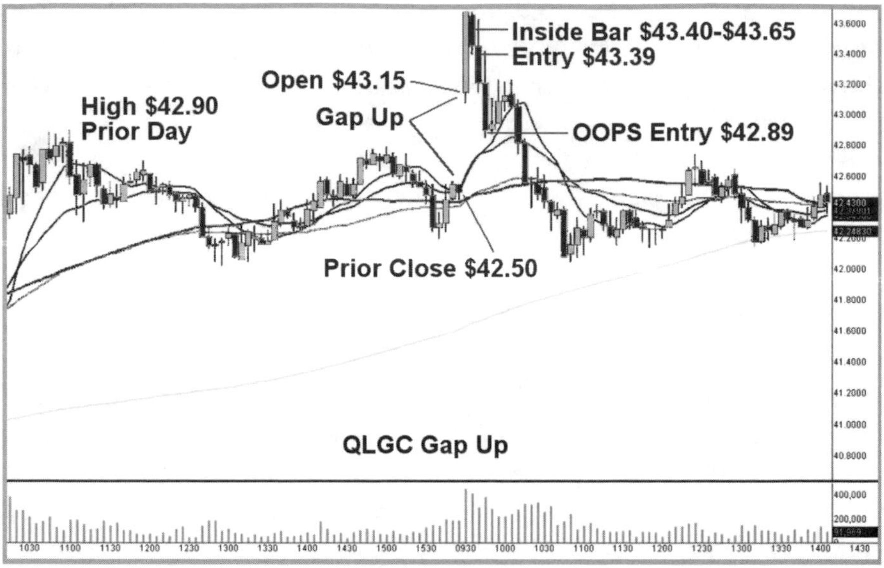

The next illustration shows a close-up view of the two potential entry points from the preceding chart.

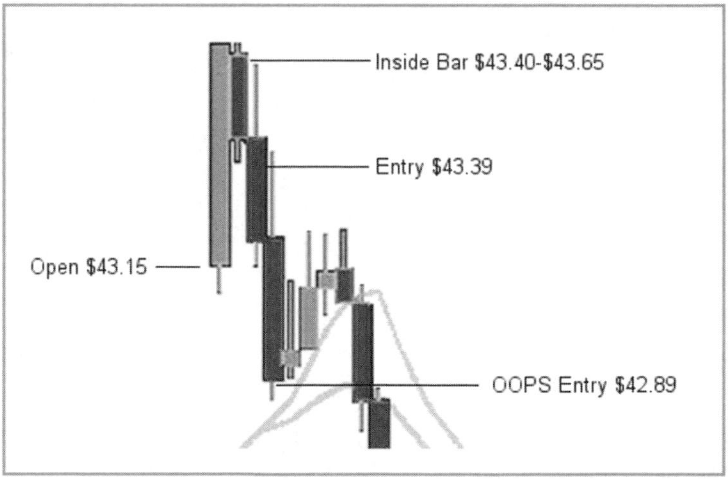

Referring to the previous chart, notice that the prior day's high was $42.90. The following day, QLGC opened at $43.15, which is higher than the prior high of $42.90. Therefore, it is a potential OOPS trading opportunity. The OOPS entry target is just below the prior day's high, or $42.89 in this case.

Also, though, the second bar that appears is an inside bar. While you could wait for an OOPS entry, my preference in this case would be to take the inside bar entry. As explained earlier, for an inside bar the entry for a gap up is just below the inside bar's low. Since the inside bar range is $43.40 to $43.65, the entry price target is $43.39. Therefore, to trade off of the inside bar target, you would sell the stock short when the price hits $43.39. Then, place a stop-loss order above the inside bar's high, or above another nearby area of resistance if the stop seems unreasonably narrow. In such cases, it's likely the stop would be just above the highest high of one of the bars immediately preceding the inside bar.

If you miss the inside bar entry, or prefer to wait for the OOPS entry, you would sell the stock short when the price hits the OOPS entry price target, or $42.89 using the preceding example.

The official point to set a stop-loss order for an OOPS trade is the high of the day. However, the high of the day can sometimes be a fairly wide stop, which is one reason I'm not a big fan of the official OOPS trade. In my opinion, you should take into account your tolerance for risk, the circumstances of the gap, and the price action ahead of the trade to determine the best setting for your stop-loss order. If the range is not too wide, you could use the official recommendation and set a stop-loss slightly above the high of the day. Otherwise, I would look for a closer area of resistance or once I had gains, I would take profits prior to a price pullback.

Another risk management alternative is to reduce your lot size so that a wider stop-loss remains within range of your maximum risk limit. Regardless of the approach, I think it's important to predetermine the amount of risk you are willing to accept on any trade, and then adjust the parameters of a trade to stay within that limit. Capital preservation is key to succeeding long term as a trader.

A gap down OOPS trade works exactly the same as for a gap up, except in reverse. The OOPS entry target is a breach to the upside of the prior day's low, in which case, you would by the stock long and use the current day's low for the official stop-loss placement. Once again, I recommend an approach that narrows the stop-loss setting when the daily low falls outside of your maximum risk tolerance for a trade.

GAP AND GO ENTRIES

Though in most cases if the market gaps large, there is a snapback price reversal, there are also days when the market gaps and just keeps on going in the same direction. I call this *gap and go*.

How do you trade *gap and go* days? These are the days that you use the 10:00 AM rule discussed in the "Intraday Timeframes" chapter as a guideline. For your convenience, here is a brief restatement of the 10:00 AM rule.

If a stock gaps up, you should not buy it long unless it makes a new high after 10:00 AM. Conversely, if a stock gaps down, you should not sell it short unless it makes a new low after 10:00 AM.

Following the 10:00 AM rule, if a stock gaps up then makes a new high after 10:00 AM, you would buy the stock long. The following QLGC chart shows an example of this type of entry.

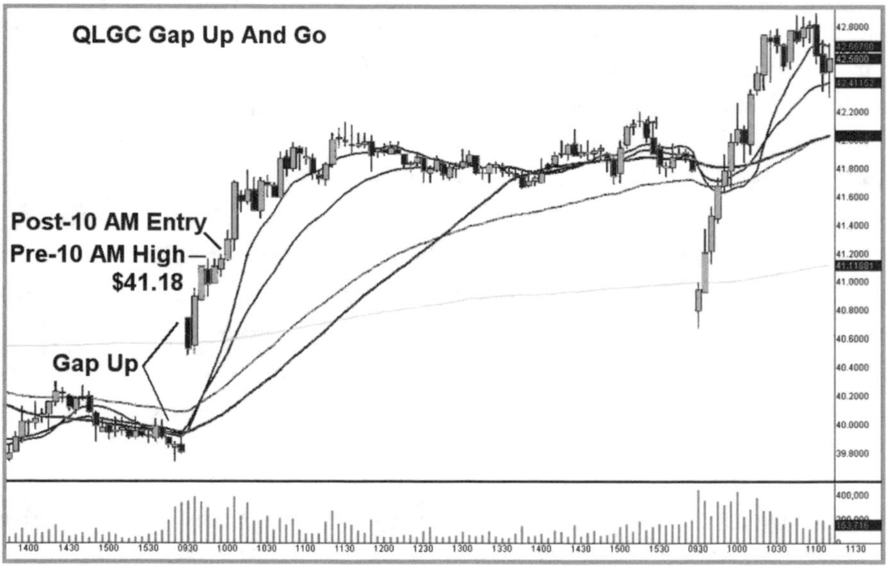

Notice on the preceding chart that after QLGC gapped up, rather than reversing, the price continued to move higher. This is an indication that buying pressure is increasing, and/or selling pressure is subsiding.

The high prior to 10:00 AM was $41.18. Upon an upside breach of the $41.18 high, or when the price hits $41.19, you could enter a long position. Afterwards, you should place a stop-loss order slightly beneath the low that occurred prior to 10:00 AM. If this would result in a stop-loss that is too wide and outside of your maximum risk limit, adjust your stop or lot size such that your maximum risk isn't exceeded (possibly to another nearby support level). Later in this chapter, the "Using Stops" section provides additional stop-loss guidelines and suggestions.

In the preceding example, you can see that an entry based upon a breach of the high that occurred prior to 10:00 AM resulted in a nice short-term trade.

Another *gap up and go* example follows.

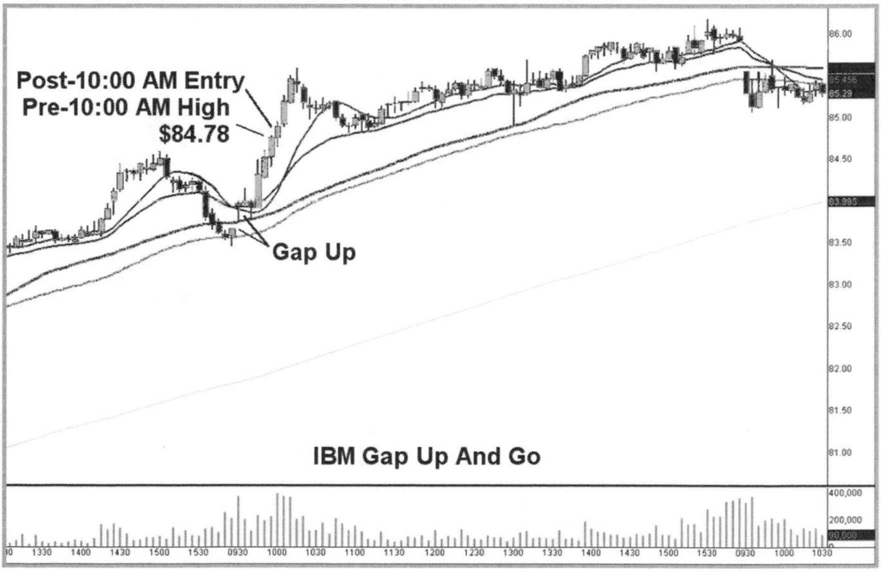

Once again, as you can see on the preceding chart, the buying pressure continued after IBM gapped up. Upon a break through the high that occurred prior to 10:00 AM, or at $84.78 in this case, you could enter a long position. Afterwards, place a stop-loss order beneath the low that occurred prior to 10:00 AM or once again, use a closer stop or smaller lot size should the low exceed you maximum risk limit.

As you likely have already surmised, you can apply the 10:00 AM rule to trading gaps to the downside as well. To do so, if a stock gaps down then makes a new low after 10:00 AM, you would enter a position by selling the stock short.

The following chart of KLAC shows a *gap and go* entry that is based upon a gap down.

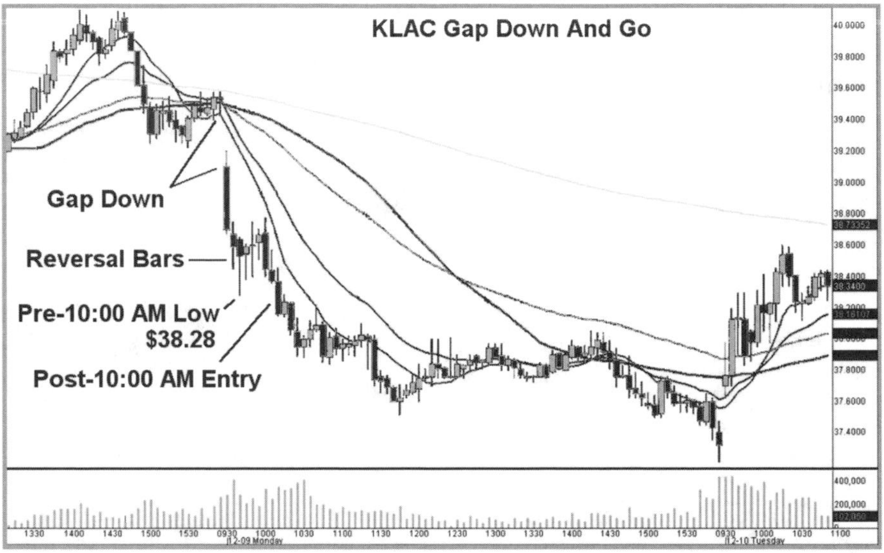

Looking at the preceding chart, it's possible that you might have entered into a long position upon seeing the reversal bars that appeared shortly after the gap down. Even though it didn't work out in this case, such an entry would not have been wrong. Later, the "Getting The Extra Edge" discusses leading indicators you can use that might help you avoid a false entry. However, if you use stop-losses, you will stop out of the trade when there is a failure of the reversal bars. Additionally, as I noted earlier, reversal bar failures can be powerful indicators for entering a trade in the opposite direction, which would have worked well in this case.

Regardless of whether you had entered a long position based on the reversal bars, once you stopped out and a breach of the 10:00 AM low occurred, you could enter a new position on the short side. Afterwards, you would place a stop-loss slightly above the high that occurred prior to 10:00 AM. As previously discussed, should such a stop setting be too wide, you can adjust the stop so that it remains within your maximum risk limit (possibly to another nearby area of resistance).

Following is a chart of ADTN that shows another gap down example.

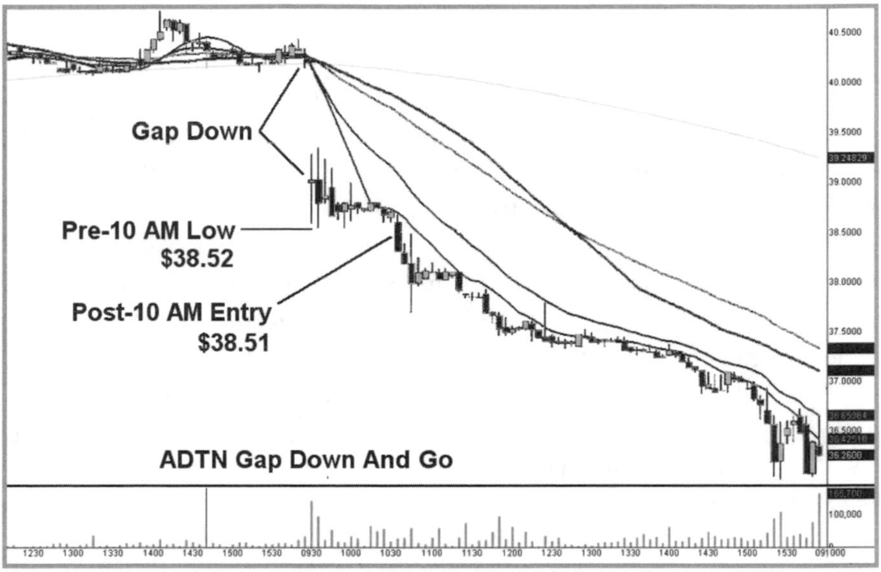

Once again, after ADTN gapped down, there was no resulting snapback price reversal. After a brief period of consolidation, the price continued lower. The low prior to 10:00 AM was $38.51. Upon a breach of the $38.51 low, you could sell the stock short then place a stop-loss order slightly above the high that occurred prior to 10:00 AM.

After entering a *gap and go* trade, you should trail any favorable price movement with your stop-losses, and take profits when appropriate. For more information about these topics, see "Taking Profits" and "Using Stops" under "Exit Strategies" later in this chapter.

Small Gaps Or Flat Opens

On days when the market essentially opens flat, or a gap is very small, it's best to wait for the market to establish a directional trend, or bias, before entering a position.

Once again, as described in the preceding "Gap And Go Entries" section, you can use the 10:00 AM rule as a guideline. If the market (or your stock) makes a new high after 10:00 AM, then you would trade it long. Similarly, if it makes a new low after 10:00 AM, then you would sell it short.

Exit Strategies

Now that you've read about charting techniques to determine gap trade entries, how can you use technical analysis to determine price targets for your exits, and hopefully, exit your trades with a profit? This section explores a few strategies for this purpose.

Of course, even though you can use charts to plan your exits, keep in mind that various other overriding factors can also influence, or even dictate, how you exit a gap trade. Your initial objectives for a trade, your expectations, and your daily trading goal can all play a role.

Other factors include the individual price action of the stocks you are trading, the behavior of the overall market, and the method you choose for taking profits. For longer trades, the 10:00 AM rule discussed in the "Intraday Timeframes" chapter and in this chapter also comes into play.

Of course, as I mentioned earlier, if the trade goes against you, your exit may be determined by where you place your stop-loss order, or in the case of trailing stop-loss orders, at the point where the price reverses and hits your stop.

If you desire to use technical indicators, there are various chart formations you can potentially use for exiting trades, and/or as warning signs where more caution should be exercised.

Following, I'll discuss various techniques that I've used to set price targets for exiting my positions and taking profits. I'll also provide examples of technical signals, or warning signs, you can watch for that might indicate a move is losing momentum or about to change directions.

Gap Fill Exits

An important area of support or resistance, depending on whether the gap is up or down, tends to occur when a gap fills. That is, when the price approaches the pre-gap price. Generally, this is the prior day's closing price.

Therefore, a gap fill is a price target where you should consider taking all or a portion of your profits, or depending on the size of the gap and your gains; you should at least move your stop-loss to breakeven on the trade. And, since gap fills are widely known as a potential points of resistance (or support depending on the direction) by other traders, as a gap fill approaches, you may want to act a bit early rather than wait for a complete fill of the gap.

If a gap is large and the gap fills, I will definitely take a portion, or all, of my profits. If a more modest gap fills (e.g., a gap of $0.40 or so), depending on how strong the trade appears I may move my stop-loss to breakeven, or I may take a portion of my profits and move my stop-loss to breakeven on my remaining shares. Regardless, I will not allow the trade to turn into a loser at this point.

The following MSFT chart shows how resistance is encountered, if only temporarily in this case, after a gap down is filled.

A clean break through the resistance could lead to a continuation of the upside move, which is what subsequently occurred. A useful tidbit to note and tuck away for future consideration is that old resistance often becomes an area of new support. Looking at the chart, you can see that once the price broke through the resistance, the old resistance became a new level of support for a period of time.

Reversal Bar Exits

Other warning signs to watch for are candlestick reversal bars. See "Reversal Bars" at the beginning of this chapter for a general description of the reversal bars discussed here.

Candlestick reversal bars often appear when a move is running out of steam. For an example of this, look at the preceding MSFT chart and the following close-up view of the reversal bars. Notice that shortly after the reversal bars appeared, the drive to the upside lost momentum and the price pulled back.

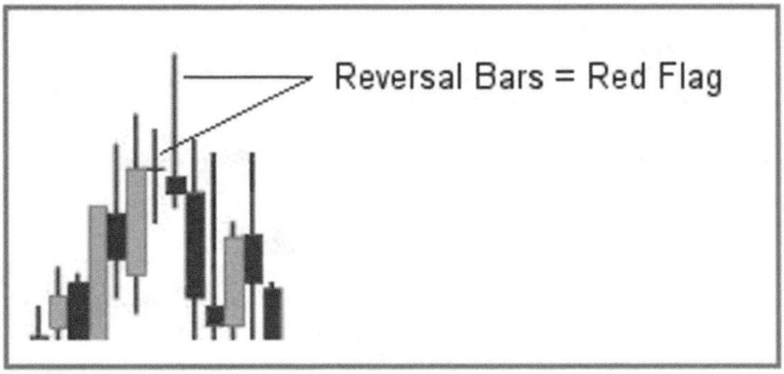

The first reversal bar, or candle, in the preceding illustration is called a Doji. It should be considered a red flag since the price opened and closed within a very tight range. The second candle is called a Shooting Star (or Inverted Hammer). One or more of these reversal bars frequently precede uptrend reversals, as they did in this case.

Reversal bars are well known candlestick patterns that are used in technical analysis. Although it's beyond the scope of this book to cover in-depth candlestick charting and the large variety of possible candle formations, if you would like to explore candlestick charting further, there are many good books devoted entirely to the topic. You can visit www.trendfund.com for our current recommendations.

Reversal bars can signal the end of a downtrend as well. For an example, see the following chart that shows a gap up of GNSS.

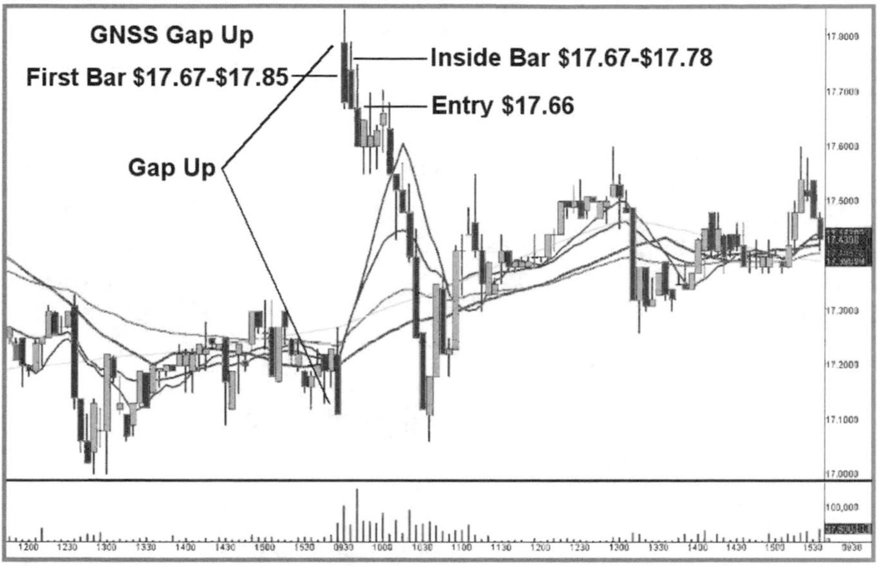

Looking at the preceding chart, after GNSS gapped up and sold off, you can see that a Hammer reversal bar appeared just before the price bounced. A Hammer often marks the end of a downtrend. Following is a close-up of the Hammer reversal bar.

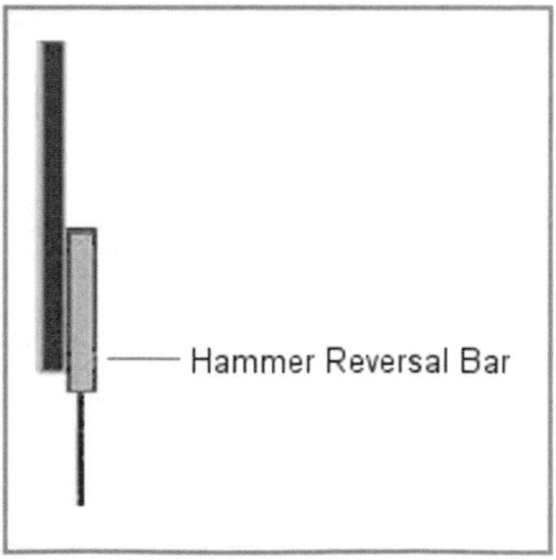

Though I don't always exit a position based solely on the appearance of reversal bars, I do consider reversal bars to be red flags. After seeing one, depending on the situation, I may take a portion of my gains off the table and watch the trade more closely, tighten my stops, or close out a position entirely.

Taking Profits

In the previous chapter, I discussed the importance of taking profits. Since taking profits applies to all exit strategies when gains are involved, including technical analysis strategies, I'm providing additional comments here that take into account the technical indicators discussed in this chapter.

In general, once a price target for your exit has been reached, it's important to be disciplined and take at least a portion of your profits. Your stop-loss should then be moved to breakeven or better on your remaining shares. At this point, under no circumstances, should you allow a winning trade to turn into a losing trade. Doing so not only erodes your trading capital, it can be psychologically devastating as well. Therefore, you should consider it a key rule that must be enforced. *Do not allow winners to turn into losers*!

As I discussed previously, I like to take profits as the trade moves in my favor. I will generally take some money off the table as the price nears the first point of resistance, which is typically the point where the gap fills. However, if I have substantial gains, I may take profits even sooner. Why take the chance of giving it back? Of course, the size of the gap and the amount of gains impact my decisions as well, so this is simply a general guideline that doesn't apply exactly the same to every situation.

What I usually do is take profits on 1/2 of my shares by the time the gap fills. Depending on how strong the play appears, or how weak, I may even take profits on all of my position. However, if I feel strongly there is more upside, I will sell 1/2 of my shares and move my stop-loss to at least breakeven on my remaining shares (including commissions), or slightly better than breakeven when the situation permits it. I will sometimes tighten my trailing stop at that point as well. For example, suppose I initially have a $0.75 trailing stop. After selling 1/2 of my shares, I may tighten my stop to $0.30 or $0.40.

If I achieve significant gains on my remaining shares, I'll either take profits on the rest of my shares, or I may once again sell 1/2 of my remaining shares and continue to trail the move until I stop out of the trade. However, if I see any reversal bars, I will likely take profits right away, or at the very least, tighten my stops.

Obviously, there are many potential variations for how you can take profits, especially when taking your own tolerance for risk into consideration. Many traders take all of their profits at once whenever they have any significant gains, or as a gap fills. My preference is to take money off of the table a piece at a time as I achieve gains, but you can take whichever approach works best for you.

The most important point is that you must take profits! Otherwise, you risk giving back all of your gains. Don't beat yourself up if you could have had more gains by staying in a trade longer. It could just as easily have gone against you. If you made money on the trade–you did good! You've likely heard the familiar adage, *no one ever goes broke taking profits*! This applies to trading gaps as well.

Similarly, no one ever picks perfect tops and bottoms either. If you executed the trade according to your plan, you either made money or got stopped out and preserved your capital, so don't beat yourself up over it. Learn whatever you can from the experience, change your plan, if applicable, and then move on to the next trade.

Using Stops

This section discusses some specific approaches you can consider for setting stop-loss orders. However, as always, you should always limit any loss to the maximum you are willing to accept according to your own tolerance for risk.

As I've mentioned elsewhere about trading gaps, since gaps tend to be more volatile, I generally use slightly wider stop-loss settings than I might use for other types of trades. Still, the precise setting is subjective and dependent on a variety of factors related to a specific trade. Therefore, you can consider the recommendations here general guidelines then make adjustments according to the specific circumstances and your own risk limits.

Initial Stop

When planning a gap trade, I typically have a predetermined maximum stop-loss limit in mind for the trade. As market valuations, volatility, gap sizes, and sentiments change over time, I make adjustments to my initial stop-loss settings accordingly. Of course, I make allowances for the size of a specific gap, and the stock's price and historical trading range as well.

For example, I would obviously use wider stops for a stock that is trading at $50.00 than I would use for one that is trading at $2.00. Generally, a higher priced stock will have a larger trading range. It may move $2 or $3 or more during a day, whereas a $2.00 stock might only move $0.05, $0.10, or $0.20. So, you obviously need to take these factors into consideration when placing your stop-loss orders.

If a stock is gapping by $0.50 or $0.60, I might use something like $0.40 or $050 for an initial maximum stop-loss limit. For example, if stock XYZ is gapping up by $0.50 and I enter the trade at $50.30; I might place a stop at $49.90 ($50.30 - $0.40 = $49.90). One psychological area that support or resistance is frequently encountered, if only temporarily, is at round dollar amounts such as $49, $50, $51, and so on. With that in mind, if it's within an appropriate range for a stop, I will often set my stop slightly beneath nearby round dollar amounts.

For smaller (or larger) gaps, I would adjust my stop setting accordingly, within reason. Meaning, I don't want to arbitrarily set it too tight, or too large. I might use up to a maximum of about $1 for higher priced stocks that have gapped fairly large, but it's not likely that I would allow a gap trade to go against me by much more than $1.00. The best bet is to test and track the stocks you are playing for gaps and see what they trade like over a period of time at the open. Stocks usually have patterns (trends), so you can see what an appropriate stop might be for any given stock.

Daily lows and highs are also price targets that I frequently use for setting my initial stop-losses. Since prior lows and highs often establish areas of support and resistance, a break of these could mean a gapping stock's price is not reversing as expected, in which case, I would want to stop out of the trade. When using lows and highs, however, if the stop seems too narrow or too wide, then I would make adjustments so that it falls within a more reasonable range as described above.

Other potential levels of technical support and resistance you might consider for stop-loss settings are gap fills, Fibonacci grid points, or key moving averages. Some key moving averages to keep an eye on for this purpose are the 10-, 20-, 50-, and 200-day moving averages. If you use technical areas of support and resistance for your stop settings, in most cases, it's best to place the stop slightly beyond (or wider than) the desired price target since they are frequently exceeded slightly before holding. A technical area of support or resistance could be a useful alternative when a stop-loss based upon the approaches described earlier is either too tight, or too wide. When possible, a setting that is comprised of multiple technical indicators is even better, since it tends to be stronger. For example, a setting that coincides with a recent high, a 200-day moving average, and a gap fill is likely to be stronger than any single indicator.

When using technical analysis to plan your entries, a good general guideline to keep in mind for setting stops relates to a failure of the specific pattern that is used for the entry. In other words, you should stop out of a trade when the price movement causes the chart pattern to fail.

Stop-losses can also be based on the total amount of money that you are willing to lose on a trade. For example, if the most you are willing to lose on a trade is $500 and your lot size will be 1000 shares, then your maximum stop-loss setting shouldn't be more than $0.50 from your entry price ($500 / 1000 shares = $0.50). Of course, you must also consider what makes sense for a specific trade based on the total purchase price and percentage loss. For example, you wouldn't want to buy 1000 shares of a $1.00 stock for a total cost of $1000 and still use $500 as your maximum loss, or a $0.50 stop-loss setting. You would lose $500, or half of your money, before you stopped out of the trade! Of course, this example is only for illustration purposes. As a general rule, we don't play stocks that are under $10.00 for gap trades. I've found that stocks under $10.00 usually don't trade consistently using this technique (or most techniques). The higher the stock price, the more consistent the gaps is a general rule of thumb. Higher priced stocks tend to be the most volatile as well. Don't be afraid to trade 100 shares of a $70.00 stock as opposed to more shares of a $7.00 stock. Frankly, more often than not, you'll find that you get more bang for your buck with the $70.00 stock!

10:00 AM Stop

As time passes or when there is any significant movement in your stock's price, you need to adjust your stop-loss setting. At the very least, the first review of your initial stop-loss setting should occur at 10:00 AM. At this time, you can use the 10:00 AM rule as a guideline for determining where to place your stop. Although the 10:00 AM rule is covered elsewhere in the book, for your convenience, here is what it says.

If a stock gaps up, you should not buy it long unless it makes a new high after 10:00 AM. Conversely, if a stock gaps down, you should not sell it short unless it makes a new low after 10:00 AM.

To use the 10:00 AM rule as a guideline, adjust your stops to the lows, or highs as the case may be, that were put in prior to 10:00 AM.

For example, if the market gaps down and you enter a long position, when 10:00 AM comes move your stop-loss setting for the stock to, or slightly beneath, the low that occurred prior to 10:00 AM. Conversely, if the market gaps up and you enter a short position, when 10:00 AM comes move your stop-loss setting for the stock to the high, or slightly above the high, that occurred prior to 10:00 AM.

You might be wondering why I'm suggesting that you use the 10:00 AM rule for stop-loss placement. The main reason has to do with the way market makers and specialists manage order flow. As orders begin to come in during pre-market trading when volume is light, there may be a lack of either buyers or sellers on a given day. Market makers and specialists must then make a market by taking the other side of the trades with their own inventory. Since they must make money as well (if they want to retain their jobs), they push prices up or down according to the buy or sell bias. After the market opens, during the first 30 minutes of trading there is a higher degree of uncertainty and fluctuation in the market as market makers readjust their inventories. As a result, the market gaps and is more volatile initially. Then once the market makers clear out their inventory imbalances and have made their money, the true market trend begins to develop for the day according to the actual buyers and sellers in the marketplace. Therefore, it's appropriate to review and reset stop-losses relative to the market's true directional trend.

Trailing Stop

A trailing stop-loss order is a stop that either automatically trails the price of a stock as it moves, or is manually adjusted to trail the price movement. You can use trailing stops to trail the price of your long positions as they move higher, or to trail short positions as they move lower.

Many of today's trading platforms provide the capability to place stop-loss orders that trail price movements by a specified amount for you automatically. However, if your broker doesn't provide this feature or if you prefer to have greater control over the process, you can also manually adjust stop-loss orders to trail a stock's price movement.

Here's an example of how an automatic trailing stop-loss order works. Suppose that you enter a long position at $50.00 with a plan to stop out of the trade should it initially go against you by $0.50. You also want to use a trailing stop-loss order, rather than a fixed stop-loss that doesn't change, so you can immediately capture any gains should the price move in your favor.

After entering a position at $50.00, you would place a trailing stop-loss order at $49.50. If the stock's price immediately moves against you and falls to $49.50, you'll stop out of trade with a $0.50 loss. However, if the price goes up $0.25 before pulling back, your stop-loss setting would also automatically go up by $0.25 as well. You would now stop out of the trade with a $0.25 loss, if the price fell to $49.75. Similarly, if the price goes up to $51.00 before pulling back, you would stop out of the trade at $50.50 (the high of $51.00 - $0.50 = $50.50) for a gain of $0.50. As you can see, the stop-loss trails any upside movement of the stock's price, minus $0.50, but the stop-loss price does not fall when the stock's price falls. Of course, you can electively choose to sell and take profits at any point you choose. In the preceding example, you would have obviously come out further ahead by taking profits closer to $51.00, rather than waiting to be stopped out of the trade. Therefore, it's best to use trailing stops, or any stops for that matter, as a method of limiting risk and protecting gains rather than as your sole strategy for taking profits.

An advantage to using an automatically trailing stop-loss order is that it shifts a large portion of the responsibility for managing stop-losses to your trading platform, which can be a big help when managing multiple, quickly moving trades at once. On the other hand, an automatic stop doesn't take into account any unique circumstances that might apply to a trade. For example, there might be occasions when you have achieved significant gains, but for one reason or another, you would like to stay in the trade even if it pulls back by $0.55 or $0.60 rather than strictly enforcing the $0.50 trailing stop you initially placed. For instance, maybe you noticed there is a strong level of support $0.10 below where the trailing stop will trigger. Unless you are paying close attention and quickly adjust your trailing stop or change it to a fixed stop, you will be stopped out of the trade if the price falls sufficiently to trigger the stop.

In the case of fixed stops, you assume all responsibility for making any adjustments after placing the initial stop-loss order. As you achieve gains, you need to manually reset your stop-loss order to the desired price. On some trading platforms, you might need to cancel your existing stop-loss order and place a new order, while other systems let you change an existing order without first canceling it. Since this varies, you'll need to check with your broker for the specifics on the types of features that are supported, but regardless of the specifics, it becomes your responsibility to manually adjust your stop-loss orders to trail any upside movement on your trades.

It's really a matter of personal preference regarding which type of stop to use. When playing gaps, you can start with an initial stop that is fixed as described earlier and adjust the stop as the trade evolves, or you can begin with an automatically trailing stop. Another option is to begin with a fixed stop initially then switch to a trailing stop later. Whichever method you choose, at the very least, you should begin trailing your gap trades more closely as the gaps fill, or as they take out the prior lows or highs of the day (and recent prior days). And as previously mentioned, it's a good idea to take a portion of your profit at this time and move your stops to breakeven on any remaining shares.

Stop Versus Stop-Limit

Before leaving the topic of stop-loss orders, I'll discuss a question that I frequently receive about which type of stop-loss order is best to use, a stop-limit order or a standard stop-loss order. Some trading platforms don't provide an option to specify stop-limit orders. If your trading platform doesn't offer such an option, then you may have no alternative but to use a standard stop-loss order.

Since a standard stop-loss order executes as a market order once triggered, in a fast moving market your order could fill at a price that is worse than your intended stop price. If you want to be certain that your order fills after your stop-loss triggers, then you can't do anything to avoid this potential outcome. While you can use a stop-limit order that fills only if your limit price is met, this could leave you exposed to additional risk. If a rapidly moving price does not precisely hit your limit price (i.e., it jumps over your limit price), your order will not execute.

For example, if you place a stop-limit order on a long position with a stop price at $25.35 and a limit price at $25.35, when the stock's price hits or falls below $25.35, your stop will trigger and your order will execute as a regular limit order at $25.35. If the stock's price is moving quickly and falls to $25.36, then to $25.34 or lower without specifically hitting $25.35 (or for whatever reason, the price gaps below your limit price), your stop will trigger but your limit order will not fill. The $25.34 price would be lower than your specified minimum limit of $25.35, which prevents the execution of the limit order. The price could subsequently fall to $22.00 or lower and you will not stop out of the trade.

A regular stop-loss order that executes as a market order ensures you will stop out of a trade. Though there is no guaranty your order will fill precisely at the specified stop price, your order will fill. Practically speaking, when trading liquid stocks, in most instances your order will fill reasonably close to your stop price. On the other hand, with fast moving low volume stocks you could experience worse fills. Regardless, using the preceding example, I would prefer to stop out at $25.20, or whatever, rather than not stop out at all. Since that's my preference, I use and recommend using a standard stop-loss order that executes as a market order once triggered.

As always, though, you should take the specific circumstances of a trade into account. There may be unique situations where a stop-limit order is appropriate, like when holding swing trades overnight and a gap could take out your stop before you've had a chance to review the situation. This isn't a concern for me because as I mentioned under

"Swing Trades", I remove all of my stops before the market closes each day and reset them the following morning, which avoids the possibility of gaps taking out my stops.

Another approach you could consider is to set the limit price of a stop-limit somewhat lower than the stop price to help ensure your order fills, but for general trading purposes, I still prefer to use a standard stop-loss order over a stop-limit order.

Getting The Extra Edge

Traders are always looking for a way to achieve an *extra edge*, that is, a way to stay a little ahead of the rest of the crowd. Anything that might provide an early indication of a potential change in a stock's price movement, or the overall direction of the market, could be quite beneficial, and profitable. Leading indicators, or those that tend to lead the market, are one method by which traders can obtain an edge.

The futures are one type of leading indicator. They are a great way to get a sense of the market's directional bias, which is one reason you commonly see them displayed on business oriented news broadcasts. Virtually all professional traders watch the futures. Since the futures are leading indicators, if the futures are roaring higher, or falling off a cliff, then the market is likely to follow. Trader's predominately watch the Nasdaq 100 and S&P 500 index futures. Most direct-access brokers provide a way to track the futures. However, the method for doing this can vary between brokers. You can check with your broker for more specific information about how to obtain futures quotes and charts using their trading platform.

The Nasdaq Composite can also be used as a leading indicator for the directional bias of technology stocks. The Nasdaq is comprised predominately of technology stocks, and technology frequently leads the market. Why? Technology is the future and everyone wants to bet on the future rather than the past. So, overall, technology is a leading indicator.

Similarly, you can use the Semiconductor Index (SOX) as a leading indicator as well. Computer chips are increasingly being put into a larger variety of products, and this trend is currently expected to continue indefinitely into the future. Therefore, the SOX is also a leading indicator.

When used as tools for directional guidance, you generally don't trade the leading indicators themselves (although, it is possible to trade them using options or futures in some cases). For the intended use discussed here, the idea is to watch leading indicators for an indication of how stocks are likely to move.

If you want to use leading indicators such as the SOX or Nasdaq for guidance, you need to watch stocks that tend to move along with the SOX or Nasdaq. A few current examples include technology stocks such as KLAC, AMAT, QLGC, and EBAY. These are only a few examples for illustration purposes, and not specific recommendations. The best stock choices change over time. However, you can simply watch some good candidates for a few days. If you repeatedly observe that whenever the leading indicators you are tracking are going up or down, certain stocks are also up or down, then they are potential trading candidates. In situations where the leading indicators have begun to move but the corresponding stocks you've identified are lagging the move for no apparent reason (news, etc.), there is a good chance the stocks will play catch-up at some point, and as a result, they could provide potential trading opportunities. The "Trading Laggards" chapter discusses topics similar to this as well.

Two chart examples follow that show the Nasdaq and SOX.

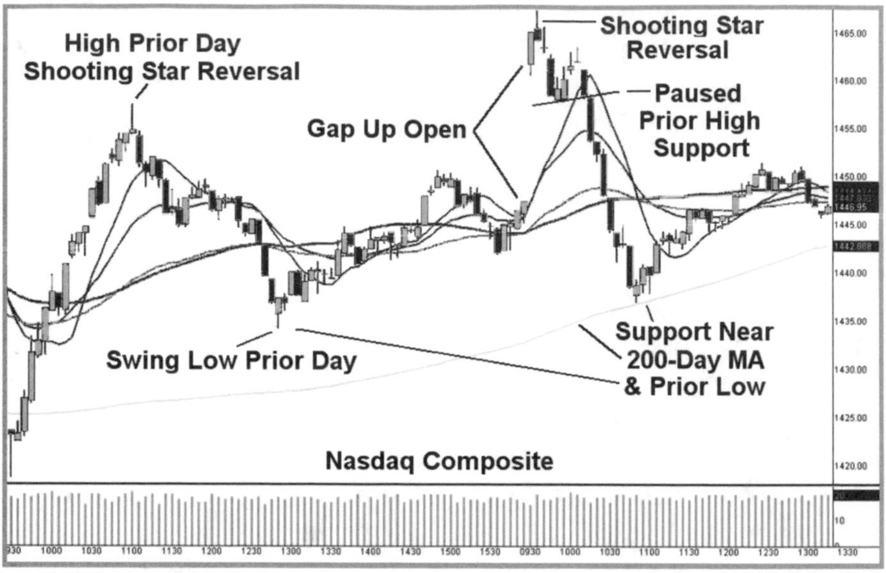

Referring to the preceding Nasdaq chart, notice the Shooting Star reversal candle that not only signaled a potential market reversal and the high of the day, it marked an area of potential future resistance. The next morning, the market gapped through the resistance of the prior high, but then it temporarily paused on a pullback as it encountered support in the same area as the prior resistance. Old resistance frequently becomes an area of future support, even if only temporarily. Also notice that once again, a Shooting Star reversal bar signaled the reversal that occurred shortly after the gap up. Another key area of support is a 200-day moving average, as well as prior swing point lows. Support tends to be even stronger when more than one indicator is involved. Looking at the chart, you can see that support was encountered near these levels.

The following chart shows how the SOX behaved during the same time period as the preceding Nasdaq chart.

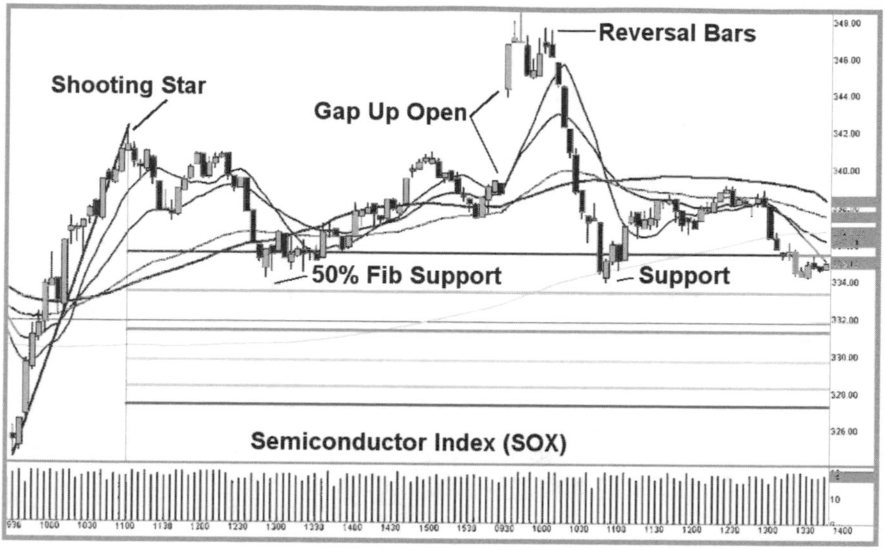

Notice the similarities between the two charts. Similar to the Nasdaq, the SOX formed a Shooting Star reversal bar that also marked the high of the day. After the gap up the next morning, additional reversal bars signaled the subsequent pullback. I've also included a Fibonacci grid on this chart (most good charting software provides the capability to overlay Fibonacci grids). Fibonacci grid lines are widely used in technical analysis to indicate potential areas of support and resistance, or potential price pivot points. Though it is beyond the scope of this book to provide in-depth descriptions of Fibonacci grids, there are many good books on technical analysis that explain their use (you can check www.trendfund.com for our latest recommendations). In this case, just note that a level of support was established near the 50% Fibonacci grid line, which subsequently held the next day as well.

By watching the futures, the Nasdaq Composite, and the SOX for reversal signals or areas of support and resistance, you can get an extra edge, or advance warning of what may lie ahead for your stocks. If you see a reversal bar or notice the market is approaching an area of support or resistance, you should at least pay closer attention to your trades. And in some cases, you may even want to consider entering positions, exiting positions, or tightening stop-losses on positions based upon what you observe using leading indicators.

6

Trading Laggards

The prices of stocks that are in a similar business, industry or sector will often move together. When the price of one goes up or down, the price of other similar stocks may go up or down as well.

For example, if you look at their charts, you'll see that the price action of two closely related biotech stocks, such as Amgen (AMGN) and Biogen (BGEN) often move together. One of the best examples no longer exists since both stocks were bought out by Barry Diller's IACI, but we'll use them to prove out the point. These were two travel industry stocks; Expedia (EXPE) and Hotels.com (ROOM). They were known to move so closely that a good trader could often catch $2 - $3 moves by following them and using the laggard techniques we'll be discussing in this chapter.

What Is A Laggard?

When a stock's price action is lagging behind its peer stocks, which are stocks in a comparable business, industry, or sector, it is called a *laggard*.

A price divergence between a laggard and a peer stock frequently corrects itself at some point, either intraday or within the next day or so. The price action of a laggard often catches up with the price action of a peer stock, but this is also subject to the specific circumstances, news, or overall market conditions. In some instances, the price of the peer stock will move back toward the price of the laggard.

To help judge which stock is most likely to make a corrective move, you can look at the strength and direction of the overall market. If the market is moving higher and a laggard's peer stock is moving higher, the lagging stock is likely to also move higher to catch up. Conversely, if the market is moving lower and a laggard's peer stock is moving lower, the lagging stock is also likely to eventually move lower.

Laggard Examples

Laggards can provide great intraday trading opportunities. For example, maybe the biotech sector starts getting attention. You could start watching some biotech stocks that tend to move together. Once again, I'll use AMGN and BGEN as an example, but this could apply to other stocks as well. Suppose you notice that AMGN is up $2 but BGEN is essentially flat. Since BGEN is lagging behind the AMGN move, unless there is some type of bad news out about BGEN, which you should check, BGEN may eventually take off and catch up with AMGN. Therefore, you might look to buy BGEN long for a trade.

There are many intraday trading opportunities such as these. If you identify and watch stocks that tend to run together, you can watch for intraday price divergences between them. Later, I'll provide suggestions for setting up your watch list for this purpose.

Here is another example of two stocks, Expedia (EXPE) and Hotels.com (ROOM), which have similar price action. Both sell hotel and motel reservations online, although EXPE also sells airline tickets, travel vacations, and other travel services. Since both stocks are in similar online businesses, news or other announcements that affect the price of one frequently affects the price of the other.

Take a look at the following chart. The chart compares the intraday price action of both stocks. Notice how the overall price action of one tends to coincide with the price action of the other.

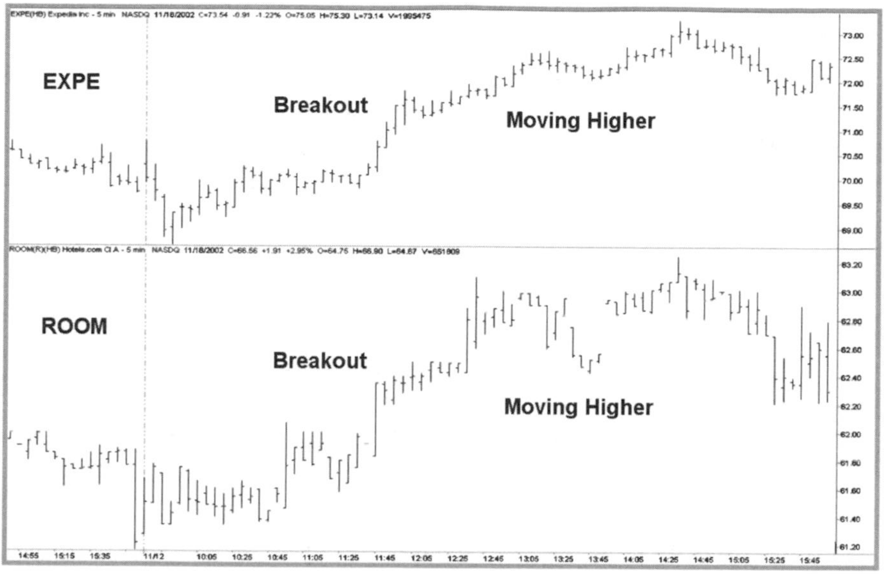

This is only one example among many stocks that behave this way. I watch and trade these two stocks frequently, and also many others. When I see price divergences between them, I try to determine the cause. If there isn't any apparent reason for the divergence, such as company-specific news that isn't applicable to the other stocks, it presents a trading opportunity since one or the other will usually play catch up, either to the upside or downside.

For example, if EXPE is up $2 while ROOM is flat or down slightly, and if the overall market is in an uptrend, I would likely be a buyer of ROOM for trade. Upon entering the trade, I would set a stop-loss order just under the low of the day, or according to a near-term level of support, but also taking into account my overall risk tolerance for the trade. If ROOM subsequently began to run, I would trail the price up with my stop-loss order, and/or take profits at an appropriate time.

I might also consider taking profits on half of my position, then move my stop-loss order to breakeven (including commissions) on the other half. From there, and with profits already locked in, I could continue to trail any additional upside move on the other half of my position with a trailing stop-loss order, and eventually stop out of the trade or take profits at my own discretion.

Following is another EXPE example.

Notice on the preceding chart how EXPE is in a strong uptrend all day. It begins the day with a strong upside move then continues with a steady gain throughout the afternoon. It finally ended the day at its highs after another strong upside move. Now, compare EXPE to the price action of ROOM on the following chart.

Similar to EXPE, ROOM began the day strong but it subsequently fell back and made lower lows or traded sideways throughout most of the day. It was noticeably lagging behind EXPE. Then, near the end of the day, it took off and began catching up with EXPE. It subsequently closed the day at its highs as well.

During the period where ROOM is lagging the EXPE move, you could trade ROOM by entering a long position with a stop-loss order placed slightly below the low of the day, or a recent support level, depending on the specific circumstances and your own risk tolerance.

A chart of the following day also shows similar price action between EXPE and ROOM.

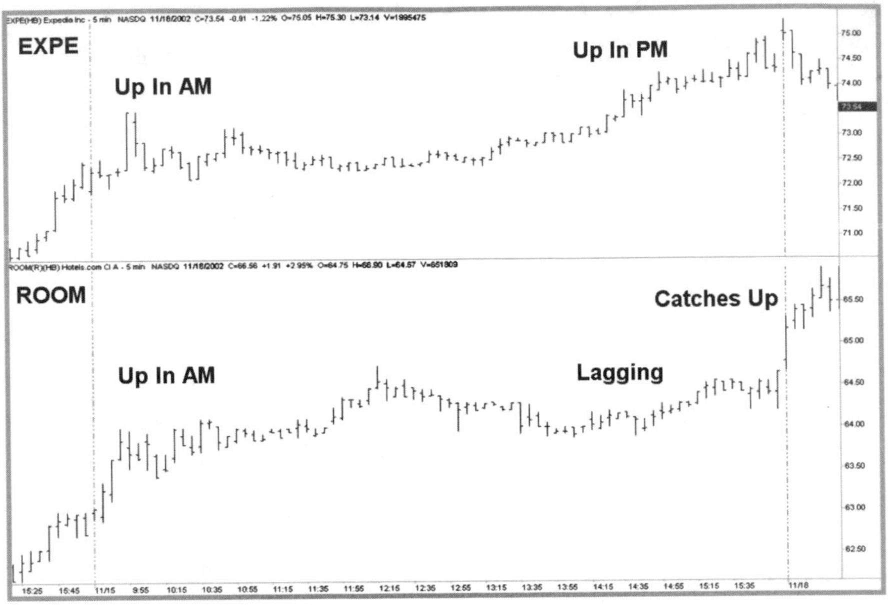

Notice on the chart that even though both stocks started out the day strong, ROOM began lagging behind during the afternoon. Just before the market closed, ROOM took off and attempted to catch up with the EXPE move.

The chart also shows how ROOM, after lagging EXPE the prior day, continued to catch up with EXPE after the market first opened the next morning (the vertical lines on the chart are session break lines). Sometimes, a laggard may carry over into the next day before catching up. However, since I don't like the additional risk exposure associated with holding a position overnight, I prefer to play laggards intraday and rarely hold them overnight.

Laggards make nice trades because they tend to be high percentage plays with minimal risk. For example, on a stock like ROOM or EXPE you can place a relatively tight stop-loss order of about $1 to minimize risk, but the stock could potentially run $4 or $5 on an intraday move, which is a great risk/reward ratio. When the Nasdaq market is really screaming, either of these stocks is a good candidate for a fabulous intraday ride, and profit.

Though there used to be many more of these high-flying stocks during the bull market of the late 1990's, you can still make money by trading laggards in today's market. To help spot laggards, try setting up your watch list according to sectors. I like to set mine up with stocks from similar sectors grouped together. For example, I'll group together the Semiconductor stocks such as KLAC, NVLS, INTC, MXIM, LLTC, BRCM, AMCC, PMCS, etc.; the Fiber Optic stocks such as CSCO, JNPR, CIEN, JDSU, GLW; the Biotech stocks such as PDLI, HGSI, CRA; the Drug/Biotech stocks such as AMGN, BGEN, IDPH, DNA; and so on. Note that the mentioned stocks are just for illustration purposes. Though I often use them, the actual make up of my watch list changes according to market conditions and my intraday needs, and many other momentum stocks are available from which you can choose your own favorites.

7

Trading The News

A variety of news stories break each day that could potentially impact the stock market or specific stocks. They range from world news events to national news events to news about individual industries or companies.

When the state of the economy, an earnings announcement or other news impacts the performance of a company, the market often anticipates that other similar companies will be impacted as well. Even though there may not be a sound reason for the news to affect other companies, just the perception that it could may be sufficient to move stock prices. As a result, when positive news comes out about a company that drives its stock price higher, traders and investors may begin looking for other similar stocks they can buy at a cheaper price. Alternatively, the same is true when the news is negative and a stock's price falls. Traders may look at other similar stocks for shorting opportunities.

For example, if a stock in the biotech sector such as Amgen (AMGN) releases a huge upside earnings announcement or other positive news, it could be perceived as good news for other stocks in the biotech sector. If you knew that the price of another biotech stock such as Biogen (BGEN) and the price of AMGN tended to move together, you could watch BGEN for a possible trading opportunity.

Eventually, the linkage between some popular momentum stocks may become so pervasive that the prices may move in sync with one another without a specific reason. If the price of one moves, particularly if it is a significant move, traders that are familiar with its competitors start watching them for potential trading opportunities. The "Trading Laggards" chapter provides more information about this type of behavior as well.

By having a historical perspective about how a given type of news has impacted individual stocks or the overall market in the past, and whether other similar stocks were also affected, you can potentially profit from trading the news. This chapter discusses issues related to trading the news and provides examples of how various types of news releases impacted the market or individual stocks.

Guidelines For Trading News

When trading the news, there are two overriding factors that go into my decision-making.

- The overall condition of the market.
- The historical context of the news.

Market Conditions

I always take current market conditions into account when deciding whether, or how, to make trades that are based upon breaking news events. Generally, but depending on the specific circumstances, I prefer not to fight the direction of the market and possibly more importantly, I don't want to fight the psychology or perceptions of the market.

If positive news comes out about a company but the market is in a strong downtrend, I am less likely to trade the news. Alternatively, if the news is positive and the market is also in an uptrend, I would be more inclined to trade the news by entering a long position. Of course, the same applies to negative news. If the market appears weak and the news is negative, then I would be more likely to trade the news by entering a short position.

However, market psychology is equally as important and may even override the preceding market trend considerations in some circumstances. If the market has little tolerance for a particular type of negative news, then the impact on a stock's price will likely to be more dramatic. In situations such as this, the price of an individual stock could easily move contrary to the direction of the market. An example of this is provided later.

The potential for the market or individual stocks to react differently to similar news events at a given point in time is the reason you need to not only have a historical perspective, which is discussed in more detail next, you also need to be in tune with the current mood of the market.

The best trading opportunities come about when various factors reinforce one another. That is, when positive news comes out about a company while the market is in an uptrend, and the market sentiment related to the news has also been positive. The same applies when all of these factors reinforce one another in a negative way.

Historical Context Of News

As mentioned, an important aspect of trading breaking news is having a historical context in which to consider the impact of the news. You need to know how a particular type of news has affected other stocks that have had similar news, and preferably, how it affected their competitors, their sector, or the market at large. With a frame of reference that puts the news into a proper context, you'll be in a position to determine whether the affected stocks or their competitors are good trading candidates.

Since a historical perspective is desirable, it's a good idea to watch breaking news over a period of time and study how it affects individual stocks, sectors, and the market overall before putting your capital at risk. In time, you can develop a historical perspective to help guide your trades.

The significance of the news is also an important consideration. The bigger the news, the better because major news events result in more volatility and larger price swings, which in turn provides better trading opportunities.

Following are some examples of breaking news events and how they impacted the performance of individual stocks and/or the market overall.

News Stories

As previously mentioned, the effect of breaking news is subject to overall market conditions and market psychology. Just because breaking news has a certain effect at one point in time, doesn't necessarily mean it will have exactly the same effect at a later time. Market reactions to a particular type of news often change over time.

In the case of extensive ongoing news coverage, news may become *old hat* over a period of time. When it becomes *old news*, the impact it has on the performance of stocks may diminish. Therefore, when reviewing the following examples, remember to take current market conditions into consideration. Also, keep in mind that these examples are simply a random sampling among many other possible news stories that could have an effect on a stock or the overall market.

Stock Purchases By Co Officers (TYC)

Large stock purchases by company officers are often perceived as positive news. Here is news that came out about Tyco International Ltd (TYC).

"Announcement by company CEO and CFO of plans to each purchase 500,000 shares of stock has helped establish an intraday floor for the stock. Reversal in price momentum has also sent shorts scrambling to cover positions. High for the rebound is $32.60. CEO and CFO buy the stock to prove it was ok to do so."

Following is a chart that shows how the news affected TYC.

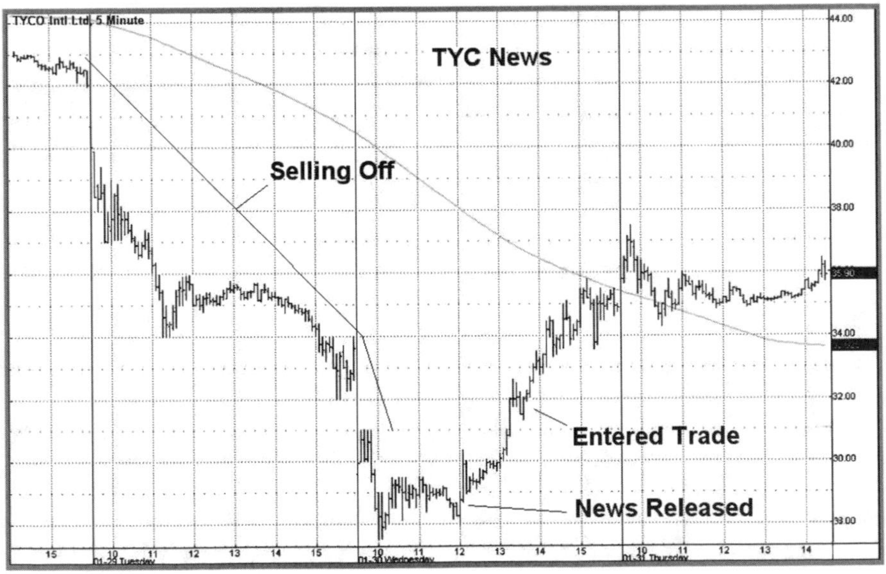

As you can see on the preceding chart, the stock only had a modest reaction to the news initially.

In this case, prior to this positive news release, the stock price had been "hammered" due to other bad news about accounting irregularities. The preceding bad news came at a time when the market had little tolerance for these types of problems. As mentioned, knowing the current market sentiment for a particular type of news is a key factor in gauging how a stock will react to the news.

Since the stock had been getting "trashed" day after day in the news, and fund managers had been dumping the stock by the busloads, the risk/reward seemed quite favorable to me. The bulk of the sellers were likely already out of TYC, so any positive news had a better chance of pushing the price higher. And the CEO and CFO coming out in the defense of the stock by purchasing such a large number of shares is generally perceived as positive news.

Additionally, since the stock had been selling off hard, I knew there were likely a large number of short positions in the stock. In fact, I had a short position in it myself at one point. So, any positive news that pushed the price higher would likely result in a *short squeeze*. A short squeeze occurs when people are short a stock and have to buy it back in order to cover their positions as the price goes up. This drives the price even higher, which results in even more short covering, and so on until equilibrium is found.

Taking all of the preceding conditions into consideration, I decided to trade the news and called it long for my clients when I saw that interest in TYC was increasing. A short time later, the stock moved almost $5 in a little over an hour for a fantastic intraday trade.

Keep in mind that just because I bought the stock long intraday didn't mean that I thought the positive news indicated it was a good long-term investment. In fact, I thought the price would ultimately go lower. I simply considered the risk/reward favorable for a short-term trade. By setting a stop-loss order slightly below the low of the day, the risk was only about $1 and the potential profit was much higher, as demonstrated by the eventual outcome of the trade.

Insider Trading (MSO)

News related to insider trading can also impact the performance of a stock. Following is a news report that came out about Martha Stewart Living Omnimedia, Inc (MSO).

"The New York Times reports that Martha Stewart, CEO of MSO and a close friend of the former CEO of IMCL, sold all her shares in IMCL a day or two before the co announced an unfavorable ruling by the FDA, according to people close to a Congressional Investigation of the co. The House Energy and Commerce Committee is Investigating IMCL and has asked for information on which relatives and friends of former IMCL CEO Dr. Waksal had sold shares in the days before the FDA decision."

Here is a chart that shows the stock's reaction to the news.

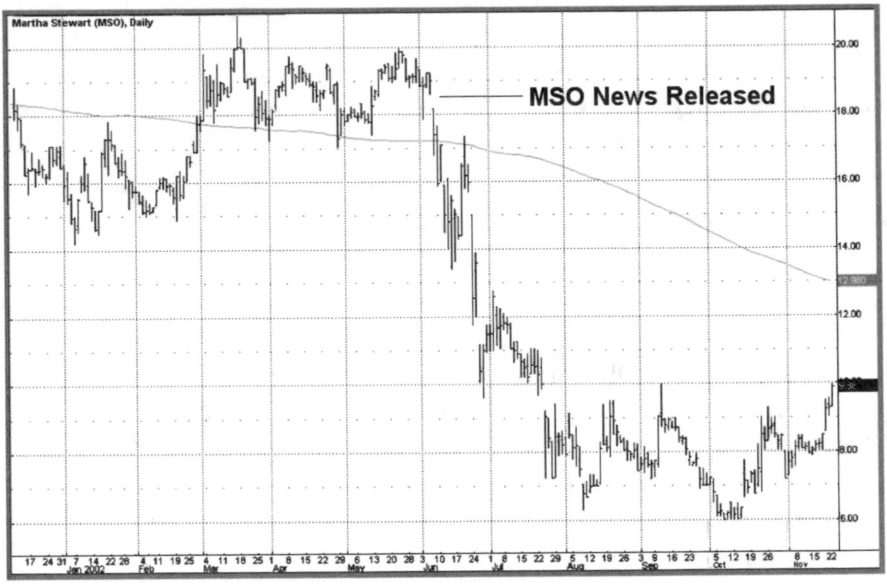

Once again, this news came out at a time when the market had a low tolerance for company scandals. There had been a string of large companies whose top management was under investigation for illegal accounting practices, insider trading, fraud and more. Making matters worse, MSO is a unique situation where the company's image, its name, and the brand of its products are all tied to the credibility and prestige of a single individual, the CEO of the company. The company's name is the CEO's name, and the CEO's name is on the company's products. Therefore, if the CEO's reputation is questioned, it has a greater likelihood of adversely impacting the company's sales and its stock price.

Even though many analysts were coming out in defense of both the stock and the CEO, I felt the stock couldn't possibly hold up in the face of such news, particularly when the company's name and its product brands are so closely tied to the reputation of its CEO. I also knew how the market had been reacting to this type of news. So, I decided to trade the stock and called it as a short trade for my clients, betting the price would fall, which it subsequently did as can be seen on the preceding chart. This was a situation that I felt justified a longer-term swing trade, so we bought PUT options on the stock. However, taking a short position would have worked as well. I chose PUT options in part so we could trade the stock with a predefined maximum risk (see the "Options Primer" and "Trading Options" chapters for more about options).

Denying Claims Lawsuit (UNM)

Healthcare companies had been taking a severe beating in the news, so when the following news was reported about UnumProvident Corp (UNM), it got my attention.

"UNUM Corp sued for denying claims (UNM) 20.90 –0.13: Traders citing Bloomberg tell us that UNM has been accused in a lawsuit of systematically denying claims for long-term disability insurance by thousands of people too sick or too injured to work."

Here is a chart that shows how the stock reaction to the news.

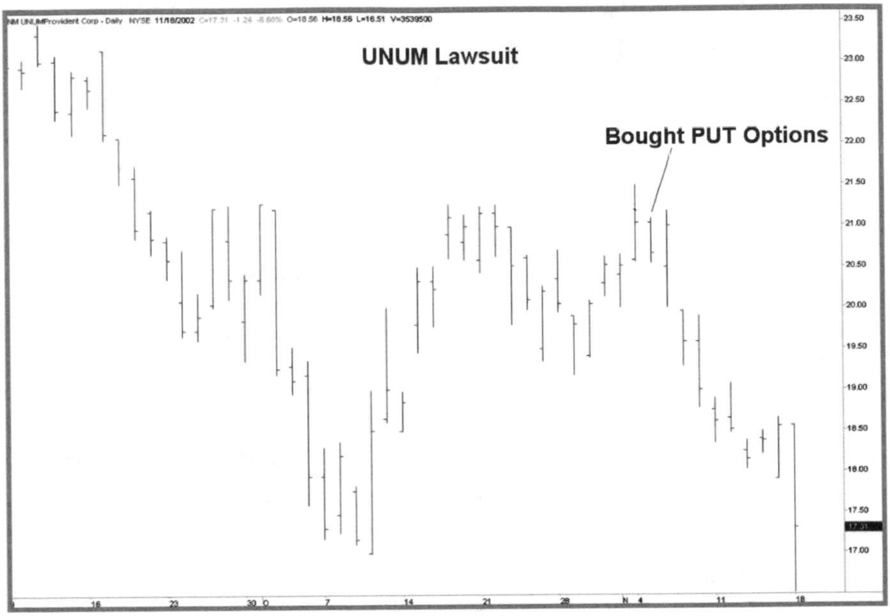

Having seen the impact that negative news had on other stocks in the healthcare sector, I thought the news about UNM would likely cause the stock to sell off. Therefore, I called the stock short for clients. We played the news by buying PUT options.

I decided to play the news with options this time because I wanted to trade a fairly large number of shares and the liquidity of this stock was low, meaning I could have a more difficult time getting out of the trade quickly. Low liquidity adds additional risk. Since the most you can lose with options is the premium price of the options, I decided to buy *in the money* PUT options to limit my maximum risk exposure. Plus, due to the low volatility of this stock the premium on the options was quite reasonable, so the overall risk/reward on the trade was great.

If you can't trade options, then you could also trade the stock short. Liquidity is less of a concern if your lot sizes are not excessively large, as was the case with mine. As you can see on the preceding chart, the stock subsequently sold off, which resulted in a nice profit on the trade.

ABSURDLY CHEAP NEWS (THC)

This was another play similar to the TYC trade discussed earlier. The Tenet Healthcare Corp (THC) stock had been beaten down severely when the following Barron's news came out.

"Tenet Healthcare 'absurdly cheap. Delta Partners manager Charles Jobson has been averaging down in Tenet. The hedge fund manager, whose fund is up 25.5% this yr, began buying THC when it first broke $28 and has been buying it more aggressively at $14-$15. 'However bad it can get, it can't get as bad as the decline in the share price suggests. The stock is absurdly cheap.' Jobson is also bullish on PacifiCare (PHSY) as a turnaround play."

Here's a chart that shows how the THC stock reacted to the news.

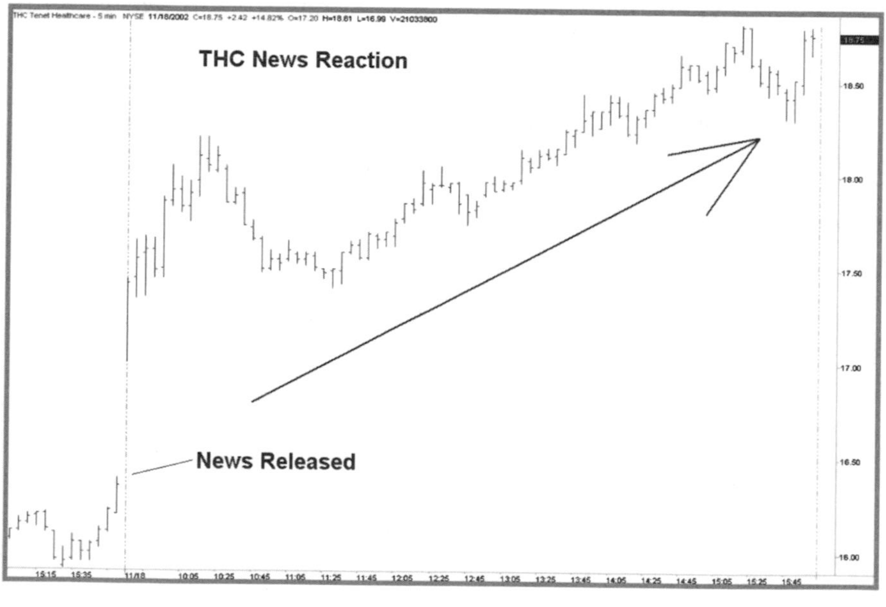

As with the TYC example shown earlier, there was considerable short interest in the THC stock due to prior bad news. Therefore, any good news could potentially trigger buying that results in a short squeeze and strong upside price movement.

As always, you want to consider the risk/reward potential for a trade. Does the news reflect a real or perceived change in the value of the company? On a short-term basis for that particular day, it did, so the overall risk/reward was favorable for a trade. Once again, I wasn't interested in taking a long-term position in the stock. I was only interested in whether it could be traded for a profit intraday. Even though this news wasn't phenomenal, since the stock was so heavily beaten down and heavily shorted, the news was sufficiently positive for a profitable intraday trade.

Iraq War News

The market and individual stocks also react to major world news events. News that came out before the Iraq War is a good example. Once a war appeared inevitable, the following news was released.

"Hearing Iraq accepts UN resolution on inspections."

Here is a chart that shows how the Nasdaq market reacted to the news.

Notice how volatile the market became after the release of the news. Initially, the market took off with a large impulsive move to the upside, but as people realized that statements released by Iraq weren't necessarily credible, there was a corrective pullback. Subsequently, the market resumed its upside move.

The market appeared confused. It wanted to believe a war was less likely but on the other hand, Iraq had a reputation for deception. This is another example of how market psychology comes into play. People want to believe that everything will work out okay. It's human nature. There is an inherent desire for things to get better. So when news comes out that provides the potential for a positive outcome, the market has a position reaction, at least initially. After reality sets in, the initial enthusiasm may subside.

Regardless of how events ultimately unfold, the volatility that is generated from news like this provides intraday trading opportunities. One way to trade this type of news is to look for laggards that have not yet reacted to the news. If you haven't read it yet, please refer to the "Trading Laggards" chapter for information about laggards.

This example also demonstrates how major news releases can affect both individual stocks, and the market at large. Compare all of the following charts and notice the similarities. The first chart shows how the news affected the S&P 500 Index.

The next chart shows how the Dow Industrials reacted to the news.

Individual stocks had similar reactions to the news. Here is a chart for Microsoft, Inc (MSFT).

And the following chart shows the reaction of KLA Tencor Corporation (KLAC).

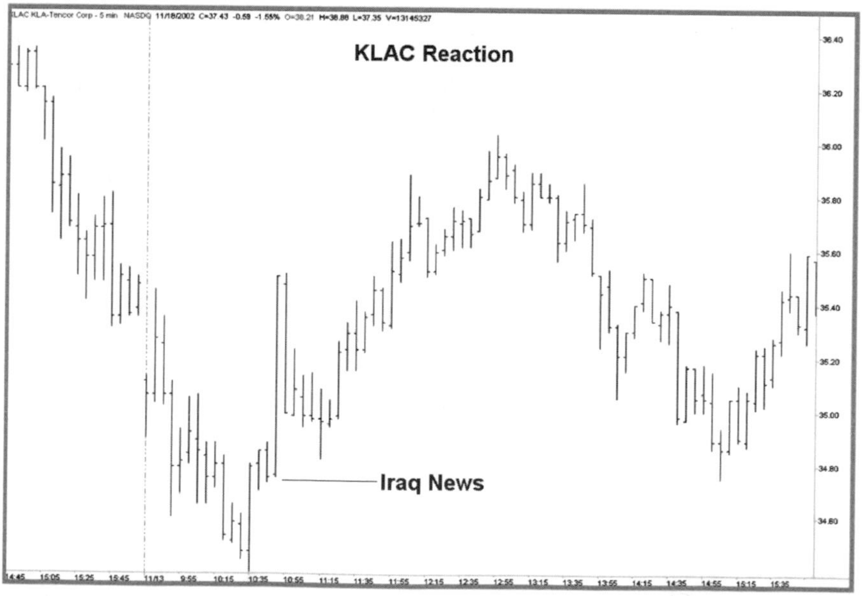

As you can see on all of the preceding charts, the Iraq news affected both individual stocks and the overall market similarly.

Earnings Guidance (GE)

Earnings announcements may also provide trading opportunities. Here is an earnings-guidance news release for General Electric Co (GE).

"General Electric guidance, charge expected (24.30) – Update.

Charge announced this morning for co's ERC biz had been well-advertised. On Tues, the WSJ reported that a charge of $1-$2 bln would be announced at today's investor meeting. Solly cut 2003 estimates the same day to $1.65 from $1.70 and also predicted co would take a billion dollar charge. This morning, before the announcement, Deutsche lowered its 2003 est to $1.70 from $1.80 ahead of the investor meeting, predicting that GE would cut guidance to the $1.65-$1.70 range. In sum, GE's 2003 guidance of $1.55-$1.70 was pretty much in-line with analysts' lowered outlook and the $1.4 bln charge fell within the range of expectations. What may be considered somewhat of a surprise is the reduced 2002 guidance to $1.51 from the $1.65. GE shares are trading up 1% in pre-market."

Here is a chart that shows how GE reacted to the news.

Even though the preceding news wasn't particularly positive, the stock didn't sell off as a result of the news. Instead, the stock gapped up and kept on going. Why? The news appears to be bad!

This is a classic case of "sell the rumor–buy the news". The problems related to this news were well known in advance, and the stock had been selling off in the days prior to this news release. Once the news was finally released, there was a relief rally and the stock traded higher.

The way the news is presented also contributes to a more optimistic perception. It was pointed out that the charge had been "well-advertised" in advance and "fell within the range of expectations", and even though the reduced guidance was presented as "somewhat" of a surprise, the overall tone of the news report was positive. This, combined with the fact the stock had already sold off heavily ahead of the news, resulted in the relief rally rather than more selling. Had the news been presented with a negative connotation, the stock might have sold off on the news.

I provided this example primarily to illustrate how market psychology and perceptions come into play. You need to know how the market and individual stocks have recently reacted to a given type of news, and also take into consideration whether the *spin* on the news is positive or negative. Plus, you should take into consideration the stock's price action leading up to the news, and whether it correlates to prior news about the same subject matter. That is, whether it is "old" news or "new" news.

The timeframe is also an important consideration. The same news might have resulted in a sell off three months earlier. Under different market conditions, companies may sell off even when they give upside earnings guidance, so you want to base your decisions on relatively recent market conditions and reactions to recent news.

In this case, since the initial gap up was so large, it might have been difficult to enter a long position. However, you would have at least known not to short the news, just because it *seemed* bad, as many traders might have done. If you take all of the issues discussed above into consideration, you are less likely to find yourself on the wrong side of a news related trade.

Rumors

A lot of traders play rumors, and I occasionally play rumors as well. The idea is to find an "edge" so if I think it will make my clients money; I'll play almost anything.

However, it has to be a rumor that is based in reality and something that I feel other traders might pick up on, which could potentially drive the price action. If there's just a rumor on Joe Blow's web site that *Bill Gates is going to step down,* then I'm not going to play it. It's not likely Bill Gates is going to step down based on a rumor put out by Joe Blow. On the other hand, if it's a rumor coming from a credible service from which we've had good success in the past playing rumors, then I might play it.

Of course, a rumor needs to be playable. For example, virtually every week you hear rumors that this company or that one is going to buy out some other company. In most cases, these types of rumors result from someone posting them on web sites simply to try and get a stock moving. A rumor needs to be reasonably credible and based in reality. Otherwise, I just don't play it.

8

Trends Are Your Friends

Trends can be your best friend–or your worst enemy!

You may have heard the phrase *trends are your friends*, but what does it mean? Well, a trend is your friend when you trade in the same direction as the trend. The momentum of a trend can help drive price movement further in your favor.

Alternatively, when trading on the opposite side of a trend, it can just as easily propel the price action against you. In this case, the trend is your enemy. Therefore, it is preferable to trade with a trend rather than against it. Your friends have "got your back" most of the time.

What Is A Trend?

Those of you with exposure to the stock market likely know the meaning of the term *trend* as it applies to the direction of price movement. For example, if the general direction of price movement is upward over a period of time, it is called an *uptrend*. Conversely, if the price movement is downward, it is called a *downtrend*.

In addition to uptrends and downtrends, the term *trend* also applies to the historical tendency for certain market behavior, price action, or patterns to repeat.

There are a variety of trends, and some reoccur with more predictability and reliability than others. Trends may be associated with certain events, time periods, perceptions, or other factors. The duration and frequency of trends vary as well. For example, gap trends occur intraday while earnings trends occur quarterly, and the January Effect trend occurs only once a year.

As with the ever-changing market, trends also change. New trends appear, and trends that were once reliable may no longer work as well, or may quit working altogether. Some trends may only work for a relatively short period of time while others may endure for years (e.g., "buy the rumor–sell the news", the January Effect and earnings trends). The reason for this varies. It may be because too many people learn about a trend so it no longer works reliably, or because market psychology or overall market conditions that were once conducive to a trend change.

For example, during the bull market of the late 1990's, the first trend I discovered and built a reputation upon was IPO spin-offs. Another IPO related trend was quiet-period expirations. Both of these trends could be traded with a high degree of reliability. A few years later, due to changing market conditions, IPOs were in short supply and those that did make it to market weren't traded with the same level of excitement and enthusiasm. The market no longer reacted the same way to IPOs (see the next section for more about market psychology). Consequently, trading the parent companies that spun-off IPOs or IPO quite-period expirations no longer worked reliably.

Although trends are not foolproof, trading in harmony with *current* trends rather than against them provides an additional "edge" that can result in a higher percentage of winning trades. Many trends are very high percentage plays with great risk/reward ratios!

Trend Psychology

People often ask me what books I read on the stock market. Actually, I haven't read many. It may seem unlikely but it's true. What I do read are a lot of psychology books. I like to know what people are thinking, and how they are thinking. The reason why the market exaggerates moves and allows us to make money is because people are always anticipating *something*. They are either anticipating good news or they are anticipating bad news.

For a long time after the 9-11-01 terrorist attacks, the market ran down on terrorist threats. Any time there was a new terrorist threat, the market tanked! People were shell-shocked, for good reason obviously, but people were expecting the worst! Whenever someone came on CNBC and said there was a terrorist alert, the market sold off, until it finally got to a point where people became immune to it. Finally, the market could go up. The terrorist alerts didn't matter. The mindset of people had changed. They were over it. They had heard it all before, and they no longer believed in the threats. Therefore, they just discarded them.

Conversely, whenever the market is running up, people are afraid to miss the boat. Though it's obvious the market can't keep going up forever, the bottom line is, people will keep on buying as long as they are afraid that they may have missed the bottom!

One of the guidelines I like to use for market sentiment is when CNBC gets bullish. When everybody starts thinking the same thing, that's the time when you want to be more cautious! It's a contrarian indicator. The *last guy in the pool is the one that swims with the turd,* right? Usually what happens is, when everyone is positive again, that's when we go back down. Everyone is back in the market, so there aren't sufficient numbers of new buyers coming into the market to sustain prices or drive them higher.

Anyway, my point is, human psychology is what drives the market and trends. Yes, there are computerized "buy" and "sell" programs, but human beings initiate them. They aren't initiated by some *dog* barking, or some *parrot* squawking "buy, buy, buy"! They come from companies run by human beings like you and me. Well, actually, some may be *subhumans,* but that's another matter. By and large, they are companies run by people that have blood, *we think,* and it's the people that decide to put in a buy or sell program.

Similarly, trends work because enough people, but not too many, learn about them and believe in them. To a large degree, it becomes a self-fulfilling prophecy. The "buy the rumor–sell the news" trend, earnings runs, the use of moving averages as support, and many other trends work because people know about them and believe they will work. For example, the 200-day moving average is perceived as a very strong level of support. So when a stock's price falls to its 200-day moving average, people start buying the stock expecting the underlying support. The additional buying causes the price to bounce, which further reinforces the trend. The same process applies to other trends as well.

The idea is to stay one step ahead of the market. In the best-case scenario, we can find trends that only a relatively small number of other people have found, since trends historically work when some people, but not everyone, knows about them. Trends tend to stop working once everyone does know about them. Once everyone knows about a trend, they anticipate it and rush in to play the trend, which leaves no more buyers or sellers to propel the trend forward. If a trend quits working, I don't try to play it anymore. When a trend doesn't play out, I want to know why, so I do research to determine if there are any variables that might have affected the trend. If I don't find any and the trend was just a "dud", it raises a caution flag but it doesn't necessarily mean a trend is no longer valid. So, I watch the trend the next time. If it's a loser a second time then I don't play it any longer until subsequent tracking confirms whether the failures were just temporary blips, or whether the trend is no longer valid.

At any rate, I track these types of things, trend behavior, the overall market sentiment, market psychology, and human nature, and I factor them into my trading plan. My goal is to find proven trends and to take advantage of them for the added "edge" they provide.

The following sections discuss trends that I've traded very successfully. However, as previously discussed, trends come and go or change over time with changes in market sentiment. Before trading any trend, it's best to watch it for a period of time to confirm the trend is still valid under current market conditions.

Window Dressing

Window dressing is a strong trend that tends to occur with a high degree of reliability.

Since fund managers are required to report their portfolio's makeup at the end of each calendar quarter, as the end of the quarter approaches, they often buy and sell certain stocks to give the appearance they held stocks that performed well throughout the entire quarter.

Stocks they currently hold that performed poorly during the quarter may be sold, and stocks they don't own that performed well may be bought. After the quarter ends, and depending on how favorably they view a particular stock, managers may buy back stocks they previously sold, or sell those they previously bought. The buying and selling of stocks for this purpose is called *window dressing*.

Timing The Trade

You can trade this trend by watching for poorly performing stocks that sell off hard for no apparent reason (i.e., with no other bad news, etc.) during the last 7-10 days of the quarter. Once the selling appears to have subsided, you can enter a long position just before the end of the quarter. During the first week of the subsequent quarter, these stocks tend to bounce back as fund managers buy them back, and/or as other people take advantage of the beaten down prices.

Conversely, you can consider entering a short position on stocks that have run up hard near the end of the quarter due to window dressing, since these are likely to pullback once the quarter is over.

Managing Risk

Frequently, this trend applies to entire groups or sectors of stocks, or even the entire market. For example, the biotech or semiconductor stocks may have performed well, or poorly, during a given quarter. In these cases, another way to play the trend is to buy indexes (QQQ, SPY, OEX, etc.) or holders (BBH, SMH, etc.) that correspond to a particular group of stocks. This is a good alternative when you want to further reduce your risk exposure by not trading an individual stock. To define your risk even more, you can consider buying CALL or PUT options as well.

One of the nice things about this trend is the relatively short-term timeframe that's involved for a trade. You'll know the outcome of the trade within a few days or a week. And since it tends to be a high percentage trend, by using stop-loss orders to limit and define your overall risk, you can make a potentially powerful trade with a great risk/reward ratio.

Window Dressing Examples

The following chart of Zoran Corp (ZRAN) shows an example of window dressing, or a *dress up* in this case, resulting from a strong quarterly performance.

On the preceding chart, notice how well the stock performed during the quarter. Since it performed so well, fund managers that wanted to show ZRAN on their books for the quarter started buying the stock near the end of the quarter, which caused the price to run up further. See the "Mark Up" time period on the chart. The week after the quarter ended, as shown by the "Take Down" time period on the chart, the stock sold off as fund managers that really didn't want to own the stock long-term exited their positions, and/or other profit takers exited positions to take advantage of the excessive run up in price.

Here is a chart of Brocade Communication Systems, Inc. (BRCD) that shows another example of window dressing, a *dress down* in this case, which resulted from a poor quarterly performance.

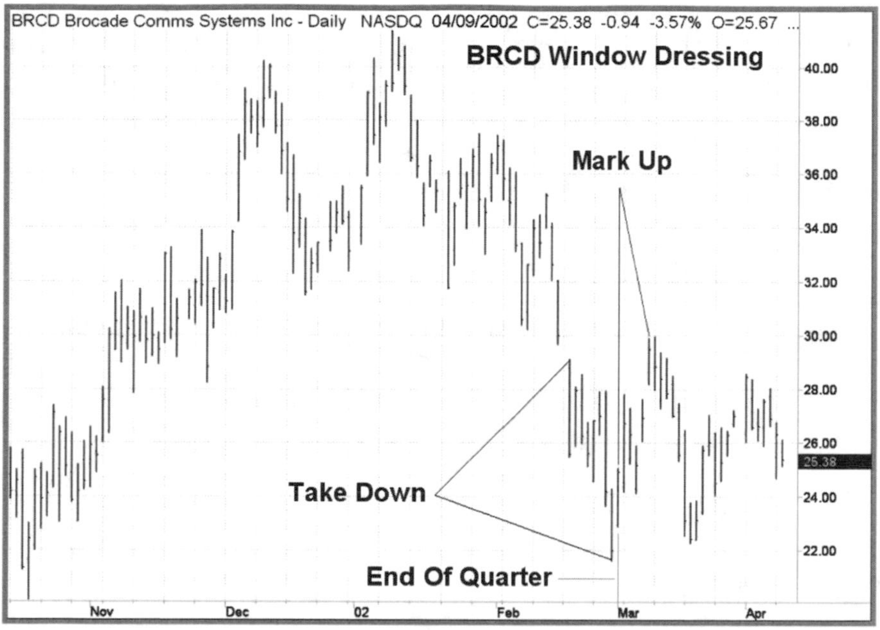

Notice on the chart how BRCD performed poorly during the quarter then sold off further due to window dressing as the quarter ended. See the "Take Down" time period on the chart. During the first week of the next quarter, as shown by the "Mark Up" time period on the chart, the stock bounced back. In this case, fund managers that sold BRCD for window dressing purposes before the end of the quarter, but still wanted to own the stock longer term, bought the stock back once the new quarter began, and/or other buyers took up positions to take advantage of the beaten down price.

From an investors' point of view, window dressing really isn't in the best interest of those that own the funds. Meaning, managers will often buy back a stock for more than what they sold it a short time earlier, or conversely, sell a stock for less than what they paid for it. And many times, there are additional commission fees associated with the trades. Regardless, window dressing is a common quarterly practice, or trend, from which traders can potentially profit. We've made many successful window dressing calls for our clients.

As mentioned earlier, this trend often applies to the overall market. In instances where it does, you can use it as an additional indicator of how the market may perform near the end of a quarter, or the beginning of the next quarter. For example, if technology stocks have collectively performed poorly throughout the quarter, the last week of the quarter will frequently be a down week for the Nasdaq market.

Earnings

The earnings trend has been a very powerful and reliable trend ever since I began tracking it years ago. Often, popular momentum stocks will run up 20-30% or more ahead of their earnings report each quarter. In most cases, but not always, they will pull back after their earnings report is released, even when the reported earnings are good. It is often a case of "buy the rumor–sell the news".

Timing The Trade

The trend is to buy a stock for a potential run ahead of earnings, generally about 5-14 days ahead of its earnings report as you begin to see signs of increased upside interest in the stock, which is indicated by an increase in the stock's price and volume You sell the stock before the market closes on the day that earnings are reported, or by the end of the prior day when earnings are reported in the morning.

In cases where the market is strong, you can consider entering your positions earlier. Conversely, if the market seems week, you may want to limit your time-based risk exposure by waiting until the earnings report is nearer.

I rarely ever hold stocks all the way into their earnings report. Holding a stock into earnings is gambling because there is no way to know what will be reported. If you hold into the earnings and the earnings are worse than expected, you could get crushed (see the NVDA chart later for an example of this). And as I mentioned earlier, a high percentage of the time stocks will sell off after earnings even when the earnings report is good. Repeatedly, I've seen instances where a company blows out earnings and still sells off afterwards. There are times when the stock will continue higher after earnings, particularly if a very large upside earnings surprise is reported and the market overall is in a strong uptrend. But since you can't know for certain in advance what the earnings will be, in my opinion, it isn't worth the risk. The play is to sell before the earnings report comes out. That is the trend!

Managing Risk

You should always consider the risk exposure from unexpected news events, and not overexpose yourself with too many earnings plays at once. Actually, that applies to trading any trend. Even though the earnings trend is a powerful trend, unexpected major news events like the 9-11-01 terrorist attacks can take the market and your stocks down regardless of the strength of a trend. The same is true of individual stock news. If a company announces it is going out of business two days ahead of earnings, the stock price isn't likely to go up. Therefore, you should only use a portion of your total funds to trade any single trend.

Similar to the window dressing trend, earnings plays are nice because once again, you have defined risk over a relatively short timeframe. You define and limit your risk two ways, by using a stop-loss order to define your monetary risk, and by controlling the length of time you are in the trade.

To reduce your time-based risk exposure further, you can wait until the earnings report is closer before entering a trade. And as with any trade, upon entering a position you should immediately place a stop-loss order according to your own risk tolerances to guard against excessive monetary losses should the trade go against you for any reason.

The Historical Perspective

Part of trading earnings is becoming familiar with the history of the individual stocks you intend to play. I pick momentum stocks that I know from experience have historically run up ahead of their earnings report. Though I adapt my actual picks to the circumstances each quarter, a few examples of stocks I might watch are CSCO, ORCL, INTC, MSFT, DELL, BRCD, NVDA, and so on. However, there are many other stocks that you might also consider.

In most cases, stocks tend to begin a run up ahead of their earnings about one to two weeks out, but this can vary depending on the stock and market conditions. For example, I've tracked Oracle (ORCL) and noticed that it frequently begins to move up ahead of earnings as much as a month out. With a historical perspective, you'll be in a better position to time the entries and exits of your individual trades.

Earnings Trend Examples

Following is a chart that shows the price action of Cisco Systems, Inc. (CSCO), an earnings play that we called for Trendfund.com members.

About one week ahead of earnings, CSCO made a brief corrective pullback then ran until the day of its earnings report. The brief pullback provided a great opportunity to enter a long position for the earnings run. Notice on the chart that CSCO gained 30% in only one week, which is a huge move for a big stock such as CSCO.

In this case, you could also have entered a long position a week or so sooner. However, as mentioned earlier, the longer the time until earnings, the greater the risk that bad news or changing market conditions could cause the trade to go against you. So, the precise timing of the entry depends on your risk tolerance, overall market conditions, and how a given stock has historically traded ahead of its earnings reports.

Here is another example that shows the price action of Dell Computer Corp (DELL) ahead of its earnings report.

Notice on the chart that DELL gained about 10% in the two weeks prior to reporting earnings. At first glance that may not seem like much, but for a stock with the market capitalization and volume of DELL, it is a very large move. The fact that large stocks like DELL and CSCO could move so profoundly in a relatively short period of time demonstrates the strength of earnings trends.

Since the earnings trends are so powerful, I will frequently trade the "big" stocks for earnings, however, my preference is to trade other momentum stocks that have a somewhat smaller market capitalization. However, I'm not referring to small illiquid stocks. The momentum stocks I generally play are still large enough to have substantial market capitalizations and liquidity, as I want to be able to get in and out of trades easily. Momentum stocks that have a smaller market capitalization, relative to the largest stocks/companies, tend to make larger moves ahead of their earnings reports.

Take a look at the following chart that shows the price movement of Nvidia Corporation (NVDA) ahead of earnings. This is another stock we called for an earnings trade.

As you can see on the chart, NVDA had a huge run ahead of earnings. In this case, we entered a long position at $11.25 and sold at the highs ahead of earnings for a 40% gain in only seven days.

This stock also serves as a good example of why you should always exit your trade prior to the earnings reports. Just take a look at what happened after NVDA reported earnings. The stock gapped down large, so anyone that held the stock through earnings took a major hit. I don't like taking risks where I have no control over the outcome. I don't know whether a stock will blow out earnings or not, so why take the risk? It's best just to exit the trade. If the stock goes up, so what? There will be many other trading opportunities. It's better to manage your risk exposure and preserve capital than gamble on unknown factors out of your control.

Index Additions

Another high percentage trend occurs when stocks are added to major indexes such as the S&P 500 and the Nasdaq 100. At one time this trend worked with some of the smaller indexes as well but since this isn't as reliable anymore, I'm primarily looking to trade stocks that are being added to the major indexes.

Index funds, which number in the thousands, track the performance of their corresponding index. For example, the S&P 500 Index is comprised of 500 stocks. Though the precise formula used by individual S&P 500 Index funds may vary slightly, generally, the funds contain a proportional amount of the same 500 stocks that are in the S&P 500 Index. If the S&P 500 Index changes, the thousands of individual S&P 500 Index funds must change to remain aligned with the index. Therefore, the managers of S&P 500 Index funds must buy or sell the affected stocks to rebalance their portfolios when stocks are added to, or removed from, the S&P 500 Index. The same process applies to other index funds as well. This puts upward pressure on a stock's price when it is added to a major index, or downward pressure on the price when is dropped from a major index.

Index funds are popular due to the belief that over a period of time, the market will go up, and investing in an index, as opposed to an individual stock, is a relatively safe, low cost way to the invest in the market. For that reason, index funds are held widely through IRAs, pensions, and so on.

Timing The Trade

I used to trade this trend by looking to go long anywhere from a few days to a week ahead of the date the stock was to be added to an index. However, as with all trends, they change over time. Since this trend has become more widely traded, fund managers have started waiting longer to buy the affected stocks.

The fund managers want their funds to reflect a stock's price as closely as possible at the time it is added to an index. Due to increased price volatility, if they buy too soon, there could be a significant price change by the time a stock is added to an index, which could impact how closely their fund tracks the performance of the index. For example, if a stock is selling at $65 at the time it is added to the S&P 500 Index, fund managers don't want to own it at $70 from days earlier.

Consequently, I now see the largest price moves from this trend occurring just before the market closes on the date a stock is officially added to the index. Many of the funds buy during the last 15-30 minutes of the day, which is usually accompanied by a corresponding spike in volume. As a trader, the shorter length of the trade actually works better in that it reduces the time-based risk exposure for the trade.

When trading this trend, you want to exit your position prior to the market's close on the date the stock is added to the index. The buying generally subsides after the index addition, so the risk/reward for holding longer isn't favorable. In fact, stocks will often pullback afterwards as profit takers come in due to the large run up ahead of the addition. Therefore, you should be sure to close your position prior to the close of the market on the day of the addition to the index.

As always, the precise timing of the move ahead of an index addition can vary. There are exceptions where a move begins sooner rather than later, or when a pullback occurs ahead of the addition as traders that are already in a position take profits, particularly if there has been a strong run up in a stock's price. Therefore, you should watch the stock's price action and trade the trend according to the specific circumstances of a given index addition.

Index Addition Examples

The following chart shows how eBay, Inc. (EBAY) traded ahead of being added to the Nasdaq 100 Index. Notice that the price went up $2.73 in the last 15 minutes of trading.

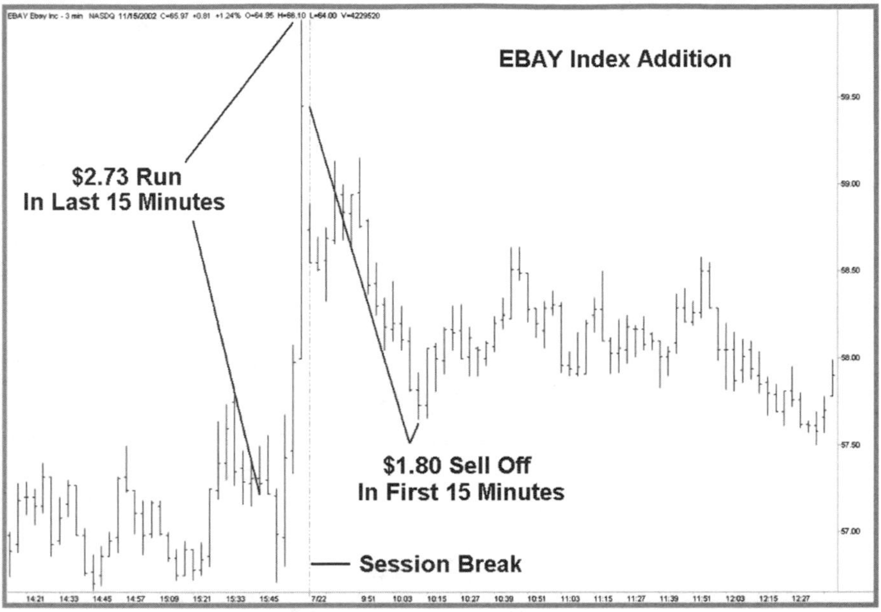

As you can see, EBAY provided a powerful trading opportunity with limited downside risk. You could have entered a long position as interest in the stock started picking up, as determined by increased volume and trading activity, for a very profitable 15-minute trade. Notice that the price pulled back after the addition to the index, which is why you should exit your position prior to the close of the market. The following day, EBAY was down $1.80 during the first 15 minutes of trading.

After entering the trade, you should immediately put in a stop-loss order to define your risk should the price pullback rather than run up as anticipated. Stocks tend to be very volatile and trade fast during this time so even though it's a very short trade, it's still a good idea to manage your risk by using stop-loss orders.

Here is another example of an index addition for Teva Pharmaceutical Industries, Ltd. (TEVA).

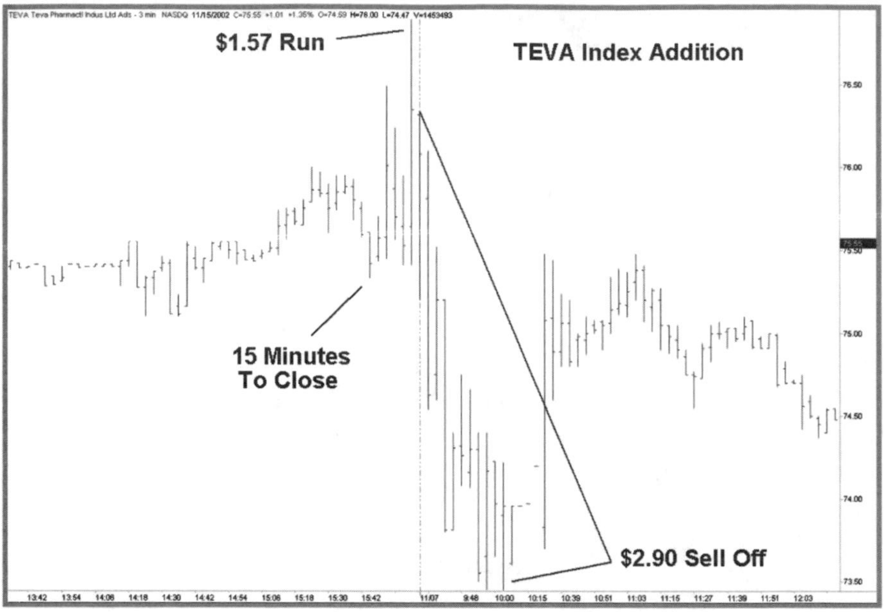

Notice on the preceding chart that TEVA ran up during the last 15 minutes of trading to close at its high for the day. It ran up $1.57 in only 15 minutes on huge volume for a great, profitable trade! However, similar to the preceding EBAY example, look what happened after the index addition when the buying pressure subsided. The stock sold off by $2.90 the next morning, giving up all of its gains and more. Once again, this illustrates the amount of price volatility that can occur, and why you should exit your position before the market closes.

As always, no trend is 100% foolproof. The goal is simply to give yourself an extra edge. By watching and taking advantage of trends such as these, you can use the extra edge they provide to improve the overall risk/reward ratio of your trades. Or conversely, by being aware of trends you might also avoid getting caught on the wrong side of one.

FOMC Runs

The FOMC (Federal Open Market Committee) is a 12-member committee that is responsible for setting interest rate and credit policies.

Another trend that has been powerful recently concerns stock runs and pullbacks surrounding FOMC meetings related to interest rate or other monetary policy announcements. Particularly, when people expect an FOMC announcement that will be viewed as beneficial to the market.

You can often trade the time before and after FOMC announcements in multiple ways. The dynamics surrounding FOMC meetings are interesting because they are associated with multiple interrelated trends, all of which have the potential to be traded.

Timing The Trade

An FOMC run tends to get underway one or two weeks ahead of an FOMC meeting. And on the day of the meeting you'll frequently see additional intraday trends come into play, which may also be followed by another multiple day countertrend reaction.

Generally, the day of an FOMC meeting tends to be volatile so once again, you need to take current market conditions into account. What frequently occurs is the market will either run up or down ahead of the meeting, depending on the perceptions of the outcome of the meeting and whether it is positive or negative for the market. Once an FOMC announcement is made, there is typically a very fast-paced knee-jerk, or impulsive, reaction to the news, which is then immediately followed by another countertrend corrective snapback. This trend has been virtually100% effective since I began tracking it. I frequently trade the countertrend snapback resulting from the initial impulsive move that follows the FOMC news announcement. I call this *fading the first move*, or *fading the first spike*. Regardless of whether the first impulsive move is to the upside or downside, it tends to fade back in the opposite direction.

It is possible to trade all of these trends but to trade the intraday news announcement; you need to be nimble and have a direct-access trading platform. You should be prepared for very fast-paced price action and trade it accordingly. Web based brokers generally don't have the order entry and order execution speeds that are needed to reliably trade the intraday FOMC moves. Although the length of an intraday FOMC move could last 5-10 minutes, it could also be over in a matter of seconds to just a few minutes.

When trading the FOMC trend, I look for popular momentum stocks such as KLAC, QLGC, EXPE, or even MSFT. I want stocks that tend to move with the market and preferable, outperform the market. If you prefer to lower your overall risk exposure rather than trading an individual stock, you can also consider trading the overall market or segments of the market using indexes or exchange traded funds (ETFs) such as QQQ, BBH, SMH, SOX, SPY, or others.

FOMC Trend Examples

The following chart shows an example of how the Nasdaq market behaved ahead of an FOMC meeting.

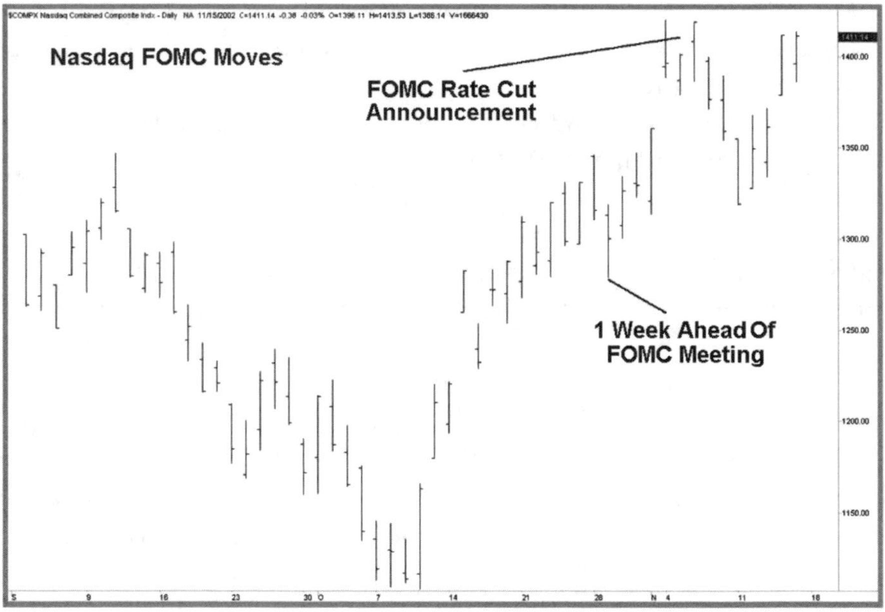

Notice on the chart a huge move took place during the week that preceded the FOMC meeting. In this case, the market actually began running up even sooner with the expectation that the Fed would lower interest rates by 25 basis points.

In cases where there is a strong run up ahead of the FOMC meeting, the market tends to sell off after the meeting. It's another case of "buy the rumor–sell the news". See the next chart of the Philadelphia Semiconductor Index (SOX) for an example.

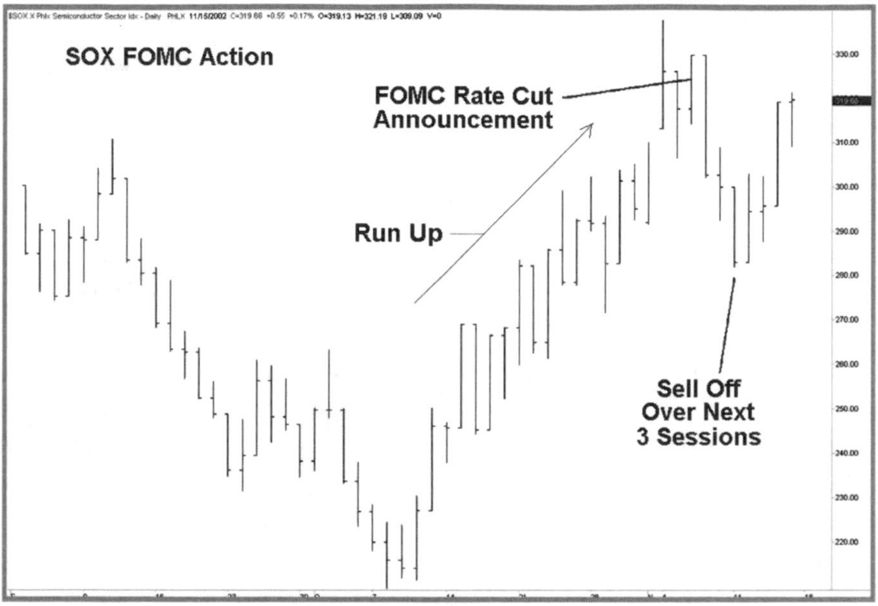

In a surprising move, the Fed actually lowed interest rates by 50 basis points. Even with such positive news the market still pulled back in subsequent days due to the excessive run up that preceded the FOMC meeting. In this case, we played the sell off with PUT options for a great trade! This illustrates the power of trends. The "sell the news" correction occurred in spite of the positive move by the Fed to cut interest rates by 50 basis points.

Another index to watch ahead of FOMC meetings is the bank index, particularly when there may be an interest rate cut. Since people feel that a rate cut will help the banks, the bank index often does well and may outperform other sectors.

An example of trading the actual FOMC announcement on an intraday basis is provided in the "My Favorite Strategies" chapter.

January Effect

The January Effect trend is another strong trend that has worked every year since I've been tracking it.

The January Effect is a well-known and widely followed trend. It is similar to the window dressing trend. In fact, you might think of it as a form of yearend window dressing. Once again, fund managers don't want to show stocks on their books that have done poorly during the year, so they frequently sell them at some point during the last quarter of the year.

Other factors contributing to the January Effect include tax loss selling, new money coming into the market at the beginning of the following year, and funds buying back their favorite beaten down stocks, especially since they are now more attractively priced as a result of the yearend selling. You'll often see very large percentage gains as a result of the January Effect.

Timing The Trade

Generally, though sometimes it may be earlier or later, the stocks that have sold off earlier in the quarter will start a January Effect run about the 20th of December.

Once again, you don't want to hold January Effect stocks long-term into the new year. January Effect stocks tend to start selling off about the 5th day of the new year. By this time, the bulk of new money and prior sellers are in the market so the buying pressure begins to wane.

I like to play stocks that have sold off but have not yet bounced back significantly. Though the actual stocks I pick each year varies depending on market conditions and the price action of individual stocks, recent examples of stocks we have played for the January Effect include GLW, CSCO, INTC, and SUNW. Additionally, I also look for small cap opportunities.

I like to trade the January Effect using options as well. Not only does it let me precisely define my risk, I can often achieve even bigger percentage gains. In some cases, I've achieved gains in the hundreds of percent using options.

January Effect Examples

The following chart is an example from the January Effect list. It shows how Corning, Inc. (GLW) performed during the January Effect time period.

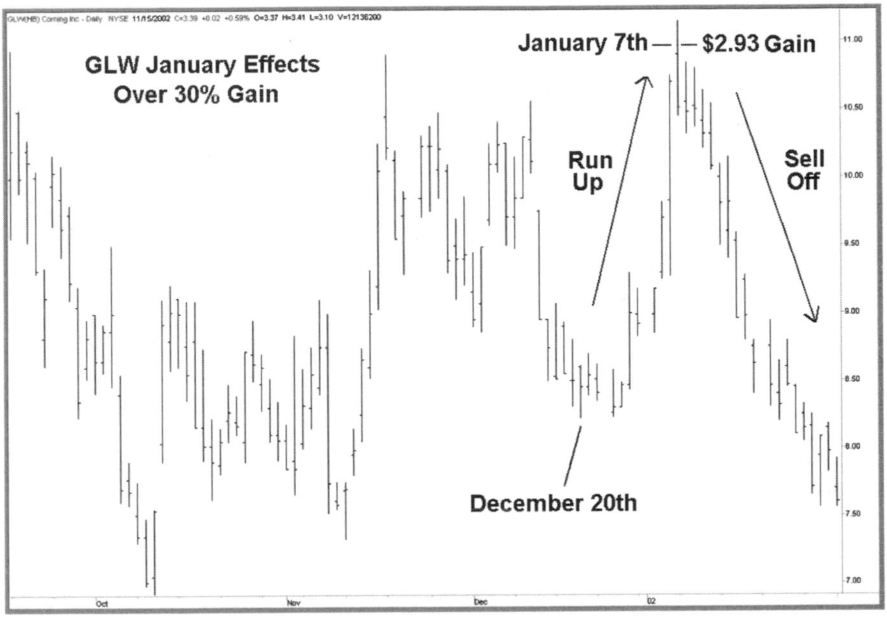

Notice on the chart that GLW moved 30% in only 14 days, which is a nice move by anyone's standards, and some of my clients that played the trade using options made hundreds of percent on the trade. The stock subsequently gave back all of its gain during the first part of the new year, serving as an example of why you don't want to hold a stock more than a few days into the new year. I've seen the January Effect impact many other stocks essentially the same as shown in this example.

While I will occasionally go short to trade the downside move of a January Effect play during the first week of January, it is always subject to specific market conditions and the potential risk/reward of a trade. Generally, shorting the downside move isn't as reliable as trading the upside move.

9

Options Primer

This chapter provides a general overview of options, what they are, the definitions and terminology pertaining to options, and the basics of buying and selling options. Once you have a general understanding of options, you can read next chapter for additional information about trading options.

It's best to read the information contained in this chapter sequentially from the beginning to the end, since the concepts introduced later build upon those introduced earlier. If you haven't had any exposure to options, your first introduction to the definitions and terminology surrounding options may seem a bit confusing or intimidating. Should a given topic not seem completely clear, I recommend that you continue reading through the remainder of the chapter. As you gain a broader perspective, the discussed concepts become easier to understand.

What Are Options?

An option is the right, but not the obligation, to buy or sell an underlying asset (stock, index, or other security) at a specified price on or before a specified date.

A *CALL* option is the right to buy the asset, and a *PUT* option is the right to sell (or for stocks, sell short) the asset. Whether it's a CALL or PUT option, the person that purchases the option is the *buyer*, and the person that originally sells the option is the *seller*.

Similar to buying a stock long or selling it short, you could buy a CALL option for a stock when you think the price is going higher, or a PUT option when you think the price is going to decline. If you are right in either case, you can potentially make money on the trade. However, unlike stocks, there is also a time-based value associated with trading options. In addition to gaining or losing value based upon the price of the underlying stock, an option can lose value over time. These issues, and others, related to trading options are covered in more detail later in this chapter, and in the next chapter.

Though the preceding definitions may make options seem somewhat mysterious and more complex to trade than stocks, they can actually be relatively simple to trade. Although it's possible to employ more complex option strategies, once you've learned the basics, you can also choose to simply buy and sell options in much the same way that you buy and sell stocks. You specify the desired option symbol then buy at the best ask and sell at the best bid. Of course, just as with stocks, there are also risks associated with trading options. Therefore, before you actually begin trading options, you should understand both the pluses and minuses associated with trading them.

It's beyond the scope of this book to provide comprehensive information about all possible permutations of options trading. Instead, this book provides introductory options information in this chapter to help get you started, and then builds upon it in the next chapter with practical techniques that I've actually used to profit from trading options. After reading the information provided here, if you would like to learn even more about options, there are numerous good books dedicated entirely to options. You can also visit www.trendfund.com for a list of our recommended reading resources.

Options are commonly used for hedging, arbitrage plays, speculation, leverage, risk management, and more. However, options are also growing in popularity among active traders for other reasons. Active traders that are identified as pattern daytraders are now subject to SEC regulations specifying minimum account funding requirements.

You are considered a pattern daytrader if you trade in and out of stocks during the same day more than a certain number of times over a specified number of days. Since the specific requirements are subject to change, you can get the latest information about these requirements from your broker.

Currently, options aren't subject to these regulations. Therefore, options provide a means for people to trade actively even when their account size would otherwise fall under the minimum requirements for pattern daytraders. Another big advantage for people that fall into this category is the powerful leverage benefit associated with trading options. By trading options, traders with limited capital can still control a meaningful quantity of shares in a stock.

Underlying Assets

There are a variety of underlying assets for options, including the following examples.

- Stocks
- Indexes
- Commodities
- Futures

To simplify these descriptions, I'll refer to the underlying asset as stock, since stocks are the most popular form of options currently traded. Just keep in mind that the underlying asset could be indexes or other types of securities as well.

A stock option gives you the right to buy (CALL options) or sell (PUT options) 100 shares of the underlying stock at a specified price on or before a specified date. You also have the right to exercise stock options, that is, to take possession of the underlying stock. However, in most cases, traders simply sell the CALL or PUT options. It's less complicated and they usually have more value due to the way premiums are determined (there's more about this later)

In the case of index options, you can't buy or sell actual indexes since they consist of more than one asset. Instead, you buy options that represent the value of the underlying assets. Each option represents 100 shares of the index. Some traders will occasionally buy index options like the S&P 100 (OEX), or others, to hedge other positions. Another potential use for index options is to quickly take advantage of an anticipated move in a sector or the overall market without taking the time to select an individual stock, or to spread risk among a collection of stocks.

Commodities options are for commodities such as corn, wheat, and so on. Since I don't use commodities and futures options as trading tools, I won't be discussing them in this book. I'm simply mentioning them in the interest of completeness and to let you know there are underlying option assets other than stocks.

Rights And Obligations

Buyer Rights

With options, all of the rights belong to the buyer. Buyers have the right to buy or sell short the underlying stock at the specified price on or before the expiration date.

Practically speaking, although they have the right to do so (and occasionally do), most options traders don't actually take possession of the underlying stock. Instead, they simply hold onto their options for a desired period of time, and similar to stocks, they sell the options, realizing any gains or losses accordingly. Or in some instances, the options may expire worthless.

Seller Obligations

All option obligations belong to the seller. The seller is obligated to provide the underlying stock. This applies to the original seller of the options (not to someone that purchases CALLS or PUTS and later sells them to close their position).

Once again, however, sellers rarely have to provide the actual underlying stock to the buyers. Still, buyers do occasionally exercise their options (more about this later), so sellers must be prepared to provide the stock, if required to do so.

Option Contracts

Option contracts consist of standardized terms that provide the rights (as described above) to buy or sell underlying stock. Option sellers are obligated to perform according to the contract terms. They must provide the underlying stock to the owner of the contract should the owner desire to *exercise* his or her options. There is more about this later under "Exercising Options".

You trade options by buying and/or selling one or more option contracts. Each contract represents the right to buy or sell short 100 shares of underlying stock. A working example of buying options is provided a bit later, under "Strike Price". For the moment, just keep in mind that an option contract represents 100 shares of the underlying stock.

Premium

Similar to paying a specific price when you buy a stock, you also pay a specific price when buy an option contract. The price of an option is called its *premium*. It's the price you pay for the right to buy or sell short shares of the underlying stock.

The premium is based on what is perceived to be the *value* of the option. A variety of factors go into determining the value of the premium. These are discussed later under "Intrinsic Value" and "Extrinsic Value".

The total cost of a contract is the premium multiplied by 100, since there are 100 shares of underlying stock per option contract (excluding broker commissions). A working example of this is provided in the following section.

Strike Price

When buying options you pay a premium for the right to buy or sell short the underlying stock at a specific fixed price called the *strike price*. An example that illustrates this follows.

Option Price Example

For purpose of illustration, following the next paragraph is a sample listing of CALL option price quotes for a hypothetical stock symbol called XYZ. However, the discussed concepts can be applied to any stock. The actual format for providing option price quotes varies from broker to broker. You can display options quotes using your own brokerage account to see how your particular broker displays the quotes.

The XYZ stock price is shown first. Beneath the stock's price are three CALL option quotes for the month of August. Note that only three quotes are shown below to conserve space and simplify this explanation, but many additional quotes are actually displayed when you access them through your broker. The next chapter, "Trading Options", provides additional examples of actual option price quote screens. A complete list of price quotes is sometimes referred to as an *options chain.*

Stock	Price	Bid	Ask	Last	Volume
XYZ	46.00	45.95	46.02	46.00	12,284,561

XYZ Aug-01-Calls

Symbol	Price	Bid	Ask	Last	Volume
XOEHV	42.50	3.50	3.80	3.70	458
XOEHI	45.00	1.75	1.80	1.75	843
XOEHW	47.50	0.45	0.55	0.55	1042

Referencing the preceding example, the XYZ stock is currently selling for $46.00. Option symbols let you specify which options you want to trade in the same manner as stock ticker symbols let you specify stocks. The option symbols, which are sometimes a variation of the underlying stock's ticker symbol, change on a month-to-month basis. The strike prices for the three XYZ CALL options range from $42.50 to $47.50. The premiums, or last prices at which the options traded, range from $3.70 to $0.55. Notice the rate at which the premiums change the further they get away from the current XYZ stock price. How the premiums are determined is explained later. The current best bids, best asks, and volumes are also shown. Many brokers display, or provide the option to display, additional data as well. Once again, you can get information related to any additional option data from your specific broker.

In this case, if you wanted to buy 10 Aug XYZ CALL options (contracts), according to the asking price of $1.80, you would pay $1800.00, less commission charges. To derive the total, you multiply 1.80 by 100 shares per contract by 10 contracts ($1.80 x 100 x 10 = $1800).

Expiration Date/Month

Options expire on the 3rd Saturday of each month; however, the last day for trading them is the 3rd Friday. You choose the desired expiration month when you purchase an option.

For example, the expiration month shown in the preceding example is August, but you could also purchase options for September or October. You can even purchase long-term option contracts, called

LEAPS. LEAPS are any option that is 9 months or more away from the current expiration month. The greater the time until expiration, the higher is the time-based portion of the premium (explained below under "Extrinsic Value").

If the CALL or PUT options you buy expire without "value", then they expire worthless, and you lose the entire premium. However, your original premium is the most that you can lose. Though many brokers SELL options on the expiration day and deposit any proceeds into your account, some may not. In this case, you may need to sell options that have value on or before the expiration date. Check with your broker to find out how they handle option expirations.

Intrinsic Value

The *intrinsic value* of an option is the difference between the underlying stock price and the strike price of the option. For example, if the stock price of XYZ was $55 and you bought a $50 CALL option, the intrinsic value would be $5 ($55 - $50 = $5). Therefore, when the underlying stock price of a CALL option climbs higher than the strike price, the intrinsic value (and premium) of the option goes up accordingly.

The intrinsic value for CALL options can only be a positive number or zero. If the calculations come out negative, then the value is considered zero. For example, if the XYZ stock price was $50 and the CALL option was $55, the intrinsic value would be zero ($50 - $55 = -$5 = 0).

Conversely, the opposite is true for PUT options. The intrinsic value of PUT options can only be negative (however, the negative sign is dropped). And, any positive numbers are considered to have a zero value.

Extrinsic Value

The portion of an option premium that is not intrinsic value is *extrinsic value*. Extrinsic value is determined by a complex standardized formula based on time and *volatility* (covered next). Extrinsic value is predominately a time-based value, or a time premium. It's based primarily on the length of time that remains before an option expires. As the time to expiration decreases, the extrinsic value decreases.

Volatility

Volatility is a measure of how fast the underlying stock changes price. A stock that has wide price swings in a relatively short period of time is considered to be more volatile than one whose price changes only a small amount or very slowly over time.

As just mentioned, the volatility of the underlying stock is reflected to some degree in an option's premium. Higher volatility causes the volatility portion of an option's premium to be higher. In this regard, there are essentially two types of volatility that come into play, *historical volatility* and *implied volatility*.

Historical Volatility

Historical volatility is a statistical measure of volatility for a specific amount of time (e.g., 10 days, 100 days, or another desired time period).

Implied Volatility

Implied volatility is a measure of the option market's perception of what volatility will likely be in the future.

In The Money

An option that has intrinsic value is said to be *in the money*. For a CALL option, this occurs when the underlying stock price is greater than the strike price. The opposite is true for PUT options. A PUT option has intrinsic value when the underlying stock price is less than the strike price.

For example, a $50 XYZ CALL option would be in the money by $5 if the XYZ stock price were $55. A $50 XYZ PUT option would be in the money by $5 if the XYZ stock price were $45.

Out Of The Money

A CALL option is *out of the money* when the underlying stock price is less than the strike price, or greater than the stock price in the case of

PUTS. In this case, it has no intrinsic value, that is, the intrinsic value is zero.

For example, a $50 XYZ CALL option would be out of the money by $5 if the XYZ stock price were $45. A $50 XYZ PUT option would be out of the money by $5 if the XYZ stock price were $55.

An option that is out of the money has only extrinsic value, or time-based value, which decreases as the option nears its expiration date. The option could expire worthless if it reaches its expiration date without any intrinsic value.

At The Money

An option is *at the money* when its underlying stock price is equal to its strike price. For example, a $50 XYZ CALL or PUT option is at the money when the XYZ stock price is $50.

Hedging

You can use options to preserve gains, or reduce losses, on an open stock position without selling your stock. This is called *hedging*.

For example, if the market appears weak, you might buy PUTS on your open stock position. If your stock drops in value, the PUTS will go up in value and help offset any losses. Additional information about hedging is provided the next chapter, "Trading Options".

Managing Risk

Options are a great way to predefine your maximum risk on a trade, or to limit your overall risk exposure. Though you could lose the entire premium if an option expires worthless, you cannot lose more than the premium. Therefore, your maximum possible losses can be easily determined in advance based upon the total cost of the options. I particularly like this aspect of trading options and will be discussing it more in the next chapter.

Speculation And Leverage

If you feel a stock is going up or down in value but aren't certain, or if you want to leverage your money so you can control a larger quantity of shares with a predetermined amount of risk, you can accomplish either by purchasing CALL or PUT options.

I will frequently speculate using options to limit risk when I think a stock has the potential to make a large move, particularly at times the risk/reward for a trade is favorable, and the option premiums are reasonable. Using options to speculate on earnings trends is one example. I'll go into this more in the "Trading Options" chapter.

As I mentioned earlier, options are also great for leveraging your money. For example, referring back to the prior quotes example, if you wanted to buy 1000 shares of the XYZ stock and it is selling for $46, it would cost you $46,000. However, you could control 1000 shares of the stock by buying 10 *in the money* CALL option contracts. You would buy the $45 CALL options at the asking price of $1.80 per contract for a total cost of only $1800. Now, that's leverage!

Arbitrage

Sophisticated traders can take advantage of price discrepancies between two underlying assets (such as two different options on different exchanges). This process is called arbitrage.

Options Pros And Cons

The main pros associated with options trading are leveraging, hedging, and predefining risk. You can leverage your available funds by paying a small price to control a large amount of stock for a larger potential gain; you can hedge outstanding stock positions against loss without giving up your original positions; and you can earn gains using low risk option strategies where the maximum risk is known in advance.

Another advantage to trading options is that unlike stocks, options aren't subject to the SEC regulation that applies to pattern daytraders, which requires the maintenance of a $25,000 account balance for traders that trade in and out of positions more than 5 times during any consecutive 5-day time period.

A major drawback to options is their time-based value. While stocks never expire, if there is no intrinsic value remaining, options expire at a specific date and become worthless. Time is your enemy when you own options. When you own stock, your enemy is being married to the equity.

Option Exchanges

Options are traded on four exchanges, the Pacific Exchange, Nasdaq Amex, Chicago Board Of Options, and the Philadelphia Exchange. Unless you just want to give a particular exchange the business, it really doesn't matter which exchange you use, though if you can get your fills on the Chicago, I find them the most reliable and generally the fastest fillers.

Volume

Similar to stocks, you can check option volume by the day, week, month, and so on.

You can watch for volume increases and decreases over a given time period and compare the amount of change to the average volume. If the volume is increasing then there may be something of interest going on that could put pressure on the value of the option. I'll discuss volume and liquidity more in the next chapter under "Index Options".

Open Interest

Open interest is a running measure of the number of option contracts that have been opened. For example, when trading options, you must buy or sell to *open* a position. Open interest tracks the total number of open contracts. Subsequently, when you sell to close a position, the amount of open interest decreases.

Don't confuse open interest with volume. Volume could be up as a result of traders repeatedly trading in and out of positions, while open interest reflects how many contracts are actually open. High open interest indicates a large number of people are trading the options.

Exercising Options

With American options, as opposed to European, you can exercise your rights to take possession of the underlying stock at any time on or before the expiration date. The seller is obligated to provide the underlying stock.

Since you can simply trade in and out of options like stock, most options traders never actually exercise their options. Because of the added extrinsic value (time value), the options are usually worth more than the underlying stock alone. If a situation arises where this isn't the case, or you simply want to own the underlying stock, you can choose to exercise your options and take possession of the stock.

If you don't sell or exercise an option by the time it expires, most brokers sell the option and deposit any proceeds into your account. However, since each broker determines their own policies, you should check with your broker for the specifics about how they handle option expirations.

Option Strategies Introduction

Buying CALLS and PUTS

As mentioned previously, you might buy CALLS and PUTS for a variety of reasons ranging from leveraging your money to hedging to predefining your risk on a trade.

If you feel a stock is going up, you could buy the stock and hold it, or you could buy CALL options. If you think a stock is going down, you could short the stock, or you could buy PUT options. Alternatively, if the market appears weak and you are holding a position in a stock that you don't want to sell, you could buy PUTS as a hedge. If your stock price declines, the PUTS will go up in value and help reduce losses. The amount of protection you receive depends on the strike price you choose for the options.

The closer an option is to being *in the money*, the more expensive it is due to both intrinsic and extrinsic values coming into play together. Once an option is in the money, it gains intrinsic value dollar for dollar with the stock price. Conversely, when an option is out of the money, it's less expensive because it has no intrinsic value. The extrinsic value also plays a role. Since extrinsic value is time based, the closer an option is to expiring, the less the extrinsic value.

Unlike stocks, your predefined risk is limited to the total premium you pay for the options. For example, in the example previously used, if you bought 1000 shares of the XYZ stock for $46, the total cost would be $46,000 (excluding commissions). Though unlikely, if the company abruptly went out of business, you could hypothetically lose your entire $46,000 investment. Alternatively, if you bought 10 $45 CALL options at $1.80 each for a total of $1800 (excluding commissions), the most you could lose is the $1800 premium. Of course, in either case, you should further limit your maximum risk exposure by also using stop-loss orders.

To determine which option best suits your needs, you need to consider the purpose of the option along with its premium costs. Do you want an option that is in the money at a higher cost or out of the money at a lower cost? Do you want an option that is nearing its expiration date at a lower cost or one that isn't close to expiring at a higher cost?

In the "Trading Options" chapter, I'll provide examples and discuss other ways you can consider trading options.

SELLING NAKED CALLS AND PUTS

If the original seller of CALLS or PUTS does not own the underlying stock, then it's called selling NAKED. This is riskier than simply buying or selling CALLS and PUTS.

Note: Selling CALLS or PUTS to close a position you bought is not the same thing as being the original seller that I'm discussing here, that is, the person that sells to *open* a position rather than to *close* a position.

You must have an options margin account to sell NAKED CALLS and PUTS. Selling NAKED is what the pros do when the implied volatility gets very high and the premium is overvalued. When selling NAKED, the risk is virtually unlimited while the reward is limited to the premium. In this case, time works for you, unlike buying CALLS or PUTS where time works against you. You want the options to expire so you can collect the premiums.

Here are examples that illustrate the risk/reward. If the XYZ stock price is $50 and you buy a single XYZ $55 CALL contract at $2, the most you can lose is $200 ($2 x 100 shares). If you sell an XYZ $55 CALL NAKED, the most you can collect is $200 when XYZ is $55 or under. If, however, XYZ runs to $70, you would lose $15 ($70-$55) times 100 shares, minus the premium, or $1300. Since the XYZ stock price could theoretically go even higher, the potential loss could get worse accordingly.

Selling Covered CALLS and PUTS

If the *original seller* of CALLS or PUTS owns the underlying stock, then it is called selling *covered*. In this case, the seller must own the same number of shares that are being sold as CALLS or PUTS. As previously noted, selling your CALLS or PUTS to close a position is not the same thing as being the original seller that is referred to here, that is, the person that sells to *open* a position rather than to *close* a position

Selling covered CALLS is a good way to earn income on stocks with prices that are essentially moving sideways or rising only slightly. It's approved for most option IRA accounts, and you can also do it with PUTS (but not in IRAs) by selling short the stock and selling an equal number of PUTS.

When selling covered CALLS and PUTS, the risk is limited and the reward is the premium you collect. If the stock goes down, you get to collect the premium on the covered CALL but your original investment in the stock loses value, which is why it's best suited to stocks where the price is basically flat or slightly increasing. As with selling NAKED CALLS and PUTS, time works for you. You want the option to expire so you can collect the premium.

Here is an example that illustrates the risk/reward. Say you sell an XYZ $55 covered CALL and own an equal amount of the stock. If XYZ rallies to $70, even though you are out $15 on the CALL, you made $20 on the stock – so you are covered.

SPREADS

A spread refers to buying one option, and selling another at a different strike price.

With bull spreads, you buy an option and sell another one at a price that is a strike price, or a few strike prices, higher than the one you bought, and then you collect the premium. This lowers your risk to the amount you paid for the option you bought, minus the premium you collected from the one you sold. The reward is limited since it falls between the two strike prices. However, even though the profits are limited, the risk is much lower as well.

For example, suppose you buy our hypothetical stock's XYZ $55 CALLS at $3 and sell XYZ $60 CALLS for $1. The net out of pocket cost is $2 ($3 - $1). If XYZ is $60 or above by the expiration date, the most you can make is $5, the difference between the $60 CALLS you sold and the $55 CALLS you bought, less the $2 net out of pocket cost for the options, which results in a maximum profit potential of $3. If XYZ is $55 or less at expiration, the most you can lose is the $2 out of pocket cost.

You can do the same thing with a bear spread by buying PUTS and reversing the process. Additional information about bull and bear spreads is provided in the "Trading Options" chapter.

10

Trading Options

This chapter expands upon many of the concepts introduced in the preceding chapter, "Options Primer". If you are new to options and haven't yet read the preceding chapter, or if you simply need a refresher concerning option definitions and terminology, please review the "Options Primer" chapter.

Speculative Options Trading

It's important to keep in mind that the techniques described here are speculative plays, which is why I typically qualify them as such whenever I send out applicable option email alerts. Though you can frequently achieve nice gains, you shouldn't get carried away on these trades since they are inherently speculative in nature.

Out Of The Money Options

As explained in the preceding chapter, a CALL option is *out of the money* when the underlying stock's price is less than the option's strike price, or in the case of PUTS, when the underlying stock's price is greater than the option's strike price.

Following is an options quote screen for KLAC for the month of December. The options expire for trading on the 3rd Friday during the month of December. The current stock price for KLAC is $42.85. Note that the quote screens shown here are for illustration purposes only. Actual screen formats and layouts vary among trading platforms.

KLAC $42.85							
Title	Symbol	Last	Volume	B Bid	Bid/Ask	B Ask	Open Int
KLAC Dec 30 Call	KCQLF	12.90	5	12.90	0.30	13.20	2,286
KLAC Dec 30 Put	KCQXF	0.25	616	0.20	0.05	0.25	4,734
KLAC Dec 35 Call	KCQLG	8.80	75	8.30	0.20	8.50	6,447
KLAC Dec 35 Put	KCQXG	0.70	711	0.60	0.10	0.70	6,717
KLAC Dec 40 Call	KCQLH	4.40	1,308	4.40	0.10	4.50	8,225
KLAC Dec 40 Put	KCQXH	1.70	3,941	1.65	0.05	1.70	5,513
KLAC Dec 45 Call	KCQLI	1.70	638	1.70	0.05	1.75	4,355
KLAC Dec 45 Put	KCQXI	4.00	288	3.90	0.10	4.00	1,304
KLAC Dec 50 Call	KCQLJ	0.45	630	0.40	0.10	0.50	2,107
KLAC Dec 50 Put	KCQXJ	8.00	37	7.50	0.20	7.70	234
KLAC Dec 55 Call	KCQLK	0.10	117	0.05	0.15	0.20	1,039
KLAC Dec 55 Put	KCQXK	22.80	0	12.10	0.30	12.40	55
KLAC Dec 60 Call	KCQLL	0.15	0	0.00	0.10	0.10	658
KLAC Dec 60 Put	KCQXL	32.80	0	17.00	0.40	17.40	200
KLAC Dec 65 Call	CKVLM	0.05	0	0.00	0.05	0.05	595
KLAC Dec 65 Put	CKVXM		0	22.00	0.40	22.40	2
KLAC Dec 70 Call	CKVLN	0.05	0	0.00	0.05	0.05	618
KLAC Dec 70 Put	CKVXN	34.60	0	27.00	0.40	27.40	3

Looking at the preceding illustration, under the "Title" column the CALL options that are $45 and higher are all out of the money options, since they are higher than the $42.85 KLAC stock price. Alternatively, the CALL options that are $40 and under are all in the money.

Conversely, the PUT options that are $40 and under are out of the money, since they are lower than the $42.85 KLAC stock price, and the PUT options that are $45 and above are in the money.

Notice that the further out of the money an option is, the cheaper it costs. See the "Last" price column in the preceding example. The $40 in the money CALL option last traded at $4.40 while the $45 out of the money CALL last traded at $1.70. Though the option costs are lower, trading out of the money options is more speculative because the stock's price has to move farther to hit the option strike price (e.g., the $45 strike price in this case).

Regardless, trading options that are somewhat out of the money is a great way to trade momentum stocks with limited, predefined risk. For example, if you thought KLAC was going to have a big move up in the near future but you weren't sure or you just wanted to precisely define your maximum risk exposure, rather than buying the stock, you could buy the $45 KLAC CALL options at $1.75 (the current asking price shown for the $45 CALL in the preceding illustration).

If you held the options until expiration, to make money the KLAC stock price would need to rise above $46.75 (the $45 option strike price plus your $1.75 option premium/cost). Your maximum risk, if the stock price remains below the $45 option strike price, is the $1.75 option cost (multiplied by 100 shares per contract, or $170.50 plus commissions per option contract). If, at options expiration, the KLAC stock price were between $45 and $46.75, it would defray some of the option costs and lessen your losses accordingly. For example, if the stock's price were $45.50 when the options expired, you would lose $1.25 per contract share rather than the original $1.75 cost. The closer options get to expiration, the lower the time based value of the options, so at expiration the value is determined by the intrinsic value, which based upon the difference between the option price and the stock price.

Of course, the prior examples apply to holding options through expiration. Often, except possibly for very cheap or small "all or nothing" option plays, you sell your options prior to expiration. Just like when a stock trade goes against you, rather than waiting for it to fall to zero, you can sell the stock at the time of your choosing. Or, you can take profits at any time. Similarly, you can do the same with options, assuming the options you have chosen are reasonably liquid and someone is available to take the other side of the trade. Additionally, you can potentially limit losses by using stop-losses on option plays as well.

Using the preceding example again, if the KLAC stock price went to $45 rather than $46.75 or higher, rather than holding your CALL options through expiration, you could sell them for a very nice profit. You could even potentially double your money. If KLAC went from $42.85 to $45, you would mostly likely get over $3.00 for the $1.75 CALL options you purchased, which would be a nice trade indeed!

We have actually achieved similar results playing options on momentum stocks during earnings season. A recent example is PMCS. We played the MAY $7.50 CALL options at $0.35 for an earnings run when the stock price was around $6.90. Brocade (BRCD), which is in a similar industry, had recently reported positive earnings and the stock responded quite favorably. As a result, PMCS seemed like a good risk/reward speculative play for options. To make money on the trade, we needed the stock price to break $7.85 ($7.50 + $0.35 option premium). The price subsequently moved up to a range of $7.90 to $8.00, which took the options to $0.70 for a short-term double!

As I mentioned, historically speaking, options are a great way to speculate on momentum stocks such as the Semiconductors, Internet, and Biotech stocks (KLAC, PMCS, NVLS, EBAY, EXPE, ROOM, etc.) when you anticipate a strong near-term move. I particularly like playing options during earnings season when prices tend to be more volatile. I'll discuss this more later.

Similar to speculating with CALL options, if you think a stock's price is going down rather than up, you can buy PUT options. As when shorting stocks, you want the underlying stock price to go lower after buying the PUT options.

Referring to the prior illustration again, you could play the KLAC $40 out of the money PUTS for roughly the same price as the $45 CALLS, or $1.70 (see the best ask column). Notice that the $42.85 KLAC stock price is near the midpoint between the $40 PUTS and the $45 CALLS, meaning both the CALLS and PUTS are a similar distance out of the money, which resulted in a comparable option premium for both.

To make money on the $40 KLAC PUT options, you need the stock's price to move toward the $40 option strike price near term, or below $40 by option expiration. If the stock's price stays substantially the same over time or until the options expire, the time-based portion of the option premium will decline, resulting in a loss on the trade.

Following is another December options quote screen for EXPE. The current EXPE stock price is $75.08

EXPE $75.08							
Title	Symbol	Last	Volume	B Bid	Bid/Ask Sprea	B Ask	Open Int
EXPE Dec 60 Call	UEDLL	15.10	4	15.60	0.30	15.90	698
EXPE Dec 60 Put	UEDXL	0.70	112	0.65	0.10	0.75	1,283
EXPE Dec 65 Call	UEDLM	11.50	73	11.20	0.30	11.50	1,469
EXPE Dec 65 Put	UEDXM	1.20	115	1.15	0.15	1.30	2,188
EXPE Dec 70 Call	UEDLN	7.50	56	7.20	0.30	7.50	1,881
EXPE Dec 70 Put	UEDXN	2.20	494	2.20	0.20	2.40	2,835
EXPE Dec 75 Call	UEDLO	4.10	327	4.00	0.30	4.30	1,507
EXPE Dec 75 Put	UEDXO	4.20	430	3.90	0.30	4.20	824
EXPE Dec 80 Call	UEDLP	2.00	285	1.90	0.15	2.05	1,287
EXPE Dec 80 Put	UEDXP	7.10	31	6.80	0.20	7.00	315
EXPE Dec 85 Call	UEDLQ	0.75	186	0.70	0.20	0.90	704
EXPE Dec 85 Put	UEDXQ	10.70	17	10.50	0.40	10.90	87

Looking at the preceding illustration, notice that both the stock price and the option premiums are considerably higher than those for the preceding KLAC example. Additionally, EXPE tends to be more volatile and trades in larger price ranges than KLAC. As explained in the preceding chapter, volatility is also a factor in calculating the extrinsic, time based component of an option's premium. To some degree, this is reflected in the higher option premiums for EXPE. See the $4.30 and $4.20 premiums for the $75 EXPE CALLS and PUTS, respectively, in the preceding illustration.

In this case, to play options that are out of the money, you would need to go about $5.00 out of the money. For example, the $80 EXPE CALL options are $2.05, which is more expensive than the $45 CALL options at $1.75 in the preceding KLAC example. Even though the EXPE options are further out of the money, the premiums are higher.

In this case, if you bought the EXPE $80 CALL options at $2.05, the EXPE stock price would need to move from $75.08 to above $82.05 (the $80 option strike price plus the $2.05 premium) in order to make money at the time the options expire. However, once again, you could still potentially make money prior to option expiration, if the EXPE stock price moves sufficiently higher in a sufficiently short period of time. For example, if EXPE moved up by $3.00 the day after you bought the options for $2.05, considering the volatility, your options would likely be worth over $3.00. If desired, you could sell them (or a portion of them, which is what I frequently do) at this point for a nice profit.

The potential rewards of this type of scenario, along with the limited predefined risk, is one of the reasons I like speculating with options when I anticipate the possibility of a large near-term price move. Since momentum stocks tend to be volatile and make large moves during earnings season due to the earnings runs, earnings warnings, breaking news, upgrades/downgrades, and so on, this is a great time to speculate using options.

However, using the previous example, if you held the options rather than taking profits, the time-based premium would continue to decrease at an ever-accelerating rate as the option expiration date approached. Unless the stock price continued moving higher, you would eventually not only lose your prior gains, you would also lose your original premium. If the stock price didn't move higher, the premiums would decrease to the point that the options would be worthless by the time they expired. During the final week prior to expiration, the preceding premiums would be considerably lower. If the EXPE stock price didn't change substantially, the premiums would likely be worth around $1.00 or $1.25 during the final week of option expirations. This illustrates the risk associated with options. If the underlying stock's price doesn't move in your favor, depending on the time until expiration, you can potentially lose your original premium at a rapid rate.

Some of the best opportunities are presented during the final week of option expirations. Due to the lower premium costs, I particularly like trading options for companies that are scheduled to report earnings at this time The anticipated earnings reports help generate the needed volatility for large near-term price moves, and by using options, you can precisely predefine your maximum risk exposure in the event a trade goes against you.

More Than One Month Out

It's also possible to buy options with an expiration date that is further out than the current month. For example, instead of buying December options like in the prior EXPE illustration, you could buy January or February options, or options where the expiration date is even further out.

As you might expect, however, the longer the time period is before expiration, the higher the option premiums, and the greater the risk. I generally buy options for the current month as short-term trades. However, there are occasions when it could make sense to consider options that are further out than the current month. For example, you might want to consider buying the following month's options when the expiration date for the current month is close (a few days to a week away), and you anticipate a stock is going to have a large price move but you can't be certain it will occur prior to the current month's expiration date.

Following are option price quotes for ERTS, which are more than a month away from expiration. These quotes were obtained during the month of December for options that expire during the month of March. The current stock price is $67.18.

ERTS $67.18

Title	Symbol	Last	Volume	B Bid	Bid/Ask Spread	B Ask	Open Int
ERTS Mar 55 Call	EZQCK	11.20	0	14.70	0.30	15.00	0
ERTS Mar 55 Put	EZQOK	2.95	0	2.40	0.15	2.55	125
ERTS Mar 60 Call	EZQCL	11.00	0	11.00	0.30	11.30	690
ERTS Mar 60 Put	EZQOL	3.80	0	3.60	0.30	3.90	799
ERTS Mar 65 Call	EZQCM	8.00	5	7.80	0.30	8.10	733
ERTS Mar 65 Put	EZQOM	5.60	11	5.40	0.30	5.70	1,071
ERTS Mar 70 Call	EZQCN	4.70	0	5.20	0.30	5.50	677
ERTS Mar 70 Put	EZQON	8.80	4	7.70	0.30	8.00	127
ERTS Mar 75 Call	EZQCO	3.30	3	3.20	0.30	3.50	255
ERTS Mar 75 Put	EZQOO	13.70	0	10.70	0.40	11.10	10
ERTS Mar 80 Call	FZQCP	2.10	0	1.90	0.15	2.05	2,441
ERTS Mar 80 Put	EZQOP	16.50	0	14.40	0.30	14.70	20
ERTS Mar 85 Call	EZQCQ	0.90	0	1.05	0.10	1.15	239
ERTS Mar 85 Put	EZQOQ		0	18.50	0.30	18.80	0

Notice in the preceding illustration that the premium of the $70 CALL option is $5.50 at the best ask, which is quite a hefty premium. Considering the option is also $2.82 out of the money ($70 minus the $67.18 stock price), the total effective premium is actually $8.32 (the $5.50 cost plus the $2.82 out of the money amount). If you were holding the options for the long run, you would need a substantial price move in your favor to come out on the trade.

As I discussed previously, I rarely make this type of long-term option trade, however, there could be an occasional instance when I might consider it. For example, maybe there is a rumor that ERTS is going to be bought out or there's some other catalyst that could potentially propel the price higher over the next few months. In instances such as these, speculating with options that are further than the current month out could be justified.

However, if I were to make this type of trade, I would likely buy *in the money* options rather than out of the money options. Instead of buying the $70 CALL, I might buy the $60 CALL at the current $11.30 asking price. At first glance, this seems more expensive but the total cost is actually less. The $60 strike price plus $11.30 is $71.30, while the $70 strike price plus $5.50 is $75.50. And, the $60 CALL is already in the money. The $70 CALL costs you $4.20 more to go further out of the money.

When buying options, I strongly encourage you to use only limit orders rather than market orders. Often, options are less liquid than stocks and they tend to have larger price spreads. Using limit orders helps ensure your order will fill according to your plan for the trade, rather than leaving you open to a potentially unfavorable price that's determined by a market maker.

Leverage And Hedging

As I discussed in the "Options Primer" chapter, you can also buy CALLS and PUTS to preserve gains or to reduce potential losses on your existing stock positions. This is referred to as hedging. You would buy PUTS to hedge long positions against losses, and CALLS to hedge short positions.

The relative importance of using hedges tends to correspond to how leveraged your account is, and its size. If you have a large account that is heavily leveraged (e.g., with a high percentage of positions leaning in the same direction, either long or short), then it is more important to consider hedging your account to protect against excessive losses should the market unexpectedly move against you.

For example, suppose you are holding large positions in stocks that you don't want to sell. Maybe you feel the stocks have more upside potential but the market overall appears to be weakening. To guard against potential losses, you could buy PUTS as a hedge. If your stocks' prices decline, the PUTS will go up in value and help reduce losses on your long positions. The amount of protection you receive depends on the options you choose and their resulting premiums, and how many options you buy.

As you might expect, there is a price to pay for the protection achieved from hedging. If a stock's price goes up, although you will gain on the stock, you will lose money on the PUT options, which reduces your overall gains accordingly. Still, if you have a large number of open stock positions that you intend to hold overnight or longer, it's a good idea to guard against a large loss from adverse news, or for whatever reason, by using a reasonable amount of hedging. If you had a $300,000 portfolio heavily leveraged on the long side, you don't want to wake up the next morning to a $40,000 loss due to unexpected bad news.

You could potentially hedge your entire portfolio against all losses, or you could simply hedge to *reduce* or limit your overall risk exposure. If your account is heavily leveraged on the long side, it implies that you are bullish and believe the market is going higher. Since your bias is to the upside, you would generally want to maintain that bias and rather than attempting to cover your entire portfolio against a downside move, you would just hedge sufficiently to limit your overall risk exposure in a worse case scenario, or in the event you are wrong about the direction of the market. With this approach, although you would still lose money, you wouldn't suffer an excessive loss or get wiped out if the market had a large move contrary to your heavily leveraged account.

In most cases, to help keep the cost of hedging within reason "traders" would only hedge on a short-term basis to temporarily limit losses rather than to protect against all possible losses, or rather than hedging over a long period of time. Since I'm a trader and rarely hold positions for a long time period, if I hedge at all, the duration of my hedging is typically less than a week, and most of my hedges only last only 1 to 3 days. I don't want to lose too much of the time-based value on option premiums. Also, since there is usually an expense associated with hedging, I generally employ hedging techniques only in cases where I have sizeable positions that I'm holding overnight and limiting losses by other means, such as with stop-losses or smaller lot sizes, may not be sufficient.

There are a variety of other methods you could consider using to hedge your account. Rather than buying PUTS for specific long positions that you are holding, you could also consider hedging with other stocks that appear weaker than the stocks you are holding long, or you might use index options to hedge against your entire portfolio. See the "Index Options" section for more about these. Additionally, you could consider taking short positions in weak stocks or the overall market as a hedge rather than using options. In an ideal scenario, you might even achieve profits on both your long positions and your hedges, though for obvious reasons, this isn't the typical outcome. Still, I've had many instances where I was holding long positions and used weaker stocks or the overall market as a hedge, and realized gains on both.

Since there is considerable flexibility in the approaches you can take to hedge, the best approach depends upon your own personal objectives and preferences, the specific circumstances, the size of your account, and your own tolerance for risk. If you don't have a large account, then it's probably best simply to manage risk by other means rather than employ hedging strategies. As I've frequently commented, you should always use stop-losses to limit your potential losses whenever possible, and you can adjust lot sizes to reduce your risk exposure. In cases where this may be less practical, as with particularly large positions or large heavily leveraged portfolios, hedging can be a useful alternative.

Index Options

There are times when you might find it more convenient to trade index options rather than individual stock options.

If you anticipate a pending sector or general market move and would like to react quickly without taking the time to pick specific stocks, you can do so by using index options. For example, if positive news came out about Semiconductor stocks and you needed to act quickly, you could consider buying CALL options for the Semiconductor Index (SOX) rather than trying to pick among individual Semiconductor stocks.

Of course, you can always consider buying the index long, rather than using options, but since many of the indexes are very expensive, using options is a more affordable alternative. As I'll illustrate in a moment, index option premiums can be expensive as well but due to the leverage provided by options, they are considerably cheaper than buying the index itself. Still, the cost of some index options may make trading them impractical for traders with smaller account sizes. Buying options for Exchange Traded Funds (ETFs), or Holders, such as SMH, BBH, HHH, and so on are another possibility you can consider.

Index options or ETFs can also be used to reduce overall risk exposure by spreading risk across the collection of companies that make up the index. And, as I discussed under "Leverage And Hedging", you can use index options to hedge your entire portfolio against potential losses. Additionally, I've frequently used index options to play other trends such as earnings trends or the FOMC runs described in the "Trends Are Your Friends" chapter.

Following are December option quotes for the SOX. At the time of these quotes, the SOX was priced at $362.64.

SOX $362.64							
Title	Symbol	Last	Volume	B Bid	Bid/Ask Spread	B Ask	Open Int
SOX.X Dec 340 Call	SOYLH	33.00	12	35.60	3.00	38.60	203
SOX.X Dec 340 Put	SOYXH	14.50	21	13.20	1.80	15.00	140
SOX.X Dec 345 Call	SOYLI	26.30	5	32.30	3.00	35.30	29
SOX.X Dec 345 Put	SOYXI	15.20	0	14.90	2.00	16.90	26
SOX.X Dec 350 Call	SOYLJ	34.90	8	30.00	2.30	32.30	99
SOX.X Dec 350 Put	SOYXJ	19.40	141	16.80	2.00	18.80	430
SOX.X Dec 355 Call	SOYLK	28.00	0	26.00	3.00	29.00	68
SOX.X Dec 355 Put	SOYXK	21.10	63	18.80	2.00	20.80	29
SOX.X Dec 360 Call	SOYLL	21.30	18	23.50	2.90	26.40	92
SOX.X Dec 360 Put	SOYXL	22.00	22	20.50	3.00	23.50	31
SOX.X Dec 365 Call	SOYLM	8.90	0	20.80	3.00	23.80	73
SOX.X Dec 365 Put	SOYXM	24.00	10	22.90	3.00	25.90	13
SOX.X Dec 370 Call	SOYLN	19.90	86	18.90	2.00	20.90	166
SOX.X Dec 370 Put	SOYXN	26.50	3	25.40	3.00	28.40	30
SOX.X Dec 375 Call	SOYLO	19.00	0	16.70	2.00	18.70	121
SOX.X Dec 375 Put	SOYXO		0	28.30	3.00	31.30	0
SOX.X Dec 380 Call	SOYLP	15.80	0	15.00	1.70	16.70	74
SOX.X Dec 380 Put	SOYXP	34.60	2	31.20	3.00	34.20	2
SOX.X Dec 385 Call	SOYLQ	16.00	7	12.80	2.00	14.80	16
SOX.X Dec 385 Put	SOYXQ	64.00	0	34.40	3.00	37.40	1
SOX.X Dec 390 Call	SOYLR	12.40	512	11.10	2.00	13.10	26
SOX.X Dec 390 Put	SOYXR	43.20	1	37.70	3.00	40.70	0
SOX.X Dec 395 Call	SOYLS	10.20	1	9.80	1.50	11.30	14
SOX.X Dec 395 Put	SOYXS		0	41.10	3.00	44.10	0
SOX.X Dec 400 Call	SOYLT	9.00	37	8.40	1.50	9.90	201

Due to their cost and the rapidly declining value of the time-based portion of the premiums, I generally only use index options for relatively short-term trades, possibly up to a week or so but preferably, only one or two days. For example, notice the premiums for the $365 CALL options in the preceding illustration. The best bid is $20.80 and the best ask is $23.80. Though it's much less than the $362.64 index cost, it is still an expensive option.

Although these options are expensive, one of the things that I like about them is they tend to move in fairly large increments in a short timeframe whenever the market moves. Unlike individual stocks where it can be less certain whether you'll get a $0.50 or $1.00 move out of them when the market moves, index options are likely to move dramatically. Of course, since a move could go against you, you should take into consideration that your losses can mount up quickly as well.

A significant disadvantage to these options is the size of the spread. Looking at the bids and asks on the previous quote screen, you can see there is about a $2.00 to $3.00 difference, or premium, between them in most cases. For example, there is a $3.00 difference between the bid and ask of the $365 CALL discussed earlier ($23.80-$20.80 = $3.00). The size of the spread lessens as you get further out of the money, but even then the premiums are substantial. If you were to open a position and subsequently changed your mind, you could potentially lose 10% to 15% by simply getting out of the trade.

As I touched on earlier, when trading options I recommend using only limit orders. Though some options have a fairly high degree of liquidity, many are thinly traded. Considering the lower liquidity and wider spreads, you could receive very unfavorable fills using market orders. Though you would most likely get a reasonable fill with highly liquid options such as those for MSFT, with index options, if the price is changing and you place a market order, you are likely to get a very unfavorable price. In fact, you could easily fill $5.00 away from your intended price. Using limit orders ensures you will either get the intended price, or your order simply won't fill.

To get a better sense of the liquidity, take a look at the "Volume" column that is shown in the preceding example quotes. Notice the volume is relatively low for all of the options. On this particular day, the highest volume was 512 contracts for the $390 CALL options. Unless they were being used as a hedge, it indicates there was some bullish interest in the SOX at the time of these quotes. Though a volume of 512 results in a reasonable amount of liquidity, it is still much lower than a stock such as MSFT, which is typically in the thousands. If the price isn't moving quickly and you placed a market order to by the $390 CALLS, you might get a fill at the best ask but even you do, you will already be down about 15% on the trade due to the large $2.00 spread ($13.20-$11.20 = $2.00).

Rather than using a market order and getting filled at the best ask, or even worse, being subject to the whims of the market maker, I generally place a limit order between the best bid and best ask. I'm rarely willing to pay more than a $1.00 premium on the spread just to enter a position. I would rather pass on the trade. Using the $390 CALLS as an example, I might place a limit order at $12.20, or less, depending on how strongly I felt about the trade. I'd prefer to get a fill that is closer to the best bid than the best ask, and since indexes tend to have a much wider range intraday, there's a good chance the price will fluctuate sufficiently to get a fill.

Though I used the $390 CALLS for purposes of discussing liquidity, I actually prefer playing in the money index options rather than out of the money options. Even though they cost more and therefore, I'm risking more, I prefer the price action of in the money options. So, using the preceding example, I would be more inclined to buy the $355 or $360 CALLS rather than the $390 CALLS.

Also notice that some of the last trades on the previous SOX quote screen are outside of the range of the best bid and ask. In some cases, it could simply be the result of passing time and changing prices since the last trade. In other instances, it could mean that someone received a very poor order fill.

Here is another example that shows December option quotes for the S&P 100 Index (OEX). The index was trading at $475.02 at the time of the quotes.

OEX $475.02

Title	Symbol	Last	Volume	B Bid	Bid/Ask Spread	B Ask	Open Int
OEX.X Dec 440 Call	OXBLH	39.00	21	37.40	1.50	38.90	2,933
OEX.X Dec 440 Put	OXBXH	3.30	1,413	3.10	0.20	3.30	4,286
OEX.X Dec 445 Call	OXBLI	35.00	6	33.10	1.50	34.60	202
OEX.X Dec 445 Put	OXBXI	3.80	266	3.80	0.20	4.00	1,392
OEX.X Dec 450 Call	OXBLJ	31.00	48	28.90	1.50	30.40	2,831
OEX.X Dec 450 Put	OXBXJ	4.80	888	4.70	0.20	4.90	4,396
OEX.X Dec 455 Call	OXBLK	26.00	67	24.90	1.50	26.40	862
OEX.X Dec 455 Put	OXBXK	5.30	286	5.60	0.40	6.00	2,375
OEX.X Dec 460 Call	OXBLL	22.10	30	21.00	1.50	22.50	6,321
OEX.X Dec 460 Put	OXBXL	7.10	1,575	6.90	0.30	7.20	5,587
OEX.X Dec 465 Call	OXBLM	18.50	39	17.70	1.00	18.70	1,263
OEX.X Dec 465 Put	OXBXM	8.50	461	8.50	0.40	8.90	1,282
OEX.X Dec 470 Call	OXBLN	15.00	227	14.50	1.00	15.50	2,919
OEX.X Dec 470 Put	OXBXN	10.60	1,273	10.30	0.40	10.70	1,826
OEX.X Dec 475 Call	OXBLO	12.50	1,112	11.50	0.60	12.10	6,093
OEX.X Dec 475 Put	OXBXO	12.50	836	12.50	0.40	12.90	605
OEX.X Dec 480 Call	OXBLP	9.40	1,020	9.20	0.60	9.80	8,490
OEX.X Dec 480 Put	OXBXP	15.20	927	15.00	0.70	15.70	1,507
OEX.X Dec 485 Call	OXBLQ	8.00	3,005	7.10	0.40	7.50	2,240
OEX.X Dec 485 Put	OXBXQ	18.10	1	18.00	1.00	19.00	8
OEX.X Dec 490 Call	OXBLR	6.40	2,763	5.20	0.30	5.50	11,897
OEX.X Dec 490 Put	OXBXR	20.50	97	21.10	1.50	22.60	197
OEX.X Dec 495 Call	OXBLS	3.80	323	3.80	0.40	4.20	1,471
OEX.X Dec 495 Put	OXBXS	24.80	15	24.70	1.50	26.20	12
OEX.X Dec 500 Call	OEBLT	2.75	1,288	2.50	0.30	2.80	10,708
OEX.X Dec 500 Put	OEBXT	28.20	157	28.70	1.50	30.20	2,774
OEX.X Dec 505 Call	OEBLA	1.90	1,612	1.85	0.30	2.15	1,925
OEX.X Dec 505 Put	OEBXA	32.50	2	32.90	1.50	34.40	11
OEX.X Dec 510 Call	OEBLB	1.25	320	1.25	0.25	1.50	3,244
OEX.X Dec 510 Put	OEBXB	55.00	3	37.40	1.50	38.90	5

Since the OEX is more actively traded, notice the correspondingly higher volume and liquidity on the preceding quote screen. Unlike the prior SOX example, you'll see numerous OEX options that have trading volumes numbering in the thousands. As a result, also notice the tighter price spreads between the bids and asks, and the higher amounts of open interest.

As explained in the "Options Primer" chapter, open interest reflects the number of option contracts/positions that are currently open, where volume reflects the number of trades both in and out of positions.

Looking at the OEX "Bid/Ask Spread" column, whereas the spreads were frequently $2.00 to $3.00 for the SOX, the OEX spreads that have the highest volume and liquidity are in the range of $0.30 to $0.70. However, some of the lower volume spreads are over $1.00, which illustrates the impact that low liquidity can have on the prices.

As usual, you can see that the OEX option premiums decrease the further out of the money the options become. For example, the best ask of the $475 CALL options is $12.10, while the best ask of the $490 CALL options is $5.50 Though the cost of the $490 CALLS is considerably less, they are over 20 points out of the money ($490 option - $475 index price + $5.50 premium = $20.50). As I discussed earlier, though I trade out of the money options as well, my overall preference is to trade in the money options. If I wanted to buy CALL options in this case, I would likely buy the $465 CALLS, or possibly the $470 CALLS.

Trading index options may not be practical for traders with relatively small accounts, especially when you take into consideration that options can't be traded on margin. However, if your account is sufficiently large to make trading index options practical, they can be a great alternative for hedging, or for short-term trades when you anticipate large moves in the market. Since index options tend to move rapidly with large incremental price moves, you can achieve huge gains if you catch a dramatic market move.

I like using index options when I have a strong trend backing up my trade. For example, after a recent FOMC meeting the market gyrated wildly intraday, moving 100+ points in both directions in a matter of minutes. Large, dramatic market moves such as this provide fantastic trading opportunities for index options. Therefore, if I think there is going to be a large market move, rather than hunting for individual stocks, I prefer to be in the indexes.

LEAPS

As a short-term trader, I don't trade LEAPS (Long-Term Equity Anticipation Securities) but for those of you that might be curious about them, I'll provide a general description.

LEAPS are options whose expiration month is 9 months or more away. The following options quote screen shows a LEAP for QLGC. At the time of these quotes, the option was approximately a year from expiration, and the QLGC stock price was $43.25.

QLGC $43.25

Title	Symbol	Last	Volume	B Bid	Bid/Ask Spread	B Ask	Open Int
QLGC Jan04 25 Call	KGMAE	19.20	27	23.20	0.50	23.70	315
QLGC Jan04 25 Put	KGMME	4.70	3	4.70	0.30	5.00	442
QLGC Jan04 30 Call	KGMAF	19.70	5	20.20	0.50	20.70	543
QLGC Jan04 30 Put	KGMMF	6.60	14	6.50	0.40	6.90	455
QLGC Jan04 35 Call	KGMAG	15.20	0	17.40	0.50	17.90	886
QLGC Jan04 35 Put	KGMMG	10.50	0	8.60	0.40	9.00	256
QLGC Jan04 40 Call	KGMAH	15.50	17	15.00	0.40	15.40	1,201
QLGC Jan04 40 Put	KGMMH	11.40	8	11.10	0.40	11.50	351
QLGC Jan04 50 Call	KGMAJ	9.40	6	11.00	0.30	11.30	961
QLGC Jan04 50 Put	KGMMJ	16.70	0	16.80	0.40	17.20	167
QLGC Jan04 60 Call	KGMAL	8.60	0	7.90	0.30	8.20	1,342
QLGC Jan04 60 Put	KGMML	25.50	0	23.60	0.40	24.00	958
QLGC Jan04 70 Call	KGMAN	5.30	0	5.70	0.20	5.90	910
QLGC Jan04 70 Put	KGMMN	35.50	0	31.20	0.50	31.70	1,329

If you were bullish on QLGC and wanted to speculate long-term that the price would go up, rather than buying the stock, you could consider buying LEAP options. However, as you might expect, you would have to pay a hefty premium for the privilege of such long-term options speculations. In fact, it's questionable whether the premium costs justify using the options over simply buying the stock outright.

Looking at the prior quote screen, you can see that the best ask for the $40 in the money CALL is $15.40. Upon expiration, the stock price would need to be $55.40 ($40 + $15.40) or higher to make money on the trade. If you felt there was going to be a large bull run on the stock, you could consider using out of the money options at a lower cost. For example, the best ask for the $50 CALL is quoted as $11.30. Though the initial cost is less in this case, you would need the price to climb to $61.30 ($50 + $11.30) or higher to come out on the trade at options expiration.

It's not likely that I would ever speculate that far out by using LEAPS. Regardless, considering my personal objectives and short-term trading style, it really doesn't come up as a consideration for me.

Straddles

One of my favorite options strategies, and one that I use often, is called a *straddle*. A straddle is buying equal amounts of CALLS and PUTS for the same stock, using the same expiration month, and at the same strike price.

Straddles are a great way to potentially profit from large near-term price moves. In situations where you anticipate a large near-term move but you aren't sure which direction the price will move, you can take advantage of the expected price volatility by using straddles.

Even though I do play them at other times, and for other reasons, I particularly like playing straddles during earnings season when the risk/reward for straddles is quite favorable.

It's common for a stock to move dramatically one way or the other after a company reports earnings, but the direction of the move depends upon the specifics of the earnings report, which generally isn't known in advance. If a company blows out earnings estimates, its stock price may be propelled dramatically higher. Conversely, if there is bad news and a company misses earnings estimates or releases an earnings warning, its stock price may plunge. Most stocks will move one direction or the other to some degree after reporting earnings, and an option straddle is a strategy you can use to take advantage of these moves.

Since it is possible, or even probable, that you will lose on one side of a straddle play, you need a sufficiently large move on the other side to make up for the loss and make a profit overall. However, there have been occasions when I've made money on both sides of the trade. For example, a company might initially run higher after blowing out an earnings estimate, which lets you roll out of your CALLS, and then it could sell off later providing the opportunity to exit your PUTS with a profit as well. Still, this doesn't occur often so straddles work best when the combined option premiums are sufficiently low to make the trade practical.

I've found the best opportunities occur for stocks that are reporting earnings during the week of option expirations. Option premiums are lower as their expiration dates approach and the earnings reports generate the needed price volatility. In fact, since the goal of traders is to obtain an "edge", or advantage, whenever possible, I've found option expirations week to be one of the best times for trading options. It's one of the few times that you have an edge when trading options because the earnings volatility isn't fully priced into the value of the options.

During earnings season, I typically perform considerably more research, especially just ahead of option expirations week. Not only am I continuing to look for the opportunity to trade stocks long for an earnings run, I'm researching option premiums for potential straddles.

I review earnings calendars and do historical research for the momentum stocks that are scheduled to report earnings during the last week of option expirations. The most promising trading candidates are stocks that have a historical tendency to move dramatically after reporting earnings.

Once I find some stocks that look appealing from a historical perspective, I check the option premiums for those stocks. The combined premium for playing a straddle has to be reasonable, which isn't always the case. I'm not going to pay $6.00 to play a straddle *at the money*, since I would need a ridiculously large move to make money. However, when the option premiums are attractive and a stock otherwise looks like a good straddle candidate, then I will trade the straddle. For example, I recently traded an EMC straddle with a total cost of about $0.50 and sold it for around $0.70 or so overall. To me, that was a nice risk/reward for a straddle play.

I've made a considerable amount of money trading option straddles over the years, as have many of my clients, especially when the market traded at the lofty levels that it did in the late 1990s. I recall making about $26.00 per contract, or about $140,000 total, on an overnight PMCS straddle. We've also had numerous other great straddle trades. Of course, not all trades are profitable nor do they all net such nice gains, but it's still not uncommon to achieve 15% or 20% gains overall, or $5.00 to $10.00 moves, and even an occasional double or better can occur when a trade goes particularly well. Regardless of the specific amount, whenever it's a gain rather than a loss, I'm happy to take whatever the market gives me!

Though the majority of my straddle trades take place during earnings season and the last week of option expirations, whenever attractive premiums and sufficient volatility allow, I will trade straddles at other times.

For example, I've used straddles to trade FOMC meetings. Since the market is often volatile when the results of FOMC meetings are announced, you can sometimes trade it using a straddle and profit from a move in both directions. Essentially, anytime there is the potential for a lot of volatility in the market, it could be a good opportunity to use a straddle. In a best-case scenario, a volatile up and down market could let you roll out of both your CALLS and PUTS with a profit.

Following is a December options quote screen for EBAY. The current stock price is $70.10.

EBAY $70.10

Title	Symbol	Last	Volume	B Bid	Bid/Ask Spread	B Ask	Open Int
EBAY Dec 50 Call	QXBLJ	16.30	0	20.10	0.20	20.30	312
EBAY Dec 50 Put	QXBXJ	0.10	4	0.05	0.10	0.15	1,905
EBAY Dec 55 Call	QXBLK	15.10	10	15.20	0.20	15.40	524
EBAY Dec 55 Put	QXBXK	0.20	398	0.15	0.10	0.25	4,164
EBAY Dec 60 Call	QXBLL	10.70	107	10.40	0.20	10.60	2,568
EBAY Dec 60 Put	QXBXL	0.40	233	0.40	0.10	0.50	7,770
EBAY Dec 65 Call	QXBLM	6.20	251	6.10	0.10	6.20	7,139
EBAY Dec 65 Put	QXBXM	1.00	1,108	1.00	0.15	1.15	4,879
EBAY Dec 70 Call	QXBLN	2.80	1,322	2.75	0.10	2.85	11,854
EBAY Dec 70 Put	QXBXN	2.80	1,134	2.65	0.10	2.75	1,061
EBAY Dec 75 Call	QXBLO	0.80	919	0.80	0.10	0.90	9,563
EBAY Dec 75 Put	QXBXO	5.80	217	5.70	0.10	5.80	664
EBAY Dec 80 Call	QXBLP	0.20	825	0.15	0.10	0.25	1,456
EBAY Dec 80 Put	QXBXP	10.30	42	10.10	0.10	10.20	272
EBAY Dec 85 Call	QXBLQ	0.10	0	0.00	0.10	0.10	22
EBAY Dec 85 Put	QXBXQ		0	14.90	0.20	15.10	0

I prefer straddles where the option strike prices are very near or *at the money*. Meaning, the strike price for both options is as close as possible to the stock's price. This lets you pay roughly an equal amount for both the CALLS and PUTS.

Looking at the preceding quote screen, notice that the EBAY stock price is $70.10 and the $70 CALL and PUT options are closely priced at $2.85 and $2.75, respectively. To play a straddle, you would buy an equal amount of the $70 CALLS and the $70 PUTS for a total combined cost of $5.60 for the straddle ($2.85 + $2.75 = $5.60).

Note that I'm simply using this quote screen for illustration purposes only. In my opinion, the premiums in this case are actually still too high, since the options were more than a week away from expiration at the time of the quotes. During the final week of option expirations, the premiums would be somewhere in the range of $1.20 or so, which would make them reasonable to consider for a straddle. The total cost of the straddle would be around $2.40, so EBAY would only need to move about 5% to make money on the trade, and it is fairly common for momentum stocks such as EBAY to move by 5% or more following an earnings report.

Even though there is risk associated with playing straddles, you generally don't lose an unreasonable amount. You can typically roll out of the trade on one side or the other with at least most of your original investment, or more. Still, if EBAY were to open essentially flat, you would lose on both sides of the trade due to the short timeframe until the options expire, and the resulting loss of the time-based portion of the option premiums. You might even lose half of your money in such a scenario. Fortunately, this rarely occurs with volatile momentum stocks such as EBAY. Volatile stocks tend to move up and down sufficiently to let you roll out of your positions. Still, the potential for loss is a reality that you should take into account before making the decision to speculate using a straddle.

Ideally, as mentioned earlier, unless you intentionally have a bullish or bearish bias, you should use CALL and PUT options for a straddle whose strike prices are as close as possible to the stock's price so that the premiums for each position are reasonably close in price as well. Otherwise, your straddle will have an inherent bullish or bearish bias. For example, if the preceding EBAY stock price were $69 rather than $70.10, you would have a bias toward the short side since the $70 PUTS would already be in the money, and would be more expensive than the $70 CALLS.

STRANGLES

Strangles are similar to straddles, except you use out of the money strike prices that are different from one another. A *strangle* is buying equal amounts of CALLS and PUTS for the same stock, using the same expiration month, at two different out of the money strike prices that surround the stock's price.

For illustration purposes, I'll use the EBAY quote screen that was shown earlier.

EBAY $70.10

Title	Symbol	Last	Volume	B Bid	Bid/Ask Spread	B Ask	Open Int
EBAY Dec 50 Call	QXBLJ	16.30	0	20.10	0.20	20.30	312
EBAY Dec 50 Put	QXBXJ	0.10	4	0.05	0.10	0.15	1,905
EBAY Dec 55 Call	QXBLK	15.10	10	15.20	0.20	15.40	524
EBAY Dec 55 Put	QXBXK	0.20	398	0.15	0.10	0.25	4,164
EBAY Dec 60 Call	QXBLL	10.70	107	10.40	0.20	10.60	2,568
EBAY Dec 60 Put	QXBXL	0.40	233	0.40	0.10	0.50	7,770
EBAY Dec 65 Call	QXBLM	6.20	251	6.10	0.10	6.20	7,139
EBAY Dec 65 Put	QXBXM	1.00	1,108	1.00	0.15	1.15	4,879
EBAY Dec 70 Call	QXBLN	2.80	1,322	2.75	0.10	2.85	11,854
EBAY Dec 70 Put	QXBXN	2.80	1,134	2.65	0.10	2.75	1,061
EBAY Dec 75 Call	QXBLO	0.80	919	0.80	0.10	0.90	9,563
EBAY Dec 75 Put	QXBXO	5.80	217	5.70	0.10	5.80	664
EBAY Dec 80 Call	QXBLP	0.20	825	0.15	0.10	0.25	1,456
EBAY Dec 80 Put	QXBXP	10.30	42	10.10	0.10	10.20	272
EBAY Dec 85 Call	QXBLQ	0.10	0	0.00	0.10	0.10	22
EBAY Dec 85 Put	QXBXQ		0	14.90	0.20	15.10	0

Looking at the preceding quotes, if you wanted to buy an EBAY strangle, you could buy the $65 PUT and $75 CALL options. You are splitting the difference between the stock price and the option strike prices. In this case, the $65 PUT is roughly $5.00 less than the $70.10 stock price, and the $75 CALL is roughly $5.00 greater than the stock price. By playing a strangle, you are betting that the stock will either go lower than $65.00 or higher than $75.00.

The combined cost of the strangle would be $2.05 ($1.15 + $0.90). As before, these quotes are just for illustration purposes and are more than a week out away from the option expiration date. The actual combined cost would be about $1.00, if you waited until the final week of option expirations, which is the approach that I generally use.

Since you are further out of the money when trading a strangle, you typically need the stock's price to move farther in order to come out on the trade. Rather than about a 5% move, as described earlier for the EBAY straddle, you now need EBAY to move around 10%. In order to cover the hypothetical $1.00 option premium and the desired $5.00 price move, the stock's price needs to move more than $6.00 (i.e., about 10%) in either direction prior to option expirations. Even so, a 10% move is quite possible for a volatile momentum stock such as EBAY, so it's not unreasonable to consider using a strangle when the option premiums and other circumstances of a trade indicate the risk/reward remains favorable overall.

As I mentioned earlier, although I've made a lot of money trading these option plays, keep in mind that they are speculative in nature. Therefore, you should only use a small portion of your total funds for such speculative trades.

Bull Spread

A *bull spread* is a bullish option strategy you can use when you think a stock's price is more likely to go higher than it is to go lower.

To trade a bull spread, you buy CALL options for a stock, and sell an equal amount of CALL options for the same stock at a price that is a strike price, or a few strike prices, higher.

The CALL option you buy is typically in the money, or closer to the money, than the CALL option you sell. You pay the premium for the option you buy, and collect the premium for the option you sell. The end result is that the overall bias for a bull spread is as its name implies, bullish.

A bull spread lowers your risk for the trade to the amount you paid for the option you bought, less the premium you collected from the option you sold. The maximum reward is limited, however, since it falls between the two strike prices. Although the profits are limited, the risk is much lower as well.

I will sometimes trade a bull spread during earnings season when I think there is a greater chance than not that a stock will move higher ahead of its earnings report.

Following is a sample options quote screen for KLAC. At the time of these quotes, KLAC was scheduled to report earnings in about two weeks. The KLAC stock price was $42.85 at the time of the quotes.

KLAC $42.85							
Title	Symbol	Last	Volume	B Bid	Bid/Ask	B Ask	Open Int
KLAC Dec 30 Call	KCQLF	12.90	5	12.90	0.30	13.20	2,286
KLAC Dec 30 Put	KCQXF	0.25	616	0.20	0.05	0.25	4,734
KLAC Dec 35 Call	KCQLG	8.80	75	8.30	0.20	8.50	6,447
KLAC Dec 35 Put	KCQXG	0.70	711	0.60	0.10	0.70	6,717
KLAC Dec 40 Call	KCQLH	4.40	1,308	4.40	0.10	4.50	8,225
KLAC Dec 40 Put	KCQXH	1.70	3,941	1.65	0.05	1.70	5,513
KLAC Dec 45 Call	KCQLI	1.70	638	1.70	0.05	1.75	4,355
KLAC Dec 45 Put	KCQXI	4.00	288	3.90	0.10	4.00	1,304
KLAC Dec 50 Call	KCQLJ	0.45	630	0.40	0.10	0.50	2,107
KLAC Dec 50 Put	KCQXJ	8.00	37	7.50	0.20	7.70	234
KLAC Dec 55 Call	KCQLK	0.10	117	0.05	0.15	0.20	1,039
KLAC Dec 55 Put	KCQXK	22.80	0	12.10	0.30	12.40	55
KLAC Dec 60 Call	KCQLL	0.15	0	0.00	0.10	0.10	658
KLAC Dec 60 Put	KCQXL	32.80	0	17.00	0.40	17.40	200
KLAC Dec 65 Call	CKVLM	0.05	0	0.00	0.05	0.05	595
KLAC Dec 65 Put	CKVXM		0	22.00	0.40	22.40	2
KLAC Dec 70 Call	CKVLN	0.05	0	0.00	0.05	0.05	618
KLAC Dec 70 Put	CKVXN	34.60	0	27.00	0.40	27.40	3

Knowing that KLAC is reporting earnings in two weeks and that it historical runs up ahead of its earnings report, you might consider playing the anticipated bullish bias using a bull spread. Referring to the preceding quote screen, there are a number of ways you could play the bull spread.

One approach is to buy the $40 *in the money* CALLS at $4.50 and sell *out of the money* $45 CALLS at $1.75. Since you are selling the $45 CALLS, you would collect the $1.75 premium then pay the $4.50 premium on the $40 CALLS you are buying, so your net out of pocket cost for the bull spread would be $2.75 ($4.50-$1.75). The in the money CALLS and higher cost on the buy side reflect your bullish bias.

If KLAC is $45.00 or higher by options expiration, you would make a maximum of $2.25 on the trade, which is the difference between the $45 options you sold and the $40 options you bought, less the net cost of the options (e.g., $45.00-$40.00-$2.75 = $2.25).

Alternatively, for further clarification the value of each option could be determined. If the KLAC stock price was $45.00, you would be up $5.00 on the $40 CALLS you bought. Since the option premium was $4.50, you would make $0.50 on the trade ($5.00-$4.50 = $0.50). The value of the $45 CALLS you sold would be zero, but you would collect the $1.75 premium. The end result is the same. You would make $2.25

on the bull spread ($0.50+$1.75 = $2.25).

If the KLAC stock price is $40 or less at expiration, the most you can lose on the trade is the net premium cost of the options, which is $2.75. You would gain or lose a proportionate amount when the KLAC stock price is in between the two strike prices. Meaning, you would lose an amount between zero and the maximum of $2.75, or gain an amount between zero and the maximum of $2.25, if the stock's price remains between the two strike prices of the options.

If you were particularly bullish on the stock, you could consider using options that are further out of the money. Your potential profits would be greater, but the stock would need to move further to fully realize all of the profits.

For example, looking at the preceding illustration again, you could buy the $45 CALLS at $1.75 and sell the $50 CALLS at $0.50, which results in a net cost of $1.25. In this scenario, you would need an earnings run to propel the price to $50 or higher to realize the maximum potential profit of $3.75 ($50-$45-$1.25 = $3.75). The stock has to run further but if it does, you could potentially net 200% on your money. The most you could lose is the $1.25 net cost.

With bull spreads, if the price continues to move further above the strike price of the CALLS you sell, you would still net only the maximum potential profit. For example, in the preceding example, if the price ran to $60 or higher, your maximum profit would still be $3.75. While you would make more on the $45 CALLS you bought, you would give back the same amount in additional losses on the $50 CALLS you sold.

Determining precisely when and how to exit a bull spread is dependent upon the specifics of the trade and your own preferences. As explained earlier, you need not wait for the options to expire to exit a trade. You can take profits whenever you are satisfied with your gains, or you can exit a position simply to limit losses.

However, you generally shouldn't exit the CALLS you bought without also exiting the CALLS you sold, since doing so could leave you exposed to greater risk should the stock's price unexpectedly surge higher (this would be the equivalent of selling the CALLS NAKED). Without holding the *buy* position to cover potential losses on the *sell* position, you could incur significantly higher losses.

BEAR SPREAD

Similar to the way you use a bull spread for an upside bias, you can use a *bear spread* when your bias is to the downside. A bear spread is essentially the opposite, or reverse, of the previously discussed bull spread.

To trade a bear spread, you buy PUT options for a stock, and sell an equal amount of PUT options for the same stock at a price that is a strike price, or a few strike prices, lower.

The PUT option you buy is in the money, or closer to the money, than the PUT option you sell. As before, you pay the premium for the option you buy, and collect the premium for the option you sell. The end result is that the overall bias for a bear spread is bearish.

As with a bull spread, a bear spread lowers your risk for the trade to the amount you pay for the option you buy, less the premium you collect from the option you sell. The maximum reward is limited, however, since it falls between the two strike prices. And although the profits are limited, the risk is lower as well.

Following is a sample options quote screen for EXPE. The EXPE stock price is $75.08.

EXPE $75.08

Title	Symbol	Last	Volume	B Bid	Bid/Ask Sprea	B Ask	Open Int
EXPE Dec 60 Call	UEDLL	15.10	4	15.60	0.30	15.90	698
EXPE Dec 60 Put	UEDXL	0.70	112	0.65	0.10	0.75	1,283
EXPE Dec 65 Call	UEDLM	11.50	73	11.20	0.30	11.50	1,469
EXPE Dec 65 Put	UEDXM	1.20	115	1.15	0.15	1.30	2,188
EXPE Dec 70 Call	UEDLN	7.50	56	7.20	0.30	7.50	1,881
EXPE Dec 70 Put	UEDXN	2.20	494	2.20	0.20	2.40	2,835
EXPE Dec 75 Call	UEDLO	4.10	327	4.00	0.30	4.30	1,507
EXPE Dec 75 Put	UEDXO	4.20	430	3.90	0.30	4.20	824
EXPE Dec 80 Call	UEDLP	2.00	285	1.90	0.15	2.05	1,287
EXPE Dec 80 Put	UEDXP	7.10	31	6.80	0.20	7.00	315
EXPE Dec 85 Call	UEDLQ	0.75	186	0.70	0.20	0.90	704
EXPE Dec 85 Put	UEDXQ	10.70	17	10.50	0.40	10.90	87

Similar to the bull spread, you can choose among a number of strategies to play a bear spread. For example, you could buy the $75 PUTS at $4.20 and sell the $70 PUTS at $2.40. Your net cost for the trade would be $1.80, which is the premium you paid for the $75 PUTS minus the premium you collected for the $70 PUTS that you sold ($4.20-$2.40 = $1.80). If the price of EXPE moves to $70 or lower, you make $3.20 on the trade ($75-$70-$1.80).

Alternatively, if you wanted to go further out of the money on the trade, you could consider buying the $75 PUTS at $4.20, and rather than selling the $70 PUTS, you could sell the $65 PUTS at $1.30. The net cost in this case would be $2.90. If the price of EXPE moves to $65.00 or lower, you would make $7.10 on the trade ($75-$65-$2.90). Though the potential profits are higher when you go further out of the money, the stock price has to move further as well. My preference would be the $75/$70 spread in this case, since the associated cost and risk is less.

As with the bull spread, you need not wait for the options to expire to exit a bear spread. You can take profits anytime you choose, or you can exit a losing position to help reduce the maximum potential losses. And once again, you generally shouldn't exit the PUTS you bought without also exiting the PUTS you sold, since doing so could leave you exposed to greater risk should the stock's price fall unexpectedly (in this case, it would be the equivalent of selling the PUTS NAKED). Without holding the *buy* position to cover potential losses on the *sell* position, you could incur significantly higher losses.

11

My Favorite Strategies

With so many trading tools and strategies to choose among, new traders frequently ask me which I think are best. Well, I like and regularly use all of the techniques described in this book. After all, that's the reason I put them in the book. Depending on the circumstances and market conditions, each strategy has its moment in the sun, or a time when it shines bright.

However, for those of you who may prefer to narrow their focus, there are a handful of techniques that have slightly edged out the others over the years to earn a spot on my list of favorites. How do they earn such an honor, you might ask? They earn it from years of consistently making my clients, and myself, the big ka-chingos!

This chapter highlights my favorite trading strategies. Although the techniques presented here are also described elsewhere in the book, I thought you might appreciate having them conveniently organized in one location for easy reference. You can look here to easily see which techniques I feel are the cream of the crop. Also, the descriptions and examples provided here differ from, or further expand upon, the corresponding material provided earlier in the book, so you might pick up a few new useful trading tidbits while reviewing them.

Although only strategies that have withstood the test of time make it onto my favorites list, I should qualify it by noting that just as the market changes over time, so may my favorite trading strategies change. If market conditions evolve such that a particular trading technique no longer works well, or it quits working for whatever reason, then I would obviously cull it from my list of favorites. Similarly, I may discover new trends or techniques in the future that replace these but if their longevity up to this point is any indication, I suspect these strategies will continue to work their magic on my portfolio for the foreseeable future. Hopefully, they will do the same for your portfolio as well!

Okay, here is the list of my favorite plays.

- Gap Fades
- Earnings Runs
- Earnings Straddles
- FOMC Fades
- 10 AM Rule

I'll discuss each of these in greater detail and provide examples for them in the pages that follow.

Gap Fades

For good reason, gap fades are at the top of my list of favorite techniques. Fading gaps has worked consistently for me over a period of years in both bull and bear markets. I like fading both gap ups and gap downs but between the two, fading gap downs is the winner. The further the market gaps down, the more I like the play.

Since I provided a considerable amount of information earlier in the book about trading gaps, you can look there if a more detailed explanation is desired. For your convenience, I'll provide a brief review of gaps here.

A gap down occurs when the market or a stock opens lower than it closed the prior day. A gap up occurs when the market or a stock opens higher than it closed the prior day.

The catalyst for gaps could be breaking news, or simply an excess of supply or demand during the trading that occurs outside of regular market hours. Since volume is low during after-hours trading, any significant buying or selling pressure can result in exaggerated price moves. Once the market opens for regular trading and volume returns to normal, these exaggerated price swings frequently correct themselves, resulting in a snapback price reversal in the direction opposite to the gap.

Trading these snapback price reversals is called *fading the gap*. To fade a gap down, you enter a long position when the initial selling pressure subsides. To fade a gap up, you enter a short position when the initial buying pressure subsides. Remember that there are occasions when the market gaps, then keeps on going the same direction without a snapback reversal. Therefore, to manage risk and limit potential losses, you should immediately put into place an appropriate stop-loss order after entering a gap trade.

Since the market rarely opens at exactly the price that it closed the prior day, it generally gaps by some amount. On days when the gap is very small or when the market essentially opens flat, rather than fading the gap, you should hold back and wait for the market to establish a direction for the day, and as explained earlier in the book, use the 10 AM rule as a guideline (I'll discuss this more later in this chapter as well). You can often trade modest gaps successfully but more discretion should be used, and large gaps that are either up or down create the best trading opportunities.

A chart of the Diamonds Index (DIA) follows that illustrates a gap down.

Looking at the preceding chart, notice that the DIA gapped down significantly from its prior close. After the gap down, there was a brief period of consolidation where a level of support was established.

To trade the gap down, you would enter a long position during the period of consolidation, or when the price breaks through the high that occurred prior to 10 AM. Afterwards, you should place a stop-loss order below the low of the day, or according to your own tolerance for risk, to limit losses in the event the market continues to move lower.

If the price moves higher, you can adjust your stop-loss order accordingly and trail the upside movement, taking profits along the way as any substantial gains are achieved. At your discretion, you could take profits on all of your position, or on 1/2 of your position then move your stop-loss to breakeven on your remaining shares.

At this point, you should not lose on the trade. With profits locked in on ? of your position, you can continue trailing any further upside movement on your remaining shares until you stop out of the trade. By following this strategy with the preceding example, substantial gains were possible. As long as you didn't set your initial stop-loss setting too tight, it isn't likely you would have stopped out during the momentary pullback that took place. And if you were able to trail the move for all it was worth, you could have potentially made up to about $1.65 on the trade.

Though I frequently trade individual stocks that have gapped down as well, I chose the DIA for this example. Rather than always seeking out specific stocks, I will often simply trade indexes such as the DIAs or QQQs, and so on.

An advantage to using the DIA or other indexes is that unlike individual stocks, which don't always track the market perfectly, if the Dow bounces after a gap down, the DIA is sure to bounce as well.

The DIA not only spreads risk across more than one company, it provides a true reflection of the market's price action. Conversely, with individual stocks, there are times when the market bounces and a given stock may, or may not, follow along. For example, if you buy IBM and the market bounces, IBM could bounce, remain flat, or even go down. Another advantage to the DIA is you can short it without being subject to the uptick rule. Therefore, it also works well for shorting gap ups.

Here is another example chart that shows EBAY gapping up.

To trade the gap up, you would enter a short position when the buying pressure appeared to be subsiding. Once again, you should then place a stop-loss order above the high of the day, or according to your own tolerance for risk, to limit losses in case the stock doesn't pull back as expected. As described for gap downs, you can then trail any favorable move with your stop-loss and take profits along the way at your own discretion.

As you can see from the preceding examples, gap fades provide great opportunities to trade the market on a part-time basis. So, if you can only set aside one or two hours in the mornings for trading, gap fades could provide the desired profit opportunities.

Earnings Runs

Right next to gap fades on my favorites list is earnings runs. I've charted this trend year after year, and it has been a very reliable trend, and very profitable!

An earnings run trend refers to the historical tendency for the prices of popular momentum to run higher in anticipation of their earnings reports, which are commonly reported after the end of each calendar quarter.

The success rate of this trend is likely over 90%, although that's mainly just an instinctive "gut" estimate on my part. Due to the subjective nature of such an effort, and the fact that the best stocks to play changes on a quarterly basis, I haven't tried to precisely calculate the percentage. However, I've tracked this trend for years and I can attest that it virtually always works at some level.

As always, you should take into account overall market conditions, and any sector or stock specific circumstances when evaluating the potential for earnings to run at the end of any given quarter. Depending on overall market sentiment, the strength and timing of an earnings run can vary. If the market at large is weak going into earnings season, an earrings run may occur a week or so later than usual. If the market has already run up substantially and is in an overbought condition going into earnings, the earnings trend could be somewhat weaker as a result. In some instances, the market overall might be moving sideways or appear to be weak on the surface while individual momentum stocks are still running up ahead of their earnings reports. Other earnings run variations are possible as well.

A potentially good setup for an earnings run occurs when the market pulls back, creating a slightly oversold condition, just ahead of earnings season. Under ideal conditions, the upside potential for an earnings run can be explosive. The main point is that the precise timing and strength of earnings runs can vary, but there is generally at least some subset of individual momentum companies that run up ahead of their earnings.

In general, individual momentum stocks tend to start running up about two weeks ahead of their scheduled earnings report. Of course, as I discussed earlier, this is based on the overall historical patterns of various stocks and sectors. On any given quarter, you need to consider overall market conditions and the historical patterns for the specific stocks you are trading, and make any appropriate adjustments.

To find potential trading candidates, you can review online earnings calendars for companies that are scheduled to report earnings in the coming weeks. Various online news and stock market oriented services provide earnings calendars.

A word of caution about earnings calendars, however, use discretion because not all are created with the same due diligence, and some may contain inaccurate information. Additionally, companies sometimes change the date of their earnings reports and services that do not regularly confirm the earnings dates may not reflect these last minute changes. This is important because a key rule to trading the earnings trend is that you exit your position ahead of the actual earnings report and if you are basing the timing of your exit upon inaccurate information, it could be a very costly mistake.

Okay, here's another opportunity for a shameless plug (but it could be profitable for you). We provide earnings calendars and other related information to our clients as well; with a special emphasis on the momentum stocks that we feel are most likely to run up ahead of earnings. In fact, we often provide lists of our favorite earnings stock picks to our clients. If you are interested in exploring this further, you can visit www.trendfund.com for additional information.

Once you find some potential stocks to trade, you can pull up charts and research them to determine how they behaved ahead of theirs earnings reports in the past. I typically go back a couple of years to confirm the trend. If a stock has only run up once or twice in a row, though it may be of interest, I don't consider it a solid trend. Threes time could potentially establish an early trend, and I'd consider more than that to be indicative of a trend. Basically, the more times the trend repeats itself, the better. And though an occasional miss doesn't necessarily break the trend, you should use reasonable discretion and watch it more closely.

Since news rules, before entering a trade you should also check the latest news for each individual stock and their sectors to be certain nothing is going on that could adversely impact an earnings run.

Following is a chart of BVSN that shows how it traded leading into an earnings report. We actually traded this stock for an earnings run.

Looking at the preceding chart, notice the sideways consolidation action that occurred during the weeks that preceded the earnings season. Basing action such as this often provides a great setup for an earnings play entry. You can enter a position when you see an upside break of the range, or if you feel the trend for a given stock is particularly strong and can tolerate slightly more risk, you could even enter the trade during the basing period and place a stop-loss order just under the support level of the range. Another reason I liked this trade is because it was lagging other similar stocks that were already running up ahead of their earnings.

We entered the trade in the general range of $3.75 as buying interest in the stock picked up. As you can see on the chart, the price subsequently moved about $1.00 higher, which resulted in a gain of approximately 18% to 20% in about one week. Our profits on the trade ranged from about $0.75 to $1.00 depending on the specific entry price, which isn't bad at all for such a low priced stock.

We sold BVSN on the day of its earnings report, which is a key rule for playing an earnings trend. I don't recommend holding a stock into its actual earnings report, even when you expect a positive earnings report. In my opinion, that is gambling, since there is no way to be certain in advance what will come out in the earnings report. If earnings are bad, or a company warns or lowers estimates for future earnings, you might not only give back any gains you've achieved, you could incur substantial losses.

Additionally, stocks that have had a large upside move ahead of earnings will frequently sell off after their earnings report, even when the report is positive. It's often a case of buy the rumor, and sell the news. Though it doesn't show up on this particular chart, BVSN did sell off shortly after reporting earnings.

Although there are times when a company will blow out earnings and run higher, to me the upside potential isn't worth the risk. To play an earnings run trend, you should enter a position as appropriate ahead of a company's earnings report and exit the position on the day of the report before the market closes, or at your own discretion, even sooner. Meaning, whenever substantial gains are achieved, you can take some or all of your profits sooner. Similarly, if the risk/reward for a trade changes and is no longer favorable, possibly due to breaking news or for whatever reason, you may want exit a position early to limit losses.

As I've mentioned, my preference is to take profits along the way as I achieve any substantial gains, and that applies to earnings runs as well. What I will often do is sell 1/2 of my position, and then move my stop-loss to breakeven on my remaining shares. This locks in profits and ensures that I can't lose on the trade. Then, I will trail any further upside movement with my stop-loss order and take profits at my own discretion, or I'll simply continue trailing the move until I stop out of the trade.

Here is another earnings run example that shows the price action for RMBS ahead of an earnings report. In this case, we not only bought the stock long, we used options to play the earnings run as well, which is another technique I like to use.

As you can see on the preceding chart, RMBS had a nice run during the two weeks that preceded its earnings report. Once again, notice the basing action that preceded the run. At this point, I was watching the stock closely as a potential earnings run candidate. Notice the large, impulsive upside move that occurred a couple of months earlier. This was in part due to a short squeeze. It indicated to me that there was now a lot of interest in the stock overall. As I noticed activity picking up near the end of the basing period, I took advantage of a brief pullback to enter a position about 10 days out from earnings.

I not only played the stock for the earnings run, I decided to use options for the play as well. Not only did options let me clearly predefine my risk, the premiums were sufficiently attractive that I saw the potential for huge gains if the stock ran into earnings.

We bought $12.50 CALL options for $1.25 about 10 days ahead of earnings and sold them a week or so later for about $4.00 – ka-ching! That was over a 200% profit.

Following is another earnings run example for BRCM.

Looking at the preceding chart, the price action for BRCM was more volatile ahead of earnings. I decided to take advantage of a fairly sharp pullback that occurred a couple of weeks ahead of earnings to enter a position for a potential earnings run.

We entered a position near the lows, the $12.00 range that is shown two weeks out on the chart, which resulted in a nice profit going into earnings. Our overall gain on the trade was in the range of $1.50 to $2.00, which was a nice short-term gain for a $12.00 stock.

Earnings Straddles

Another consistently profitable, and therefore favorite, technique I like to use to play earnings runs are option straddles. Though this is based upon the same earnings run trend that I just discussed, it employs a different strategy that uses options to play the trend.

As you may recall from the "Trading Options" chapter, a straddle is a technique you can use to potentially profit from a large move in a stock's price, regardless of whether the move is up or down. To put on a straddle, you buy both CALL and PUT options at the same strike price for the same expiration month.

When playing an earnings straddle, rather than always selling prior to an earnings report, which I will still do if I achieve the desired gains, I may hold the trade or a portion of it over the earnings report. In this case, since your risk is already predefined and limited, if you don't yet have sufficient gains to profit on the trade, you can hold it over the earnings report and potentially profit from large earnings related price moves. In fact, if the option premiums are particularly low, I will sometimes speculate on the actual earnings report using options by putting on a straddle the day a company is scheduled to report earnings.

An earnings option straddle has been a high percentage play for me. In other words, the risk/reward for the play has been great! A key element of the trade is getting into the straddle at a favorable total premium. With that in mind, I usually play earnings option straddles for companies that are reporting earnings during the last week of options expirations. Since the time based component of option premiums are lowest at this time, and the spreads between the two option positions are tighter, it's more likely that I can put on a straddle at a favorable total cost.

To profit on a straddle, you need the underlying stock's price to move a sufficiently large amount in a short period of time. Earnings runs and earnings reports generate the desired volatility for such potentially sharp price swings. In an ideal situation, you might even get the opportunity to roll out of both sides of the trade with a profit.

Following is a chart of EMC for which we recently played an earnings straddle.

Generally when you play a straddle, you try to setup the position without a bias in either direction. Meaning, both sides of the trade are roughly the same value and the strike price is roughly the same as the underlying stock's price. When this isn't the case, there is a built-in bullish or bearish bias to some degree, where you either make or lose more when the price moves in one direction or the other. In some instances, this can work to your advantage if you actually desire a bias going into the trade.

In the case of the preceding EMC example, I felt it was more likely the stock would go higher rather than lower after reporting earnings, so when I noticed a slight upside bias for the straddle, I didn't mind.

Therefore, during the week of options expiration and on the day EMC was scheduled to report earnings, we put on a $7.50 options straddle for EMC by buying the $7.50 CALL options and the $7.50 PUT options. The stock was trading near $7.75 at the time, which resulted in the slight upside bias. The CALLS were slightly in the money, and the PUTS were slightly out of the money.

The combined cost of the straddle was about $0.50, so the potential risk/reward for the play was favorable. Regardless of whether EMC beat or missed earnings, I felt the stock would likely move at least $0.50, and possibly more. And if I was wrong, the $0.50 total cost was the most I could lose on the trade.

Well, as you can see on the preceding chart, after a positive earnings report, the stock moved fairly dramatically. We exited the position the following morning with about a 35% profit. Due to the short-term nature of the trade, and considering the short time to options expiration, I generally exit such a position the next morning or at some point during the following day. However, in this particular case, anyone that held the position longer could have achieved even larger gains on the trade. Regardless, I'm quite satisfied with a 35% overnight profit.

Following is another earnings straddle example using IBM.

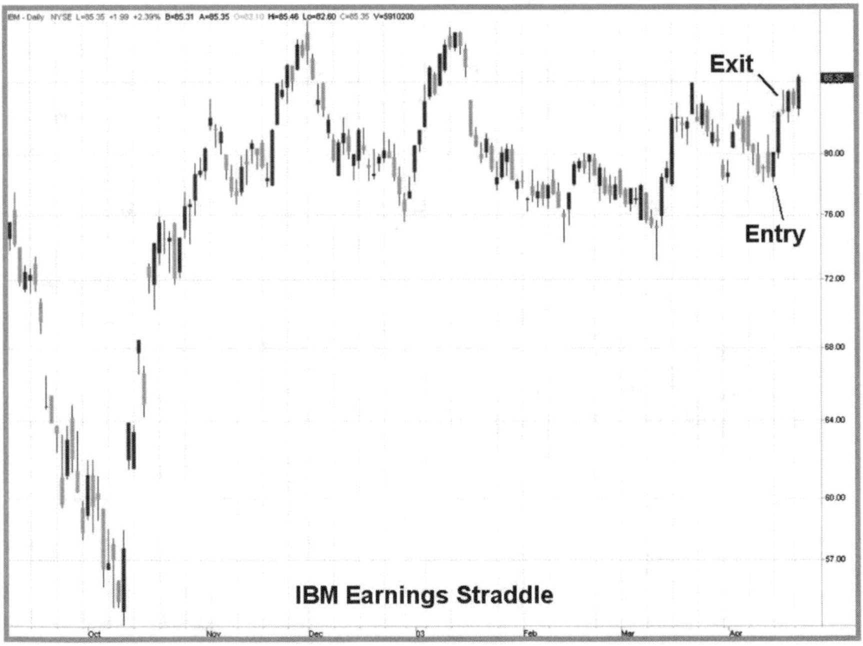

IBM is currently a high-priced momentum stock that has historically reacted to its earnings reports with a large price move. Of course, as with all of the examples in this book, this isn't a specific recommendation to trade IBM. I'm simply using it for illustration purposes. With that in mind, it's not uncommon for volatile momentum stocks such as IBM to move by 5% or more after reporting earnings, which is the type of large move that's needed in order to profit on an earnings straddle.

In this case, we put on an $80 IBM straddle for a total cost of $3.50. As you can see on the preceding chart, IBM subsequently moved about $5.00 higher. We then exited the position with about a 15% profit.

FOMC Fades

Another technique that I like is fading FOMC (Federal Open Market Committee) announcements. As explained in the "Trends Are Your Friends" chapter, the FOMC is a 12-member committee that is responsible for setting interest rate and credit policies.

When the FOMC meets the market often becomes uncertain and anxious about the outcome of the meeting. Will interest rates go up, go down, or remain the same? Will the Fed change their future interest rate bias, loosen or tighten their monetary policy, or make other comments about the state of the economy that could impact the market?

Whether it's justified or not, the market tends to react dramatically to the FOMC news releases. Depending on the announcement, sometimes the reactions are only momentary, sometimes they last the rest of day, and sometimes they carry over into subsequent days or weeks.

Regardless of the overall duration of the impact on the market, immediately after the FOMC announcement the market is typically very volatile and behaves erratically for a period of time as traders digest the news (I'll provide a chart illustration of this a bit later). On some occasions the DOW moves by 100 points or more in one direction, and then abruptly swings back in the other direction by the same amount. In extreme instances, all of this can take place in a matter of minutes, particularly in cases where there is confusion initially about the significance or meaning of an FOMC announcement. Eventually the market digests the news and begins to settle down or establish a clearer directional trend.

Although the price action can be fast paced and may require some agility, the initial volatility that follows an FOMC meeting announcement presents a great trading opportunity for traders that anticipate it. Though not always, more often than not the first impulsive move that follows the FOMC announcement is exaggerated, and perhaps more importantly, it's often based on irrational emotional trading. As a result, the first move is frequently in the wrong direction.

Therefore, similar to playing gap reversals, I generally fade the first impulsive move that occurs after an FOMC announcement. Actually, the move is frequently so impulsive that it typically results in a sharp spike on a chart. It's this first spike that I'm interested in fading. The larger the first spike is, the better.

Even in cases where the direction of first impulse doesn't turn out to be incorrect, by fading the move I'm betting that it will at least be exaggerated initially and will snapback in the other direction as a result, or that it will simply fade the other way to some degree due to the initial confusion caused by the announcement. Either way, you can potentially profit from the trade even if a corrective snapback reversal is only temporary.

To fade an FOMC announcement, I like to use volatile momentum stocks that are in volatile sectors. As an example, the chart that follows shows how EBAY reacted to an FOMC announcement.

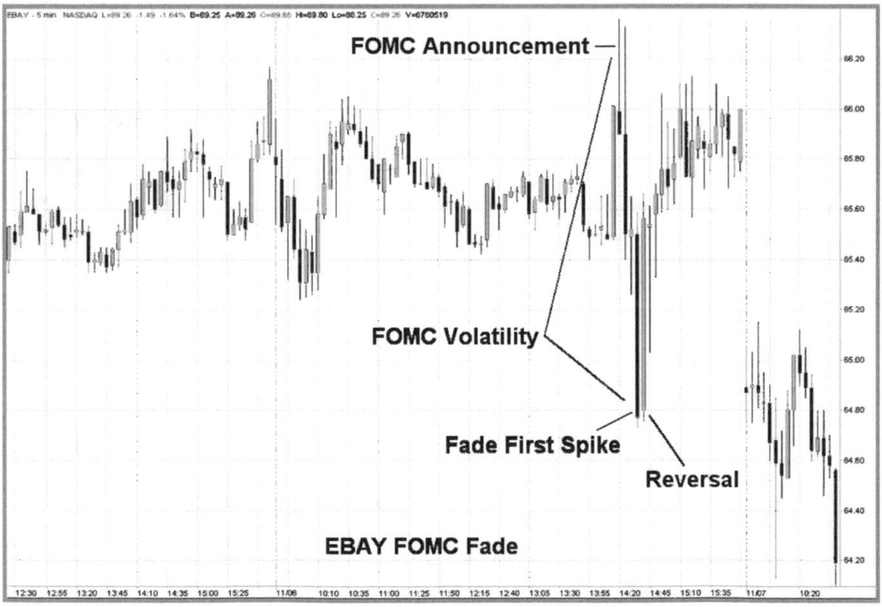

The outcome of an FOMC meeting is usually announced about 2:15 PM to 2:20 PM. It's a good idea to watch a business news channel such as CNBC for the announcement, in addition to keeping an eye on your online news service.

Looking at the preceding chart, notice the price moved higher in anticipation of the announcement. After the announcement, there was a sharp downside price spike, which was immediately followed by a snapback price reversal. The dark candlestick bar on the chart indicates the downside spike, and the very next light bar indicates the reversal. The whole process was over in a matter of a few minutes. Also note the overall amount of volatility surrounding the FOMC announcement.

To fade the reversal, you would enter a long position on the first downside spike and exit the position upon achieving gains from the reversal. As you can see on the chart, the price action can be quite rapid so you need to be prepared to act quickly. Additionally, you really need a direct access brokerage account to reliably trade this trend. Web based platforms generally don't have sufficient execution speeds to ensure you can get in and out of the trade quickly enough, and reliably.

In fact, the price action for this play is sometimes so fast that it is one of the rare situations where I have occasionally used a market order during the first spike to help ensure that I don't miss the reversal. Since I want to catch the bottom of the move for a reversal anyway, a market order will generally fill somewhere near that point. However, I must stress that you should only use a market order if you have a fast direct-access trading platform and understand what you are doing. Using the preceding example, if your trading platform is too slow or your timing isn't correct, a market order could fill after the reversal near the price top, rather than at a favorable price prior to the reversal.

Referring to the chart once again, you can see that in this case the price action settled down a short time later then resumed its prior trend for the duration of the day, which was essentially a sideways range bound trend. The prior trend doesn't always resume as in this case. Depending on the FOMC news, a rally or sell off could endure after the initial reaction.

If the initial spike after an FOMC announcement was to the upside rather than the downside, you would simply reverse the process previously described and enter a short position rather than a long position.

In addition to using stocks for the FOMC fade, I'll frequently buy Diamond (DIA) options, or options on another index such as the SOX or BKX. With this approach, you don't need to pick individual stocks and you tend to get a cleaner move with the market (I discussed using index options in more detail under the "Gap Fades" section and in the "Trading Options" chapter). However, you should only use limit orders when fading an FOMC move with options. You could easily get filled at a very unfavorable price attempting to use market orders with fast moving index options.

10:00 AM Rule Plays

I'm including the 10 AM rule in my list of favorites because it has proven to be a reliable indicator as to the near-term direction of the market, or individual stocks. Following the 10:00 AM rule has not only proven to be a consistently profitable strategy, it has also helped many traders avoid losses from entering trades prematurely.

Though I covered the 10 AM rule earlier in the book, for your convenience, here it is again.

> *If a stock gaps up, you should not buy it long unless it makes a new high after 10:00 AM. Conversely, if a stock gaps down, you should not sell it short unless it makes a new low after 10:00 AM.*

The 10 AM rule concept is actually very straightforward. Using the 10 AM rule, if a stock you are watching for a trade setup makes a new high after 10 AM, you could buy it for a long trade. Conversely, if a stock makes a new low after 10 AM, you could sell it short for a trade.

For example, suppose MSFT opened for trading at $25.00, and then between 9:30 AM and 10:00 AM, it made a high of $25.50. If at anytime after 10:00 AM the price hits $25.51, you could conceivably buy it long for a trade. As always is the case, you still need to consider overall market conditions and other circumstances applicable to a given stock but as long as these are conducive for the trade, you could potentially profit by entering a long position since a new high after 10 AM is a bullish indicator.

Alternatively, using the preceding example, suppose MSFT opened at $25.00 then made a low of $24.50 between 9:30 AM and 10:00 AM. If it subsequently hit $24.49 after 10:00 AM, you could conceivably short it for a trade since a new low after 10 AM is a bearish indicator. Once again, this assumes that any other applicable factors are conducive for the trade.

How or why does the 10 AM rule work? Well, when the market first opens for the day there tends to be more emotional trading and uncertainty. The market hasn't yet found its footing or established any type of directional bias, and worse, it could send false signals as to its true direction. Plus, there is frequently pent up demand on either the buy side or the sell side initially due to leftover imbalances from post- and pre-market trading.

All of these issues are usually resolved by 10 AM, so the price action that occurs after 10 AM is generally a more reliable indicator of the true directional bias of the market. Hence, the 10 AM rule was created. It provides guidelines to not only help avoid the early morning pitfalls, but to also potentially achieve greater profits, especially on directional trending days.

Following is a chart of NVLS that illustrates the 10 AM rule.

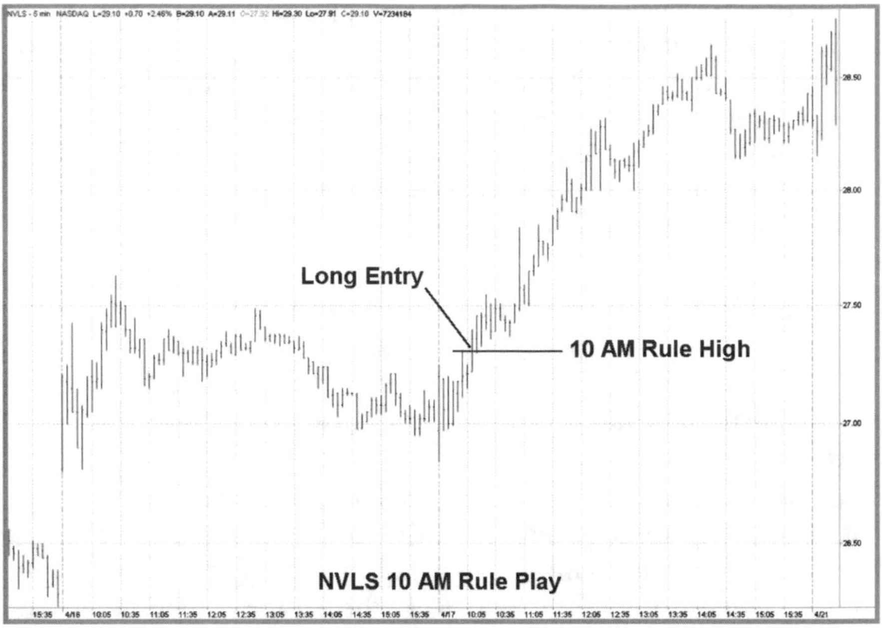

Looking at the chart, notice that the market initially began the day where it left off the prior day, essentially opening flat. Shortly after 10:00 AM, NVLS broke through its pre-10:00 AM high. At this point, you could enter a long position. You should then place a stop-loss order slightly beneath the low that occurred prior to 10:00 AM. If the market subsequently reverses directions, you should limit your losses by stopping out of the trade.

In the preceding example, you could have profited nicely on the trade by following the 10 AM rule. As the price moves higher, you should continue to trail the move with your stop-loss order. And as I've discussed before, my preference is to take profits along the way as any substantial gains are achieved. Once sufficient gains are achieved, I'll frequently take profits on 1/2 of my position then move my stop-loss to breakeven on my remaining shares. At this point, I can no longer lose on the trade. Next, I typically trail any additional gains on my remaining shares until I either stop out of the trade, or until I decide to take any additional profits and exit the position.

Here's another example of the 10 AM rule that illustrates a move to the downside using QLGC.

On the preceding chart, QLGC gapped up initially. As you can see by examining the chart, anyone that got caught up in the initially buying frenzy and went long paid the price a short time later. This serves as an example of how the 10 AM rule can help prevent premature trade entries, which is great when they would have been on the wrong side of the trade.

By following the 10 AM rule, you would either fade the gap up, or you would sell short once the stock made a new low after 10 AM. Upon entering a position, you should then place a stop-loss order slightly above the high that occurred prior to 10 AM. Afterwards, you would continue to trail any substantial gains and take profits along the way as described for the previous example. Once again, you could have achieved nice gains by using the 10 AM rule as a guideline for timing a short entry.

Of course, these examples are only for illustration purposes. There are days when the market briefly makes a new high or low after 10 AM and subsequently moves sideways or reverses direction. In the case of reversals, your stop-loss orders will trigger and limit potential losses, which is why it is important to use stop-losses. On range bound days, whether you profit on the trade and by how much would obviously depend on the specifics of the trade and the size of the trading range. Generally, the best gains are achieved when the market establishes a directional trend that lasts for the entire day.

That's when you can make the really big Ka-chingos!

12

Power Wrap-Up

I wanted to write a book that dealt with Trend Trading as a life choice. Some of you might decide you want to trade stocks part time. Some of you might Power Trade full time. You might quit your job of 20 years because you want to spend more time at home with your kids. Some of you may trade a year from now because you want to finish getting your degree. Still others might never trade because you decide it's just not for you. All of these scenarios are legitimate. And, they all deserve respect. One of the great things about life is that we're all unique in many ways. We all have different needs, different desires, and different dreams.

For those of you who are either trading now, or decide to trade, I wish you the best of luck, and the best of skill. I hope this book helps give you some of the tools, and mindset, that you need to succeed. I hope this book helps make that magic "switch" turn on, if it hasn't already turned on. Either way, you've taken a very important step in your life's adventure. You decided to learn something new. That's a VERY powerful action. In physics we learn that every action has an equal reaction. The same holds true in our life journey. If you take a positive step in your life, you will eventually get "someone" back of equal importance. Just remember that your success might not happen the way you planned, but that doesn't mean you should ever give up on your dreams.

For me, I don't believe I should ever do anything halfway. I try to do everything wholeheartedly. Why bother if I'm not going to give it my all? You can always back out and decide that it's not for you, but how would you know if you didn't give it a real honest try? If you are going to trade, TRADE POWERFULLY, as there is no other way to trade!

And, when you do achieve the success you dreamed about, be sure to be charitable. It's a spiritual law that whatever charity you do, you get back 10 times that amount in your own life. So, if you are the stingy type, you can look at charity as an investment in your own future!

And, regardless of what path you choose, LIVE POWERFULLY because in the end, what other way is there to live?

See ya on the other side,

Michael "Waxie" Parness